SOCIAL WORLDS OF SENTENCING

ော

SUNY Series in New Directions in
Crime and Justice Studies

Austin T. Turk, Editor

Social Worlds of Sentencing

Court Communities Under Sentencing Guidelines

൦ӄ

Jeffery T. Ulmer

State University of New York Press

Published by
State University of New York Press, Albany

© 1997 State University of New York

All rights reserved

Printed in the United States of America

No part of this book may be used or reproduced in any manner whatsoever without written permission. No part of this book may be stored in a retrieval system or transmitted in any form or by any means including electronic, electrostatic, magnetic tape, mechanical, photocopying, recording, or otherwise without the prior permission in writing of the publisher.

For information, address State University of New York Press, State University Plaza, Albany, N.Y. 12246

Production by M. R. Mulholland
Marketing by Theresa A. Swierzowski

Library of Congress Cataloging-in-Publication Data

Ulmer, Jeffery T., 1966–
    Social worlds of sentencing : court communities under sentencing guidelines / Jeffery T. Ulmer.
      p.   cm. — (SUNY series in new directions in crime and justice studies)
    Includes bibliographical references and index.
    ISBN 0-7914-3497-4 (hc : alk. paper). — ISBN 0-7914-3498-2 (pb : alk. paper)
    1. Sentences (Criminal procedure)—United States. 2. Sentences (Criminal procedure)—Social aspects—United States. I. Title.
II. Series.
KF9685.U43   1997
345.73'0772—dc21   96-45351
                                                          CIP

10 9 8 7 6 5 4 3 2 1

Contents

List of Tables	vii
Preface	ix
1. Courts, Sentencing, and Sentencing Guidelines	1
Research on Courts and Sentencing	6
2. Court Communities as Social Worlds	21
Processual Order/Social Worlds Theory	21
Court Communities as Social Worlds	25
Central Research Questions	29
3. Data and Analytical Strategy	35
Statistical Data	36
Statistical Data Limitations	43
Ethnographic Data	44
Ethnographic Data Limitations	47
4. Statewide Sentencing Outcomes	49
Main Effects Models	49
Interaction Effects Models	63
Summary	71
5. Metro County	75
Statistical Analysis of Conviction and Sentencing Outcomes	75
Ethnographic Analysis	82
Summary	102
6. Rich County	105
Statistical Analysis	105
Ethnographic Analysis	112
Summary	135

7. Southwest County 137
   Statistical Analysis 137
   Ethnographic Analysis 142
   Summary 159

8. Conclusion: Court Communities and
   Sentencing under Guidelines 163
   Statewide Sentencing under Guidelines 163
   Case Processing and Sentencing in
      Three Court Communities 165
   Sentencing Guidelines: Possibilities,
      Limitations, and Dilemmas 183
   Broader Sociological Issues 185

Appendix A: Pennsylvania Sentencing Guidelines 191

Appendix B: Examples of Interview Questions by Topic 193

Appendix C: Descriptive Statistics: Variables
   in State-wide Analysis 197

Notes 207

References 215

Index 229

Tables

3.1	Independent and Dependent Variables Used in Statistical Models	38
3.2	Number of Pennsylvania Counties by Court Size	39
4.1	Logit Models of Overall Incarceration, State Imprisonment, and Dispositional Departures	52
4.2	OLS Models of Incarceration Length, Corrected for Selection Bias	58
4.3	OLS Models of Durational Departures Below and Above Guidelines	61
4.4	Logit Models of Overall Incarceration, Cases With Prior Record Scores of 2 or Less and 3 or Greater	66
4.5	Logit Models of Dispositional Departure, Cases With Prior Record Scores of 2 or Less and 3 or Greater	68
4.6	OLS Models of Incarceration Length, Prior Record Scores of 2 or Less and 3 or Greater	70
5.1	Modes of Conviction by Offense Severity: Metro County	76
5.2	Logit Models of Overall Incarceration, State Imprisonment, and Dispositional Departures: Metro County	78
5.3	OLS Models of Incarceration Length, Corrected for Selection Bias: Metro County	80
6.1	Modes of Conviction by Offense Severity: Rich County	106
6.2	Logit Models of Overall Incarceration, State Imprisonment, and Dispositional Departures: Rich County	108
6.3	OLS Models of Incarceration Length, Corrected for Selection Bias: Rich County	110

7.1	Modes of Conviction by Offense Severity: Southwest County	138
7.2	Logit Models of Overall Incarceration and Dispositional Departures: Southwest County	139
7.3	OLS Model of Incarceration Length, Corrected for Selection Bias: Southwest County	140
8.1	Court Community Contextual Features by County	166
8.2	Processual Order of Case Processing by County	175

Preface

This book was conceived in James Eisenstein's seminar on courts and the legal process at Penn State University, where I was a graduate student in sociology. The central themes of Eisenstein's graduate seminar were the same as those found in the books and articles on the organization and activities of criminal courts he and his associates Herbert Jacob, Peter Nardulli, and Roy Flemming have written. First, some of the most important characteristics and processes of criminal justice are to be found at the local level, where communities and their courts enact, filter, and perhaps modify the laws and policies of larger-scale institutions of the state. Second, local courts themselves are best seen as communities, with their own formal and informal rules and norms, organizational arrangements, relationships, politics, opportunities, and constraints. Third, these local court communities set the context for, and are in turn maintained or modified by, the daily activities of individual attorneys, judges, and others within courtroom workgroups. Fourth, anyone who wants to understand criminal sentencing—and the possibilities and limitations of any kind of sentencing reform policy (like sentencing guidelines)—had better study the "contours" of local court communities, the activities and decisions of their participants, and their consequences for criminal defendants. Eisenstein et al. (1988, p. 296) put it this way: "Reform from above does not operate in a vacuum of Law. If changes occur, they must take place in the real world of criminal court communities, where the decisions have to be implemented."

These insights from Eisenstein's seminar and published works strongly resonated with other, more general themes from symbolic interactionist treatments of social organization and structure, which I had been reading under the direction of another mentor and friend, David Maines. The works of W.I. Thomas, Robert Park, Herbert Blumer, Anselm Strauss, Helena Lopata, Howard Becker, Maines himself, and many others emphasize that macro, meso, and mirco domains of social life are inherently interrelated. Macrolevel structures influence mesolevel institutional and organizational arrangements, which in turn present contexts of opportunity and constraint within which individuals interpret their situations, make decisions, carry on routine activities, and adapt to problematic situations (with varying degrees of success). These microlevel activities in turn maintain, slightly modify, or radically change meso and sometimes even macro structures. This symbolic interactionist perspective, like Eisenstein and associates' court community framework, directs the researcher to focus on the ways in which larger scale structures (state sentencing guideline policies, for example) are mediated by the local community and organizational contexts and the interaction strategies of participants. This book is therefore framed by two highly compatible conceptual agendas: the court community framework of Eisenstein and his associates, and the symbolic interactionist processual order framework. The former is specific to the organization and activities of courts, and the latter is generic and applies to organizational arenas of all kinds and the interaction processes within them.

The subject matter of this book also presents a prime example of a topic that requires both quantitative data on outcomes (convictions and sentences) and ethnographic data on court contexts and processes (case processing strategies and sentence decision making). The triangulation of data and methods in this book is also compatible with both the court community framework and the processual order approach. The works of Eisenstein and his associates are exemplars of multimethod research on courts and sentencing. Further, it is a common misconception that symbolic interactionist theory is universally hostile to quantitative research. Blumer (1969) as well as other interactionists maintain that quantitative data are appropriate for analyzing outcomes of social processes, but that ethnographic data are necessary for analyzing the social processes themselves. Any analysis of courts and sentencing must begin by addressing the question of who gets what kind of sentence, and under what circumstances? This is best answered by quantitative analysis of sentencing. The task is then to try to gain some insight into the contexts and processes that produce the sentencing statistics, and this is the methodological strategy of this book.

This book is primarily intended as a research monograph for an audience of scholars interested in crime, courts, sentencing and sentencing policy, and organizations. However, the book is also appropriate for use as a supplemental reading for graduate and advanced undergraduate students in courses on criminology, criminal justice, the sociology of law, social control, policy analysis, organizations, or other appropriate topics. Therefore, I have tried to couch the book's theoretical and methodological discussions in the clearest language that I am capable of. In particular, I have tried to explain and interpret the statistical analyses and findings in language that is accessible to students who have at least some basic familiarity with statistical methods.

Many people deserve my thanks for helping to make this book and the research it describes possible. First and foremost, this book, and the dissertation from which it derived, would have been impossible without the opportunities, resources, and guidance provided by John Kramer, Professor of Sociology at Penn State and executive director of the Pennsylvania Commission on Sentencing. John gave me access to the statistical data and invited me to be a member of the commission research staff's ethnographic data collection project. He funded me as a research assistant throughout graduate school and hired me as a postdoctoral research associate. In addition, he and I have collaborated on a number of sentencing-related research projects, and I have learned a great deal from this process. I would also like to acknowledge other current and former members of the Pennsylvania Commission on Sentencing research staff for their support, advice, and help: Cynthia Kempinen, Jody Hobbs, Carol Zeiss, Sally Babin, and Paula Brown.

I thank Darrell Steffensmeier and James Eisenstein for providing insightful critiques and advice during various stages of this and related research projects. I thank David Maines, both for his intellectual mentorship and for helping me transform a 400-page dissertation that no one would want to read into a shorter, less ponderous book manuscript that, hopefully, at least a few people will want to read. I also thank the late Anselm Strauss, the late Carl Couch, and Peter Hall for "talking interactionism" with me and helping me "get it right." The comments of the anonymous reviewers of State University of New York Press also helped improve the book a good deal, as did the comments of Susan Moe, who gave the manuscript a careful and critical reading from a student's perspective. I thank a number of my colleagues at Purdue University for helping me guide the manuscript through the confusing seas of the academic book publishing world: Ken Ferraro, Dean Knudsen, JoAnn Miller, Rich Hogan, Anthony Lemelle, and Jerry Van Hoy. Finally, I thank the judges, attorneys, probation officers, clerks, and others who allowed us into their courtrooms and offices, and trusted us enough to share their social worlds of sentencing with us.

1

Courts, Sentencing, and Sentencing Guidelines

Few public issues mobilize more interest, emotion, and fascination in contemporary American society than crime and sentencing. In an attempt to satisfy political constituencies who are increasingly fearful of street crime and demanding that the criminal justice system "get tough," nearly all fifty states and the federal system have implemented various, diverse sentencing policies aimed at achieving greater deterrence, retribution, and incapacitation of criminal offenders (Feeley and Simon 1992; Austin et al. 1994).

On the other hand, the fairness of the criminal justice system in general, and sentencing in particular, is also a long-standing concern in public and scholarly discourse about crime (Savelsberg 1992). For example, does "equal justice under law" prevail, or are criminal justice institutions biased regarding race, gender, age, and other extralegal factors? The extent and sources of unwarranted sentencing disparity have become a particular concern in recent years, given the dramatic increase since 1980 in imprisonment rates for young black males from poor backgrounds—a pattern that characterizes most states as well as the federal prison system (Edna McConnell Clark Foundation 1993). Are such trends, as Wilbanks (1987) or Kleck (1985) argue, due simply to disproportionate involvement in serious crime for certain groups— young black males, for example—or do these patterns indicate systematic bias in sentencing decisions as others maintain (Lizotte 1978; Bridges and Crutchfield 1988)?

The growing nationwide trend toward sentencing guidelines is where these two sets of public issues intersect: concern with increased certainty and severity of punishment and concern with inequality in sentencing. As Samuel Walker (1993) maintains, central to both of these issues is the use and control of sentencing discretion. As Walker notes, the history of American criminal justice policy in the twentieth century is largely the history of wrestling with these issues of discretion and disparity, which in turn invoke a basic set of sociological questions. What sanctions do various types of criminal offenders receive? What groups or institutions will a society or community trust with the discretion to determine criminal sanctions, and how much discretion will they be allowed? How will these agents of formal social control be held accountable for the use of their discretion, and to what degree will their sanctioning decisions reflect larger structural patterns of social inequality?

The federal court system, and a growing number of states as diverse as Minnesota, Pennsylvania, Washington, Oregon, Tennessee, Florida, North Carolina, Arkansas, and Utah, have or are developing presumptive sentencing guidelines to manage and control sentencing discretion in local trial courts (Austin et al. 1993). The specific goals and characteristics of these various sentencing guidelines systems are very diverse, but they all share the general aims of controlling judicial discretion and unwarranted disparity (Austin et al. 1993, Ch. 4; Tonry and Coffee 1987). Sentencing guidelines are different than the mandatory sentencing schemes adopted by most states, such as the "three strikes and you're out" measures popular in the mid 1990s, in that guidelines seek to structure, yet not remove, local court discretion in sentencing. Guidelines seek to provide formal sentencing norms that should be followed in typical cases, while allowing local courts to adjust sentences to fit unusual circumstances or defendants. The move toward sentencing guidelines is a growing, nationwide trend, and it is probable that more states will adopt guidelines or similar systems in the future (Feeley and Simon 1992; Savelsberg 1992).

Sociological issues

Research on these and other questions concerning the everyday realities of the "law in action" in local trial courts contributes a great deal to criminology, the sociology of law, and to knowledge of organizational interaction processes and decision making. This book addresses just such issues by investigating sentencing outcomes, organizational relations, and case processing in the context of Pennsylvania's sentencing guidelines, one of the nation's oldest sentencing guidelines systems.

Since courts are crucial deviance processing institutions that mete out material and symbolic sanctions, most of the courts and sentencing literature concerns the location and use of decision-making discretion, opportunities for unwarranted sentencing disparity, and the degree of such disparity. Unwarranted disparity, in turn, has become a core issue for labeling theory in criminology, given its concern with the relative influence of legally prescribed, organizational, and defendant-related factors on the differential sanctioning of offenders (Bernstein et al. 1977a; 1977b; Farrell and Swigert 1978).

Prior research, such as the ground-breaking studies by Eisenstein and associates (1977; 1988) also shows that any adequate understanding of sentencing must include a focus on the social organizational contexts of courts. In fact, researchers have used criminal courts as a context in which to study general organizational topics such as informal norms and rules (Sudnow 1965; Blumberg 1967; Rosett and Cressey 1976; Eisenstein and Jacob 1977), decision making and discretion (McDonald 1979; Emerson 1983; Padgett 1985; Nardulli et al. 1985; Farrell and Holmes 1991), negotiation (Church 1976; Heumann 1978; Maynard 1984; 1988), loose coupling (Hagan et al. 1979), and organization-environment relations (Levin 1977; Clear et al. 1978; Altheide 1992).

Another broad sociological issue is involved in the study of sentencing under guidelines. The effort to structure sentencing through guidelines involves a philosophical dilemma for agents of formal social control—the balance between the principle of uniformity (similar offenders should receive similar sanctions) vs. individualized justice (social control agents should have the discretion to tailor sanctions to the particular characteristics and situations of individual offenders). Savelsberg (1992) identifies this dilemma as part of a larger issue in the sociology of law, between Max Weber's (1954) ideal types of formal and substantive rationality in social control. Each of these ideological principles, in turn, confronts the organizational realities, such as discretion and its use of local social control institutions (Walker 1993).

Sentencing guidelines, like any broad, formal state policy, are enacted through networks of collective and individual actors with varying degrees of discretion in complex organizational and community contexts, and these contexts in turn condition different substantively rational criteria (Savelsberg 1992) in sentencing. This book addresses these issues in the sociology of law and social control by investigating local court contexts and sources of sentencing disparity under Pennsylvania's sentencing guidelines, which, as described later, leave more opportunity for the dilemma to be played out between the uniformity and structure of formal rationality and locally defined substantive rationality in sentencing. The basic theoretical framing elaborated in this book is that courts are like communities (Eisenstein et al. 1988) or social worlds with their own local processual orders of legal culture (Friedman 1977), court politics, interorganizational relations, and case processing. These features of court communities condition various locally defined criteria of substantive rationality in sentencing, which in turn may produce varying degrees and bases of sentencing disparity. Court communities are thus policy arenas (Hall 1995; Estes and Edmonds 1981) where two sets of sentencing standards meet—the formally rational ones articulated by guidelines (such as offense severity, prior criminal record) versus the substantive, extra-legal criteria deemed relevant by local court actors and local legal cultures. This argument about state guideline policies and local court cultures is analogous to Herbert Blumer's (1990) analysis of industrialization as an agent of social change: large-scale social processes and state policies are channeled through local cultures and organizational contexts, and enacted, modified, or ignored by local actors with particular substantive interests.

Contributions of the Book

The steadily growing movement across the U.S. toward sentencing guidelines, long-standing public and scholarly concern with crime and sentencing, and the above theoretical issues place a premium on empirical research on sentencing in the context of contemporary policies. Although an enormous amount of literature on sentencing has developed over the past three decades, comparatively few studies have investigated sentencing outcomes under guidelines, and most published empirical studies focus only on Minnesota's guidelines (e.g., Miethe and Moore 1985; 1988; Moore and Miethe 1986; Stolzenberg and D'Alessio 1994). In fact, most of what we know about sentencing under guidelines comes from research on Minnesota's guidelines or those of the federal system. These studies have been primarily concerned with statistically modeling unwarranted disparity in sentencing outcomes. However, I know of only one other published empirical study that specifically analyzes the role of guidelines in trial court case processing and organizational relations, and that links these to sentencing outcomes (see Nagel and Schulhofer 1992). Other observers have speculated about trial courts' organizational arrangements under guidelines and the consequences for defendants (Savelsberg 1992; Tonry 1987; Tonry and Coffee 1987; Lagoy et al. 1979), but these propositions have yet to be subjected to adequate empirical scrutiny. Further, much of the existing literature on trial courts and sentencing provides inadequate guidance concerning these issues. As I will argue, many studies are plagued by methodological limitations and/or conceptual flaws, and most are dated by their reliance on old data.

Although this book focuses on courts and sentencing under Pennsylvania's guidelines, it makes at least three broader contributions beyond simply examining one state's sentencing practices and policies. First, it fills an important gap in the literature on criminal courts and sentencing, since very few studies of this kind exist. By studying the sentencing practices, court community contexts and organization, and case processing arrangements in the context of sentencing guidelines, this research provides an understanding of contemporary courts and their sentencing processes. Research of this kind is all the more important in light of the questionable generalizability of existing sentencing research for the growing numbers of jurisdictions with sentencing guidelines (see Feeley and Simon 1992; Goodstein and Kramer 1989). Further, such research can shed light on both the possibilities and limitations of attempts at sentencing reform (see Savelsberg 1992).

Second, this research has broader relevance for interactionist-oriented organizational theory as well. Proponents of social worlds/processual order theory such as Strauss (1978a; 1978b; 1984), Hall and Spencer-Hall (1982), Hall (1995), and Couch (1986) have called for comparative research that investigates the contextual conditions under which various interaction strategies such as negotiation, conflict, unilateral manipulation, or cooperation emerge, and how these in turn maintain or alter organizational arrangements. Although some research has been done along these lines in several substantive settings (e.g., Kling and Gerson 1978; Hall and Spencer-Hall 1982; Levy 1982; Busch 1982; Thomas 1984; Seckman and Couch 1989), more is needed for the further development of social worlds/processual order theory (see reviews by Hall 1987; 1995; Clarke 1991). Comparative research on courts is an ideal arena for investigating these issues, and findings could then inform comparative research in other organizational arenas.

Finally, criminal courts are, first and foremost, deviance defining and processing institutions. Therefore, the most basic issues involved in this study are the consequences of the law in action for defendants, a core concern of both labeling theory and public policy. This study, like many others, attempts to identify the legal, organizational, contextual, and defendant-related factors that influence the differences in the allocation of criminal sanctions. However, this study is like very few others in that it attempts to go beyond the statistical modeling of unwarranted sentencing disparity to a process-oriented analysis of possible organizational and interactional sources of disparity that statistical models cannot capture. Such research is important both for a theoretical understanding of criminal labeling processes, and for efforts to fashion a sentencing policy that is equitable in both its intent and its consequences.

I begin by reviewing relevant studies of trial court case processing, sentencing, and sentencing guidelines, and noting their contributions and limitations. In chapter 2, I discuss the two complementary theoretical perspectives that frame this study: the "court community" framework developed by Eisenstein and associates (Nardulli et al. 1988; Eisenstein et al. 1988; Flemming et al. 1992), and social worlds/processual order theory (Strauss 1993). Chapter 3 describes the data sources and collection procedures, and outlines my methodological strategy, which consists of three parts. First, I conduct statistical analyses of state-wide sentencing outcomes under Pennsylvania's guidelines system, using data maintained by the Pennsylvania Commission on Sentencing. Second, I use this same statistical data to focus on case processing and sentencing in the trial court communities of three different-sized counties. Finally, I analyze ethnographic data from these three focus counties in order to explore the interface between sentencing guidelines, organizational contexts, and case processing strategies that lie behind the statistical findings.

Research on Courts and Sentencing

The literature on trial court organization, case processing, and sentencing can be categorized according to two general approaches, and each approach has its particular strengths and weaknesses (see Farrell and Holmes 1991; Levin 1977). One approach statistically models the influence of various factors on sentencing, while the other uses ethnographic or multimethod strategies to study court organization and case processing. I first discuss the statistical literature and focus on the issues of unwarranted sentencing disparity based on race, gender, and mode of conviction. After outlining some weaknesses of the statistical approach, I then discuss ethnographic studies of court organization, particularly the work of Eisenstein and associates. Finally, I identify reasons why existing statistical and ethnographic studies may provide inadequate guidance regarding sentencing and court organization under sentencing guidelines.

Statistical Studies

The most common approach centers around the statistical modeling of sentencing outcomes according to legally prescribed variables, aggregate contextual factors, and offender characteristics (see reviews by Thomson and Zingraff 1981; Hagan and Bumiller 1983; Kleck 1981; 1985; Maynard 1984; Myers and Talarico 1987; Albonetti 1991; Kramer and Steffensmeier 1993). This literature has produced some consistencies, and also several mixed and anomalous findings. Generally, research has consistently found that the primary determinants of imprisonment decisions and sentence severity are legally prescribed factors such as offense type/severity and criminal history. This broad consensus in the literature breaks down, however, concerning unwarranted disparity stemming from extralegal factors, particularly race and mode of conviction.

Since the American legal tradition rests on the principle of "equal justice under law," the issue of unwarranted disparity concerns the degree to which doctrines of fairness and equality are actually practiced in the criminal courts. Unwarranted sentencing disparity is defined as occurring when legally similar defendants receive dissimilar sentences.[1] Usually, discussions of unwarranted disparity focus on the influence of extra-legal factors on sentencing, such as race, gender, age, socioeconomic status, mode of conviction, or region (Hagan and Bumiller 1983; Myers and Talarico 1987). For example, unwarranted disparity on the basis of race would be indicated if whites and blacks convicted of the same offenses and with the same prior criminal records received differentially lenient or severe sentences.

Few would argue that legally prescribed factors such as offense and prior record are not the primary determinants of sentences. Instead, the main issue in discussions of unwarranted sentencing disparity is how much influence extralegal factors exert (see Brereton and Casper 1984, p. 52). This question is an important test of the ideologies of equality before the law, because the application of criminal sanctions is supposed to be neutral regarding the defendant's race, gender, or age, or whether the defendant exercised his/her right to trial.

Race disparity. The concern with race disparity in part stems from a basic issue for social stratification: whether racial and ethnic minorities are discriminated against in the processes of administering criminal sanctions (Lizotte 1978; Bridges and Crutchfield 1988). For example, some hold that legal institutions are inextricably tied to the economic and political order of a society. Thus, disparities in criminal punishment reflect economic and political inequalities in the larger society (see Quinney 1970; Spitzer 1975; Swigert and Farrell 1978). The fact that African Americans have traditionally been a politically, socially, and economically disadvantaged minority suggests the proposition that they will be discriminated against in sentencing (Peterson and Hagan 1984).

Findings from the very large research literature on this topic are quite mixed, and cannot be interpreted easily. Some studies find that blacks are incarcerated more often and receive longer sentences than whites, and interpret this as evidence of racial discrimination (e.g., Thomson and Zingraff 1981; Spohn et al. 1982; Peterson and Hagan 1984; Myers and Talarico 1987; Humphrey and Fogarty 1987; Spohn 1990; Albonetti 1991). Others find few substantial differences in the sentencing of blacks and whites, and argue that any racial sentencing differences that do exist reflect: (a) the failure to rigorously control for legal variables in sentencing, and (b) disproportionate participation in serious crime among blacks rather than discrimination by court actors (see Kleck 1981; 1985). Wilbanks (1987) makes these points most strongly, arguing that racial discrimination in criminal justice, and sentencing in particular, is a "myth" created by sloppy research and liberal political agendas.

On the other hand, some studies point to the importance of variation between local jurisdictions in the degree of race disparity in sentencing (e.g., Eisenstein and Jacob 1977; Bridges and Crutchfield 1988; Nelson 1992). For example, Nelson's (1992) study of sentencing in New York found that race differences varied widely between counties, but that analyses of aggregate statewide sentencing patterns masked these differences. Bridges and Crutchfield (1988) find that the degree of disparity between black and white imprisonment rates is greater in states with smaller black populations, higher concentrations of blacks in large urban areas, and greater black/white income inequality. Furthermore, these differences persisted when controlling for black and white arrest rates, leading Bridges and Crutchfield (1988) to argue that race differences in imprisonment are not solely due to differential involvement in crime.

In one of the most detailed treatments of the issue to date, Kramer and Steffensmeier's (1993) study of race disparity under Pennsylvania's guidelines finds moderate race differences in incarceration decisions (especially departures below guidelines). They suggest, however, that these differences do not necessarily reflect racial discrimination by court actors. Rather, they argue that the influence of race is confounded with a number of other factors that cannot be easily measured quantitatively, such as circumstances of offenses, aspects of defendants' prior convictions that do not show up on official records, plea bargaining strategies, and some judges' reluctance to send whites to state prisons with predominantly black inmate populations (see also Cassia Spohn's [1995] excellent review of race and criminal justice).

Gender disparity. Though not nearly as extensively studied, gender is also an important feature in the question of sentencing disparity. A fairly consistent finding in this literature is that adult female defendants are sentenced more leniently than adult male defendants (see reviews by Steffensmeier et al. 1993; Bickle and Peterson 1991; Daly 1987; Kruttschnitt and Green 1984). Explanations for more lenient treatment of women by courts are diverse, and most likely complementary. Some argue that this pattern results from judicial paternalism—predominantly male judges being more patronizing toward women defendants and failing to take seriously the crimes of women (Daly 1987). Others argue that the differential sentencing of men and women is due to the greater social costs of sending women with dependent children to prison (Steffensmeier 1980). Still others argue that court actors make sentencing decisions on the basis of typifications of offenders as more or less dangerous and/or blameworthy, and that gender stereotypes of women militate against their being viewed as a risk of future crime, or as criminally culpable as male offenders (Albonetti 1991; Farrell and Holmes 1991).

Mode of conviction disparity. The issue of sentencing disparity based on mode of conviction more directly concerns the organization of court case processing. Decades of research have established that most defendants are convicted through guilty pleas, and that trials tend to be avoided (Blumberg 1967; Rosett and Cressey 1976; Heumann 1978). The central issue in terms of sentencing disparity is whether courts penalize convicted defendants who exert their right to a trial with more severe sentences, and whether such "trial penalties" are used to coerce defendants into pleading guilty (see McDonald 1979).

Compared to the literature on race, a smaller number of studies have directly focused on sentencing differences according to modes of conviction and other case processing factors (e.g., Bernstein et al. 1977a; 1977b; Hagan et al. 1979; Ryan and Alfini 1979; McDonald et al. 1979; LaFree 1985; Humphrey and Fogarty 1987; Holmes et al. 1987; Feeley 1988; Champion 1989). As with race disparity, evidence is mixed concerning the effects of mode of conviction on sentencing. A number of studies find strong evidence of a trial penalty in sentencing decisions (e.g., Hagan et al. 1979; Uhlman and Walker 1980; Peterson and Hagan 1984; LaFree 1985; Spohn 1990), while others do not (e.g., Eisenstein and Jacob 1977; Nardulli et al. 1988; Albonetti 1991).

The interpretation of sentencing disparity according to mode of conviction is as complex as the interpretation of race differences. For example, LaFree's (1985) study of sentencing in six jurisdictions finds differences in sentence severity not only between guilty pleas and trials, but also between bench trials and jury trials. This suggests that the common strategy of including a simple dichotomy of pleas versus trials in sentence models may oversimplify the issue, and that analyses should also consider the relative influence of different *types* of pleas and trials.[2]

Overall, then, the statistical literature presents mixed findings regarding unwarranted sentencing disparity based on race, gender, and mode of conviction. Difficulties in interpreting these findings are compounded in that many studies exhibit methodological and conceptual weaknesses.

Problems with the Statistical Literature

The strength of the statistical modeling approach lies in its potential for rigorously analyzing sentencing outcomes using large numbers of cases, and for comparing these outcomes among different jurisdictions. However, most existing literature falls short of this potential due to several common limitations.

A number of studies, particularly many of those conducted in the 1970s and early 1980s, have exhibited key methodological problems. First, the statistical designs of many studies of race disparity fail to rigorously control for factors such as offense type and severity, criminal history, and mode of conviction (a few studies do not control for these at all—see reviews by Hagan and Bumiller [1983], Kleck [1981; 1985], and Kramer and Steffensmeier, [1993]). More recent studies also exhibit similar limitations. Myers's (1987) and Myers and Talarico's (1986; 1987) well-received studies provide a typical example. They use crude controls such as a dichotomous variable for criminal history (no prior convictions versus at least one prior conviction), and even these data are only included for a subsample of their cases. Further, they use limited measures of offense type and severity, such as the imprecise grouping of offenses into five broad categories: violent, robbery, burglary, property theft or damage, and drug offenses. Such limitations are also shared by other influential studies, such as Lizotte (1978), Thomson and Zingraff (1981), Unnever and Hembroff (1988), and Humphrey and Fogarty (1987). Other sentencing studies fail to examine potential differences due to different modes of conviction while examining other sources of sentence disparity (e.g., Lizotte 1978; LaFree 1985; Thomson and Zingraff 1981; Frazier and Bock 1982; Myers and Talarico 1986; 1987; Myers 1987; Humphrey and Fogarty 1987).

As a final example, Bridges and Crutchfield's (1988) influential study is often cited as evidence of racial sentencing disparity at the level of individual cases and defendants. However, their study is pitched at the aggregate level, using black and white state prison population ratios as their dependent variable and state-level demographic factors, legal characteristics, black and white arrest rates, and state prison capacity as independent variables. Since they rely on such data, they are unable to control for offense, prior record, or mode of conviction in any way. While they convincingly demonstrate race differences in state prison populations and the influence of regional characteristics on such differences, their findings do not establish that comparable individual black and white defendants receive dissimilar sentences.

Other methodological problems in this literature concern the choice of inappropriate modeling techniques. Some studies fail to control for or even consider the possibility of sample selection bias problems that can obscure or confound the effects of predictor variables on measures of sentence lengths, since length decisions follow decisions to incarcerate (Berk 1983). Further, some studies use inappropriate least-squares regression techniques for modeling dichotomous dependent variables such as convictions or incarceration decisions (e.g., Hagan et al. 1979; LaFree 1985; Spohn et al. 1982; 1987; Nardulli et al. 1985). The results of such analyses can be quite misleading when attention is not paid to possible sources of error because of inappropriate estimation techniques (Hanushek and Jackson 1977).

Finally, the large majority of studies published in the past decade use data that are quite old, despite the changes that have occurred in the criminal justice system and its political context. Very often, data used in studies published throughout the 1980s and 1990s were gathered during the early or mid-1970s. For example, at least three more recent studies published in major journals (Albonetti 1991; Bickle and Peterson 1991; Spohn 1990) use data that are more than fifteen years old. Among the many statistical analyses of sentencing, only Miethe and Moore's (1985; 1986; Moore and Miethe 1986) studies of sentencing under Minnesota's guidelines avoid most of the methodological problems noted above. Even their studies, however, rely on data collected in the late 1970s and early 1980s.

More importantly, most solely quantitative approaches of courts and sentencing share a limitation of conceptual focus. By focusing solely on modeling aggregate case *outcomes*, such studies are unable to capture the interactional, organizational, and political *processes* that generate case outcomes (see Nardulli et al. 1988; Maroules 1991; Farrell and Holmes 1991). The fact that most studies' models (even the more methodologically sound ones) only explain about half or less of the variance in sentences suggests the limitations of a preoccupation with case outcome modeling. Most statistical sentencing studies report R-squared values of .50 or less in modeling sentence lengths and incarceration decisions (Bernstein et al. 1977; Lizotte 1978; Hagan et al. 1979; Thomson and Zingraff 1981; Myers and Talarico 1986; 1987; LaFree 1985; Miethe and Moore 1986; Kramer and Steffensmeier 1993). Studies that employ logistic regression models of incarceration decisions seem to enjoy somewhat better prediction, but this is difficult to tell because most of these do not report any meaningful tests of their models' predictive power, such as the percent of cases accurately classified by the models (e.g., Peterson and Hagan 1984; Holmes et al. 1987; Albonetti 1987; Spohn 1990).

In terms of unwarranted sentencing disparity, for example, studies that rely on statistical analyses alone are unable to empirically identify the processes that give rise to disparities and the case processing stages at which they occur. As a recent example of a lack of conceptual clarity about bases and sources of sentencing disparity, Stolzenberg and D'Alessio's (1994) study of sentencing under Minnesota's guidelines models sentence outcomes by offense severity and offenders' prior criminal convictions, and assumes that any variance in sentences not explained by these two factors is unwarranted disparity. Further, the case processing and sentencing strategies of prosecutors, defenders, and judges are often not apparent from statistical analyses. Finally, analyses that aggregate statistical data from different jurisdictions into general models tend to mask important differences in local legal culture, norms, and political contexts (see reviews by Levin 1977; Thomson and Zingraff 1981; Peterson and Hagan 1984; Maynard 1984).

Ethnographies of Court Organization

The ability to capture the processual and contextual aspects of trial court organization and case processing is the strength of the second approach found in the literature. This second approach uses ethnographic strategies to analyze the organization of trial courts' case processing and sentencing in an integrated way (e.g., Sudnow 1965; Heumann 1978; Rosett and Cressey 1976; Farr 1984; Maynard 1984; 1988).

The studies carried out by Eisenstein and Jacob (1977), Nardulli et al. (1988), Eisenstein et al. (1988), and Flemming et al. (1992), which will be discussed further in the next chapter, perhaps best exemplify this approach. These studies use both ethnographic and statistical data to study the influence of courts' political contexts, formal and informal organization, and power relations between sponsoring agencies on case processing and sentencing. Such analyses enabled Eisenstein and associates to develop a grounded theoretical approach known as the *court community* framework. The most notable features of this framework are: (1) the metaphor of courts as communities based on local legal culture, members' shared workplace, and interdependencies between key sponsoring agencies (prosecutor's office, bench, defense bar); (2) attention to "going rates," or informal norms concerning routine charges, plea agreement terms, and sentences; (3) an emphasis on interorganizational relations between sponsoring agencies, not only in terms of formal bases of authority but also the informal processes by which agencies and their representatives exert influence in courtroom workgroup strategies and case outcomes; and (4) detailed attention to the guilty plea and sentencing processes as the core organizational activities of courts.

The research of Eisenstein and associates opened a wide agenda for future research. Nardulli et al. (1988, pp. 383–84) state:

> We will not learn much by continuing to conduct multivariate analyses of case, defendant, and decision-maker attributes . . . We do not suggest a total abandonment of studies that focus on case outcomes; they are still the bottom line of what criminal courts do. Instead, we suggest a move away from the preoccupation with deviation from system norms to a focus on the differences in norms across court communities. Such a reorientation...would open new vistas for court research and broaden the scope of research into these vital and complex institutions.

They also call for further development and refinement of the court community theoretical framework (pp. 369–70):

> At this embryonic stage of its development, the potential utility of the notion of a courthouse community seems significant but is still unclear...A more systematic analysis and mapping of court community norms and values could help identify key differences across court communities and perhaps lead to a fairly inclusive typology of court communities.

Eisenstein et al. (1988, ch. 10–11) expand upon these suggestions for future research. Although they collected their data before the implementation of sentencing guidelines, they do predict the impact of any court and sentencing reform policies. Generally, they hold that the influence of any type of sentencing reform will be filtered through the organizational and political contours of local court communities. It follows that the influence of sentencing guidelines on actual case processing and sentencing practices will vary according to local court system characteristics. The fact that models of statewide sentencing in guideline states such as Minnesota (Miethe and Moore 1985; 1986; Moore and Miethe 1986), Pennsylvania (Kramer and Steffensmeier 1993), and Florida (Griswold 1987) explain half or less of the variance in incarceration decisions and lengths suggests the veracity of this proposition. This study is concerned with a set of issues that flow directly from the court community research agenda: the interface between court community contexts, organizational relations, and the equality of outcomes for defendants under sentencing guidelines.

Studies of Sentencing Under Guidelines

The comparatively small body of literature on sentencing guidelines provides limited guidance concerning the issues discussed above. In fact, the story of systematic social science research on sentencing under guidelines is largely the story of research on Minnesota's and the federal system's guidelines. Generally, Miethe and Moore's (1985; 1988; Moore and Miethe 1986) studies of Minnesota's guidelines found that race, gender, and class disparity greatly decreased in the early years of implementation, but increased moderately in later years, though it did not return to preguidelines levels. In a later analysis, Jo Dixon (1995) also concluded that Minnesota's guidelines significantly reduced racial sentencing differences (though she did not examine the influence of gender or class).

Even fewer studies have statistically modeled sentencing consequences of different modes of conviction under guidelines systems, and these show mixed results. Miethe (1987), Miethe and Moore (1985; 1988) found little difference in sentencing outcomes due to modes of conviction in Minnesota. On the other hand, Griswold (1987) found that departures below Florida's guidelines were moderately more common among defendants who pleaded guilty. Nagel and Schulhofer's (1992) study of plea bargaining under the federal sentencing guidelines found that a number of federal district court organizational characteristics fostered noncompliance with the guidelines.

Further, Dixon (1995) found that while the strongest influences on sentencing under Minnesota's guidelines were offense and prior record, the effects of guilty pleas and trials on sentencing outcomes varied according to courts' levels of bureaucratization. She found that guilty pleas resulted in significantly shorter sentences in highly bureaucratized courts, but not in less bureaucratized ones. She also stated that the complexity and variability of sentencing processes necessitate more research "to examine the organization of sentencing in jurisdictions that vary in their organizational, political, policy, and social contexts" (Dixon 1995, p. 1193).

The relative scarcity of empirical research on the role of guidelines in formal and informal court organizational arrangements and case processing strategies, as well as ways in which this role is shaped by local political contexts, is a serious gap in this literature (see Goodstein and Kramer 1989). Such research is crucial, however, because court community contexts and norms may strongly shape sentencing outcomes and the potential influence of guidelines. Further, such research could address the issue of the degree to which court community organizational arrangements and sentencing norms are shaped by externally imposed policies.

A number of scholars have speculated about the role that guidelines play in court organization and case processing, and the consequences for defendants. One important potential role of guidelines concerns the balance of sentencing discretion and power between sponsoring agencies. The "hydraulic displacement of discretion" hypothesis is a commonly cited criticism of guidelines and other determinate sentencing reforms. According to this proposition, guidelines place more sentencing discretion in the hands of prosecutors by restricting judicial sentencing discretion (Alschuler 1978; 1988; Lagoy et al. 1979; Tonry and Coffee 1987). Prosecutors translate this discretion into greater power to coerce defendants into accepting guilty plea agreements, which ultimately preserves sentencing disparity in less visible ways (Rathke 1982).

Savelsberg (1992) holds that guidelines, particularly those that allow the least judicial discretion such as Minnesota's or the federal system's guidelines, foreclose the possibility of sentence bargaining in plea negotiations, and thus lead to a reliance on charge bargaining, which masks sentencing disparities (p. 1372): ". . . future research should test the hypothesis that sentencing guidelines increase the power of prosecutors in the negotiations. Since the sentence for a particular offense is clearly defined through the guidelines, negotiation about the sentence is no longer possible. . . . A shift from sentence to charge bargaining must be expected." For Savelsberg, the result is that such guidelines do not reduce unwarranted disparity, but merely shift and hide its sources (p. 1377): "Guidelines do not appear to be the remedy they were intended to be. . . . The visibility of disparities in criminal justice may be reduced as they are shifted from sentencing into other areas such as prosecution. In this case, guidelines would be a very dangerous treatment."

Miethe (1987)[3] uses measures of unwarranted disparity in guilty plea outcomes as a proxy for the hydraulic displacement of sentencing discretion to prosecutors. She finds little evidence of such disparity, and concludes that hydraulic displacement has not occurred under Minnesota's guidelines. Miethe's findings suggest that a hydraulic displacement of discretion to prosecutors, if it in fact occurs, does not necessarily produce unwarranted disparity. However, while Savelsberg (1992) and Miethe (1987) tell us about issues of disparity and the interorganizational distribution and use of sentencing discretion under comparatively restrictive guidelines like the federal systems' and Minnesota's, what about these issues in states with "looser," less restrictive guidelines, such as Pennsylvania, Louisiana, Florida, and several others? This book looks at the Pennsylvania context as an example of sentencing under "looser" guidelines, where the interplay between formally rational guideline sentencing criteria and substantively rational sentencing concerns found in local court communities is particularly salient. This focus requires discussion of some background on Pennsylvania's guidelines, their ideological/philosophical goals and characteristics, and how these compare with other states.

Pennsylvania's Sentencing Guidelines

Pennsylvania's guidelines were developed during roughly the same time as Minnesota's (1978–82), the other state which pioneered sentencing guidelines. The Pennsylvania legislature created the Pennsylvania Commission on Sentencing (PCS) in 1978, and charged it with a broad mandate to develop sentencing guidelines. The PCS then established two principles that frame Pennsylvania's guidelines system. On one hand, the PCS, like the Minnesota sentencing commission,[4] decided to develop prescriptive sentencing standards, rather than the merely descriptive ones found in some states' determinate sentencing systems.[5] In other words, the guidelines were not to establish norms based on the statistical average of past sentencing practices, but were instead to be based on the "informed judgements of those writing the guidelines" (Kramer and Scirica 1986, p. 16). Thus, the PCS did not commit itself to making its sentence recommendations congruent with preguidelines sentences.

While the PCS intended to establish prescriptive sentencing standards, however, the members realized that guidelines are a simplification of a complex decision-making process. Thus, the PCS decided that the guidelines were not to be mandatory sentencing standards, but "benchmarks" for judges' decisions (Kramer and Scirica 1986). The commission took the position that guidelines would not increase fairness in sentencing if judges applied them ritualistically and uncritically. Rather, the guidelines were intended to be applied with due consideration of the characteristics of individual cases: ". . . guidelines should assist—not replace—the court" (Kramer and Scirica 1986, p. 16). Unlike the sentencing commissions of the federal system and Minnesota, the PCS therefore decided against guidelines that greatly restricted judicial sentencing discretion.

The PCS then submitted a set of guidelines to the state legislature in 1981. These were rejected, and the legislature directed the PCS to increase the severity of guideline sentences and to further increase the judicial discretion allowed. The PCS then increased judicial discretion by increasing the upper limit of each guideline sentence range, and increased the severity of minimum sentences recommended for violent offenders. The legislature adopted this second set of guidelines, with relatively minor revisions, in 1982.

Unlike other states' guidelines, Pennsylvania's apply to both felonies and misdemeanors. But Pennsylvania's guidelines do share with almost all other guideline systems the goal of establishing sentencing standards in which the severity of the convicted offense and the offender's criminal history are the major determinants of sentencing decisions (Kramer and Scirica 1986). The guidelines establish sentence ranges for each combination of offense severity/criminal history scores in the form of a sentencing matrix, shown in Appendix A. Pennsylvania's guidelines are also unique in that they establish three sentence ranges: standard, aggravated, and mitigated. The standard ranges are intended to be the most prescriptive norm. As in other guideline states, sentences that are more lenient or more severe than the guideline recommendations are allowed, but the judge must justify any departure with written statements of the reasons for the departure. Further, both the defense attorney and the prosecutor have the right to appeal sentences that depart from guidelines in this way.

Compared to other guidelines systems such as Minnesota's, Washington's, and the federal system's, Pennsylvania's sentence ranges intentionally allow more judicial discretion (Kramer et al. 1989). In part, this is because the Pennsylvania Judicial Code embraces diverse (and potentially contradictory) sentencing philosophies: rehabilitation, incapacitation, deterrence and retribution. Thus, the Pennsylvania guidelines must allow for some flexibility in sentencing purposes to accommodate the state's Judicial Code (see Kramer and Scirica 1986). The amount of judicial sentencing discretion allowed by the guidelines varies with offense severity and prior record, with wider sentence ranges in the higher offense severity/prior record matrix levels and narrower ranges at lower matrix levels (see Appendix A). Pennsylvania's guidelines provide normative boundaries for sentences, yet their greater judicial discretion affords ample potential for disparity (Tonry 1987).

In sum, contemporary public interest in sentencing, the growing trend toward sentencing guidelines, and gaps in sociological research literature all point to the need for research on sentencing outcomes, local court organizational arrangements, and case processing strategies under different kinds of sentencing guideline systems. We have a good deal of research on "tight," restrictive guidelines like Minnesota's, but what about sentencing and local court contexts under "loose," less restrictive guidelines like Pennsylvania's? Further, what about the larger sociological issues involved, such as the role of key social statuses like race and gender in sentencing and case processing, even under normative policies like guidelines that seek to blunt their influence? What about social organizational issues, such as potential tensions between local institutional arenas—with their own normative cultures shaped by locally defined substantive rationality—and externally imposed formally rational normative standards? The next chapter provides a theoretical framework and set of conceptual tools for considering these larger sociological questions in more detail.

2

Court Communities as Social Worlds

This chapter delineates an integrated theoretical framework for studying court contexts, case processing, and sentencing. While my analysis focuses on these issues as they exist under Pennsylvania's guidelines, I argue that the framework can be applied to investigations of courts in a variety of contexts. The court community framework, developed by political scientist James Eisenstein and his associates, provides a conceptual structure focusing on the organizational contexts and processes of criminal courts. A symbolic interactionist approach to analyzing social organization, known as the processual order/social worlds perspective, provides an analytical strategy that is uniquely well-suited for capturing the court community framework's central concepts, and placing them in a more general context of sociological theory.

Processual Order/Social Worlds Theory

The processual order framework is an analytical perspective, based in the assumptions of Pragmatist philosophy (see Strauss 1993, pp. 19–22; Shalin 1986), that is explicitly designed to study social organization and structure without losing sight of the ontological importance of human agency and the interaction process. The framework has its roots in the work of Herbert Blumer (1954; 1962) Everett Hughes (1958), and Tomatsu Shibutani (1962), and was later articulated more explicitly by Anselm Strauss (1978b; 1993). The processual order framework exhibits considerable affinity with other recent social constructionist, open systems theories of social organization, such as Weick's (1974; 1979) "social organizing" framework, Giddens' (1976) "structuration" theory, and recent work on organizational culture (see reviews by Fine 1984; Manning 1992).

A key concept in the processual order approach is that of social worlds. Strauss (1978b) defines social worlds as networks of regular activity and mutual response whose boundaries are set by lines of communication and participation (see also Shibutani 1962). Further, social worlds usually encompass various sub-worlds, which are segmented according to such factors as formal organizational allegiances, professional identities, access to resources and power, or ideology (Strauss 1984). The boundaries of social worlds may be the same as those of formal organizations, or they may encompass a site or network wherein various formal organizations intersect around shared tasks (Strauss 1978b, p. 125; Kling and Gerson 1978).

According to Clarke (1991, p. 140), "Social worlds theory is especially strong in analyzing such situations where there are typically overlapping, cross-cutting, and conflicting worlds and organizations coming together around shared tasks, with strong commitments extending far beyond the confines of the immediate organizational situation." Social worlds theory "aims at capturing, describing, and rendering susceptible to analysis the multiple simultaneous organized actions of individuals, groups of various sorts, and formal organizations" (p. 131).

The processual order framework and its conceptualization of social worlds discourages static depictions of social organization by focusing on participants' activities and interaction strategies—such as negotiation, conflict, manipulation, or cooperation—as units of analysis. The analytical task is to map how these strategies are conditioned by relevant contextual features, and to trace the consequences these strategies may have for arrangements within or outside a social world. Contrary to common misperceptions, the framework does not reject quantification and statistical analysis of organizational outcomes. However, its emphasis on processual issues such as interaction strategies and interlocking contextual relationships does place a high value on qualitative methods (Strauss and Corbin 1990; Fine 1984).

Further, social worlds/processual order theory does not see micro and macro domains of social structure as separated (see Maines and Charlton 1985). Instead, this framework views micro, meso, and macro levels of social organization as inherently linked in that they mutually constitute and affect one another through chains of conditions, activities, and consequences (Hall 1995; Strauss 1993). For example, macro- and meso-level structures and processes present conditions, constraints, and consequences for people's decisions and interactions at the micro level. Activities at the micro level in turn have consequences that maintain, slightly modify, or radically change meso- and macro-level arrangements. Thus, processual order theory focuses on tracing the linkages and interrelations between large-scale structures and processes, institutional arrangements, and face-to-face interaction strategies.

The processual order approach carries with it a theory of action and interaction based in the Pragmatist philosophy of science articulated by Dewey, James, and Mead, and the sociological applications of this philosophy carried out by early Chicago School sociologists such as Robert Park, Thomas and Znaniecki, Herbert Blumer, and Everett Hughes (see Strauss 1993). Processual order theory (an earlier version of which is known as negotiated order theory) emphasizes the empirical investigation of interaction strategies, how these are conditioned by constraints and opportunities presented by larger meso and macro contexts, and the consequences of interaction processes for a social order (Strauss 1993). Various interaction strategies include negotiation, manipulation, coercion, rhetoric and persuasion, or appeals to authority.

Negotiation is a common strategy for arriving at solutions to problematic situations, resolving disputes, and especially for dealing with ambiguity in norms (Strauss 1978). Negotiation exists alongside, and often in conjunction with, other alternatives for action such as unilateral manipulation, coercion, appeals to authority, or persuasion (but see Seckman and Couch 1989).[1] The most basic propositions of processual order theory can be summarized as follows (see Strauss 1993; Fine 1984, pp. 241–43). First, the central assumption underlying processual order theory is that interaction processes and their resulting outcomes, or orders, are crucial to the development, maintenance, and change of institutional organization. A second feature of processual order theory is the proposition that "various interaction processes—negotiation, persuasion, manipulation, education, threat, and actual coercion—will each have different salience, be of greater or less significance for *particular instances of any social order*" (Strauss 1993, p. 250, emphasis in original). For example, Strauss (1978, p. ix) discusses the importance of implicit or explicit negotiation for certain social orders:

> Rules and roles are always breaking down—and when they do not, they do not miraculously remain intact without some effort, including negotiative effort, to maintain them. What we

can assent to is that when individuals or groups or organizations of any size work together 'to get things done' then agreement is required about such matters as what, how, when, where, and how much.

Further, the frequency, intensity, and degree of importance of negotiation and other strategies, as well as their consequences, vary between institutions—and across time within institutions—according to the availability and attractiveness of various alternatives for resolving problematic situations or handling disputes. For example, in some institutions negotiations are infrequent and of little consequence, while coercion, unilateral manipulation, or other strategies are more important (Hall and Spencer-Hall 1982). In other institutions, negotiations are frequent and profoundly affect organizational arrangements, either alongside or in conjunction with other strategies (Strauss et al. 1963). Negotiation and other actions are also enacted on varying levels of scale, such as at the micro level as individual strategies of adjustment (Becker 1964; Thomas 1984), or at macro levels in which representatives negotiate on behalf of organizational or political constituencies (Couch and Weiland 1986; Hall and Spencer-Hall 1982).

Third, and of chief importance for this study, social worlds both provide opportunities and set constraints on various alternative action strategies. Among the properties of social worlds contexts that potentially influence action processes and their outcomes are the following (Strauss 1978, pp. 238; see also Maines and Charlton 1985, p. 285): (1) the relative availability and attractiveness of alternative interaction strategies for participants, such as negotiation, unilateral decision making or manipulation of contingencies, conflict or coercion, coalition formation, appeals to authority, etc.; (2) the definitions, attitudes, perspectives, and ideologies of participants; (3) the biographies and backgrounds of participants (Strauss 1993), including participants' shared pasts (when participants have previously engaged in activities with each other) or common pasts (when participants have previously engaged in similar activities, but not with those with whom they are interacting in the present) (see Katovich and Couch 1992); (4) the balance of resources and power between participants; (5) the respective commitments of parties and their stakes in various outcomes; (6) the visibility of interaction strategies and the accountability of participants to constituencies (Couch and Weiland 1986); (7) the number, complexity, clarity, and novelty of issues in which participants are involved; and (8) the temporality of interaction trajectories; that is, whether they are one-shot, routinized, serial, multiple, or linked to other interaction trajectories.

Processual orders are the outcomes of past interaction processes that have become "sedimented" into institutional structure (Busch 1982; Berger and Luckmann 1967). The role of negotiation in the development, maintenance, and change of informal organizational norms provides one example. Informal norms and arrangements often emerge as negotiated solutions to problems that are not covered by existing formal or informal rules, to ambiguous or conflicting goals, or to conflicts over resources (e.g., Hughes 1958; Becker 1964; Thomas 1984; Seckman and Couch 1989). These solutions persist until new problematic situations render them inadequate. Then, new negotiation processes occur through which informal arrangements are adapted in an attempt to resolve the new problems. In other words, negotiation processes can be seen as a collective aspect of Becker's (1964) concept of situational adjustment, and the resulting orders are cemented and maintained through various types of commitments (Becker 1960; Gerson 1976). Not all institutional orders, however, are negotiated orders. Some are based in other strategies, such as unilateral decision making and manipulation or conflict and coercion. The central point is that social orders of any type, at any scale, are processual in that they owe their existence to ongoing processes of interaction.

Court Communities as Social Worlds

Although Eisenstein and associates' conceptualization of courts as communities has never been integrated with the processual order perspective, the two frameworks are remarkably compatible. What processual order theory offers is a generic conceptualization of organizational systems as social worlds that places the substantive concerns of the court community approach at a higher level of abstraction. Strauss (1993, pp. 67–68) explains the utility of combining and applying this generic interactionist framework with empirically derived concepts and propositions from specific substantive areas:

> . . . the principal function of the interactionist theory of action is not at all to supply or directly develop concepts that will constitute the evolving substantive theory about the

particular phenomenon under study. Rather, what the theory is capable of doing is so thoroughly to inform sociological perspectives that a researcher automatically thinks interactionally, temporally, processually, and structurally . . . One of the striking paradoxes of this theory of action is that just because it has been expressed explicitly and systematically [here], it can function implicitly during the course of research itself rendering systematic the researcher's ordering of explanations.

Thus, the social worlds/processual order approach provides a broader set of assumptions and concepts that encompass the substantive concepts and propositions of the court community framework. More importantly, it provides an analytical strategy that explicitly highlights features of interaction processes and contexts that are implied in the court community framework. The social worlds approach conceptualizes interrelationships between court community contexts and interaction processes at a higher theoretical level of abstraction.

The organizational characteristics of court communities make them ideally suited for the application of a social worlds perspective. For example, court actors are enmeshed in complex webs of interdependence and influence processes with each other, with political constituencies, and sometimes with news media (Levin 1977; Hagan et al. 1979; Altheide 1992). Relatedly, trial courts do not constitute a unitary organization with a single set of policies, leadership structures, or interests. Rather, trial courts are the site where distinct organizations intersect and their representatives interact around the central task of processing cases. While the major players in the court's activities are usually judges, prosecutors, and public defenders, other participants may include private attorneys, probation officers, police, administrative personnel, and news media. Thus, the boundaries of court communities are not established by formal organizational structures, but by lines of communication, participation, and influence in case processing.

As units of analysis, court communities can therefore be conceptualized as social worlds of action and communication lodged within a context of local political arrangements and statewide legal structures. Sponsoring agencies— or organizations (e.g., judges' bench, district attorney's office, public defender's office) that "sponsor" and to some degree hold accountable key courtroom workgroup participants—can be seen as segmented subworlds within the larger court community, and these sponsoring agencies and their workgroup representatives engage in action strategies of cooperation, conflict and coercion, negotiation, coalition formation, or unilateral decision making (see Eisenstein and Jacob 1977, p. 30). Though couched in generic terms, Strauss's (1978b, pp. 124–25) description of social worlds illustrates many of the characteristics of court community organizational arrangements and case-processing activities: "Within each social world, various issues are debated, negotiated, fought out, forced, and manipulated by representatives of the implicated subworlds...Some and probably most organizations can be viewed as arenas wherein members of various subworlds engage in various strategies, stake different claims, seek differential ends, engage in contests, and make or break alliances in order to do the things they wish to do."

The activities of court community members are largely structured according to formal and informal norms of their sponsoring agencies and the larger court community. Among the most important of these are informal "going rates" that surround case processing (Eisenstein and Jacob 1977). The concept of going rates expands upon Sudnow's (1965) notion of "normal crimes" and their routinized treatment by police, prosecutors, defense attorneys, and judges. Going rates are rules of thumb as to the standard charges, implicit or explicit guilty plea concessions, and sentencing outcomes flowing from routine offenses and circumstances. These going rates represent outcomes of past interaction strategies for resolving problematic cases that have been "sedimented" into informal normative structure:

> The courtroom workgroups, through their ongoing interactions among major participants, develop norms and expectations about sentences that constrain all the participants in any individual case. No defendant is sentenced out of context; the sentence he receives becomes part of the courtroom's norm. Workgroup members continuously compared defendants and cases with others that had been processed in that courtroom. Thus, the [informal] social organization in which courtroom participants operated limited the scope for arbitrary action as much as the law itself (Eisenstein and Jacob 1977, p. 286).

The norms of the court community are developed through, and in turn influence actors' choices between, the three primary case-processing strategies of workgroup members: unilateral decisions, negotiations, and adversarial proceedings (Eisenstein and Jacob 1977). The development and maintenance of local going rates as a processual order can be illustrated by examining the role of going rates in different ideal-typical modes of case processing, and the action strategies associated with them.

In what Nardulli et al. (1988) call "consensus mode" guilty pleas, workgroup members apply existing going rates to facilitate decision making and reduce uncertainty with relative ease in routine cases. Conforming to the informal norms of going rates in consensus mode plea processes reduces uncertainty and allows workgroup members to make unilateral decisions and arrive at implicit or brief negotiated agreements. On the other hand, "concessions mode" pleas involve somewhat more problematic cases where going rates are less readily applied. Negotiation between counsel, possibly with informal mediation by judges, is the main strategy here. These cases are typically associated with more intense negotiation around the exchange of prosecutorial concessions for a guilty plea. Through these negotiations, over time, new going rates can be developed, communicated through court community grapevines, and used in similar cases in the future. In very problematic cases where going rates do not seem to apply, and where plea negotiations fail, adversarial proceedings result, involving "legitimate" trial cases recognized as such by all concerned.[2] The outcomes of such adversarial proceedings can also inform future going rates. Thus, the less going rates fit a particular problematic case because of unusual features of the offense, circumstances, or defendant-related factors, the more involved and intense negotiations will become, and the more likely they will result in adversarial proceedings (Emerson 1983, pp. 439–40; Farrell and Holmes 1991, pp. 536–37).

However, the strength of court community going rates, as well as the prevalence of negotiation as a specific case-processing strategy, varies between local jurisdictions (Eisenstein and Jacob 1977). A court community's case-processing norms may not be developed primarily through ongoing negotiation processes, but may be based in other strategies such as unilateral manipulation or adversarial tactics. The strength of going rates and the dominance of one or another type of case-processing strategy depend on the court community's social world contextual features listed earlier, such as the following: (1) the availability and attractiveness of various case-processing strategies, such as unilateral decision-making/manipulation, negotiation, adversarial strategies, or appeals to higher authority); (2) the familiarity and stability of court community membership, which in turn fosters robust shared pasts (Ulmer 1995); (3) the attitudes and ideologies of various members—especially regarding issues of crime and sentencing goals; (4) the scope of plea agendas (the factors that can be manipulated or negotiated in the guilty plea process); (5) the distribution of resources and power, including the distribution of case processing and sentencing discretion (as discussed in the previous chapter); (6) the strength and types of commitments of court community members, and the incentive structures conditioned by them; (7) the visibility of case processing activities and the degree to which workgroup members are accountable to their sponsoring agencies; and (8) case processing technologies and caseload characteristics, such as docket scheduling and the routine or problematic nature of specific cases.

The interpenetration of court community contextual features and case-processing strategies, of course, may condition the degree of unwarranted sentencing disparity, and the bases for such disparity (e.g., race, gender, age, or mode of conviction). This implies that the degree of sentencing disparity and its bases may be influenced by the organizational and political features of particular court communities. In other words, the degree and sources of extra-legal sentencing differences may vary between court communities according to these contextual features.

Central Research Questions

The goals of this study are to investigate the following court community features as they exist in the context of a sentencing guidelines system with characteristics like Pennsylvania's: (1) sentencing outcomes—especially in terms of extra-legal disparity; (2) the role of organizational and political arrangements in court community contexts, including the balance of discretion and power between sponsoring agencies; and (3) case processing and sentencing practices and norms, and the dominant interactional strategies in which these are based (e.g., unilateral decisions, negotiations, adversarial strategies, and appeals to higher authority).

Case Processing and Sentencing Outcomes

Among the most basic functions of trial courts is that of deciding the punishment of convicted defendants; this is the "bottom line of what criminal courts do" (Nardulli et al. 1988, p. 383). Therefore, I start with a statewide examination of sentencing outcomes. This analysis focuses particularly on assessing the relative importance of legally prescribed, case-processing, defendant-related, and county contextual factors. The main goal of this portion of the analysis is to identify the extent and bases of extra-legal differences in sentencing under the guidelines.

One of the few consistent findings in the sentencing literature is that legally prescribed factors, such as offense type, severity, and criminal history are the primary determinants of sentencing decisions (even when these are inadequately measured). I expect these data to show this pattern also, especially since guidelines set explicit norms for the use of such factors in sentencing decisions and foster unprecedented collection and explicit calculation of information on these factors by courts (Steffensmeier et al. 1993). However, since Pennsylvania's guidelines also allow courts more discretion in sentencing (Kramer and Scirica 1986; Tonry 1987), it is not unrealistic to also suspect that sentencing outcomes will vary significantly according to extra-legal factors, such as race, mode of conviction, gender, and age. In other words, I expect legally prescribed factors to be the strongest influences on sentencing under the guidelines, but that extra-legal factors will also condition important differences. Further, there is reason to suspect that legally prescribed and extra-legal factors will interact (see Miethe and Moore 1988; Spohn 1990). For example, the influence of mode of conviction, race, or gender on sentencing outcomes may vary according to offense type, severity, or criminal history.

As political and social aggregates, Pennsylvania's sixty-seven counties are very diverse in their contextual characteristics, and these in turn may affect local sentencing patterns (Nelson 1992). For example, urbanization and a local population's racial mix are important factors that may affect sentencing (see Peterson and Hagan 1984; Myers 1987; Bridges and Crutchfield 1988). Another contextual factor that may affect local sentencing is the percentage of a county's population who are registered Republicans which could signify more conservative "law and order" attitudes among a county's electorate (Steffensmeier 1976; Eisenstein et al. 1988). Finally, the counties vary markedly in terms of the proportion of the population in younger "crime prone" age groups, and this could affect sentencing practices (Steffensmeier and Allan 1991). My analyses will therefore include the following county-level contextual variables,[3] which are taken from the 1980 and 1990 U.S. Census and 1985 and 1991 Statistical Abstracts for Pennsylvania: percent of county population residing in urban areas, percent of county population comprised of blacks, percent of county population aged 15–19, and percent of county voters registered as Republicans. Further, the role of guidelines in sentencing outcomes and case processing may vary markedly according to the factors associated with court size, as shown in the few existing analyses that address such issues (Lubitz and Kempinen 1987; Miethe 1987). Court size will therefore be included in the models as well.

This study also analyzes three focus counties and presents statistical and ethnographic data on each. Many features of trial courts' negotiation contexts (i.e., workgroup stability and familiarity, diversity of criminal dockets, balance of power and resources among sponsoring agencies, local legal culture, etc.) may be associated with court community size (Eisenstein et al. 1988, ch. 10). Thus, the analysis will focus on one large metropolitan county, one suburban county, and one rural county to enable contrasts between court communities of different sizes and contextual features. To ensure anonymity, these counties will be known as "Metro County" (large urban), "Rich County" (medium-sized suburban), and "Southwest County" (small rural).

Organizational and Political Contexts

The statistical analyses provide a picture of the sentencing and case processing *outcomes* under guidelines both statewide and in the three focus counties. The analyses of the ethnographic data, however, provide a better picture of court community political contexts, organizational arrangements, norms, and interaction *processes* that lie behind the statistical findings. These ethnographic data will enable an investigation and comparison of several interrelated issues. First, the analysis will focus on the nature of the counties' political contexts and organizational arrangements, and how these in turn color the ways in which guidelines are viewed, used, manipulated, or perhaps circumvented. Second, the analysis will examine the role, if any, that guidelines play in sponsoring agencies' organization and agencies' power relations.

Relatedly, the analysis examines the distribution and use of sentencing discretion between sponsoring agencies under guidelines. While the well-known "hydraulic displacement of discretion" proposition discussed in the previous chapter is not incompatible with the conceptualization of court communities as social worlds, it may present an incomplete picture of the role of guidelines in the organizational context of court communities. The hydraulic displacement proposition emphasizes a general tendency for guidelines to restrict judicial sentencing discretion and to shift this discretion to prosecutors. As a result, prosecutors would enjoy greater ability to coerce defendants into accepting plea agreements. This argument especially emphasizes the use of charge bargaining under guidelines; by reducing the uncertainty of sentencing outcomes attached to given charges, guidelines are said to enhance prosecutors' ability to induce defendants to plead guilty to reduced charges that carry lighter sentences (Savelsberg 1992). This argument implies that once a charge is decided upon, guidelines allow little discretion regarding the sentence to be given by the judge.

Proponents of the hydraulic displacement proposition recognize, however, that this role of guidelines in court contexts may vary across jurisdictions and types of guideline systems. Therefore, an investigation of variation in sponsoring agency relations and the distribution of sentencing discretion between local contexts, in a type of guideline system not previously studied (i.e., one that is comparatively "loose" and driven by multiple sentencing goals), would constitute a significant contribution. The view of court communities as social worlds with distinct processual orders implies that the role of guidelines in court community power relations will vary between local contexts. Thus, the degree of discretion wielded by any actor or sponsoring agency is dynamic and contingent on the nature of case situations and local contexts.

Therefore, the role of guidelines in court community power relations may vary depending on the formal and informal organization of case processing, the strength of local sentencing norms or "going rates," and the ways in which each sponsoring agency (not just prosecutors) is able to use the guidelines to their advantage (see Eisenstein et al. 1988, Ch. 10).[4] Further, sentencing disparity may stem from a variety of sources that may or may not be related to guidelines.

Conceptualizing courts as communities and social worlds may present a more complete picture of the role of guidelines in court organizational contexts, particularly in power relations between sponsoring agencies. For example, guidelines may benefit prosecutors' charge bargaining leverage and thus sentencing influence, but only where local contexts provide the means, motives, and opportunities for guidelines to be used in this way. In other contexts, guidelines may constrain prosecutors and benefit other sponsoring agencies (Steury 1987). Such variation, in fact, is just what Eisenstein et al. (1988, pp. 298-99) imply regarding the role of any externally imposed reforms of courts and their sentencing practices.

Guidelines, Processual Ordering, and Case Processing Strategies

The final analytical task is to investigate the interrelationships between guidelines, court communities' processual orders, workgroup members' case processing strategies, and sources of unwarranted sentencing disparity. In other words, how are sentencing guidelines related to the processual orders of informal case processing and sentencing norms, or "going rates" developed and used by courtroom workgroups? What is the role of guideline factors—such as prior record, offense severity, aggravated/mitigated sentence options, or departures from guideline recommendations—in plea agendas, and how are such factors manipulated, negotiated, or fought over in different case processing strategies? How do guidelines influence charge or sentence negotiation strategies? Most importantly, how do differences in court community negotiation contexts condition differences in actors' case processing strategies and the roles that guidelines factors play in them?

Sentencing guidelines provide uniform normative boundaries for sentences—boundaries set by factors that the state defines as legitimate through the guidelines' enabling legislation (offense severity and prior convictions, for example). In these terms, guidelines represent a policy that attempts to impose a system of uniform norms, albeit one that allows discretion in their application, on local court communities. However, local courts have their own formal and informal normative orders developed through ongoing processes of negotiation, unilateral decision making and manipulation, adversarial procedures, or other action strategies. Of course, the strength, content, and sources of these orders vary between court communities. A key task, then, is to analyze the relationship between the externally imposed guidelines norms and local informal norms (going rates), and how this relationship varies between different court community contexts.

I propose that court communities with greater familiarity and stability—those where actors have more extensive shared pasts (Katovich and Couch 1992)—will exhibit stronger local going rates and thus less reliance on guidelines as a source of sentencing norms (for a fuller treatment of the role of members' social pasts in court communities, see Ulmer 1995). In these court communities, informal going rates—which are grounded in the context of local politics, sponsoring agency relations, and webs of commitment between actors—would supersede guideline norms. This would be especially true if the court community is dominated by a powerful sponsoring agency or political organization that has important stakes in maintaining local norms. In fact, the domination of one sponsoring agency can produce strong informal case processing and sentencing norms even in the absence of workgroup stability and familiarity (Flemming et al. 1993). Guidelines would thus be used or manipulated in ways that fit with the local context and its dominant norms, and these norms would override guidelines when they came into conflict.

By contrast, court communities characterized by less extensive shared pasts among workgroups and less strong going rates traditions will exhibit greater reliance on guideline sentencing standards. In such court communities, guidelines would provide a ready-made system of going rates, reducing uncertainty for counsel in predicting judges' sentences, facilitating unilateral decisions, and providing explicit tools for plea negotiating agendas. In time, these types of court communities may even develop an order that revolves around the guidelines and their uses in case processing. Such a situation would be even more likely under the following contextual conditions: (1) when the dominant agency or organization in a court community views the guidelines as serving—or at least not threatening—their collective interests; (2) when there is no sponsoring agency or political organization that clearly dominates a court community; or (3) when caseloads are heavy and guidelines are seen as a tool for facilitating quicker decision making and faster disposition of cases (see Meeker and Pontell 1985, pp. 138–40).

3

Data and Analytical Strategy

A fully adequate investigation of the role of sentencing guidelines in the organization, case-processing activities, and sentencing outcomes of court communities requires both statistical and ethnographic data (see Goodstein and Kramer 1989; Farrell and Holmes 1992; Maynard 1984). Indeed, triangulation of research methods increases confidence in research findings in any social science inquiry (Glaser and Strauss 1967; Denzin 1989).

When social scientists combine qualitative and quantitative data, they most often use qualitative data such as open-ended interviews and field observations to develop quantitative measures that are supposedly more "scientific" or "rigorous," such as questionnaires or quantified observational data (see Maines 1993). My strategy here is exactly the opposite—I started with quantitative data on sentencing, which was then used to sensitize the collection and analysis of qualitative data on court community social worlds and interaction processes that produce the statistical outcomes. In using quantitative data on outcomes to sensitize a qualitative investigation of contexts and processes, this study follows the kind of "non-mechanistic determinism" and logic of causality advocated by Strauss's (1993, p. 247) application of Pragmatist epistemological assumptions (see also Shalin 1986). Thus, the methodological logic of this book rests on a symbolic interactionist premise that statistical data are useful for analyzing the outcomes of organizational and interactional processes, while ethnographic data are better suited for analyses of the processes themselves, and of the contextual influence of social world conditions on those processes (Blumer 1969). In other words, this study "works backwards" from general patterns in sentencing outcomes to the contexts and processes of interaction by which these outcomes are produced. Carl Taylor (1947, p. 7) summarized the value of methodological strategies that combine quantitative data on outcomes and qualitative data on processes: "[Qualitative] Field studies . . . place flesh, blood, and nervous system on the skeleton of statistical information. Everything they reveal adds to and none of it subtracts from the quantitative information. Furthermore . . . the quantitative analyses reveal certain contours of behavior which help to focus qualitative observations." Therefore, to address the research questions outlined in the previous chapter, this book utilizes two sources of data, both of them indispensable to its goals.

Statistical Data

First, I use statistical data collected by the Pennsylvania Commission on Sentencing (PCS) to investigate the sentencing consequences of legally prescribed, case-processing, and defendant-related variables. The Pennsylvania Commission on Sentencing annually compiles detailed and unusually complete and "clean" data for each Pennsylvania county on defendant characteristics, sentences, and case-processing outcomes following conviction.[1] The PCS sentencing data is supplemented by data on county demographic characteristics. These data will be the basis for this study's statistical analyses.

Pennsylvania Courts of Common Pleas (trial courts) are required to report information on every sentence to the PCS (see 42 Pa.C.S. 2153 [a][14][ii]). The PCS, therefore, maintains data on nearly all sentences given in Pennsylvania from 1982 to the present. The statewide analyses will use PCS data for 1985–91, with 1988 omitted because of data reporting problems.[2] Very few other studies in the sentencing literature use data as current and timely as those used here.

Table 3.1 lists the legally prescribed, case-processing, defendant-related, jurisdictional, and sentencing-outcome variables used throughout the statistical analyses. The legally prescribed variables include unusually good measures of the two factors that are supposed to be the primary determinants of sentencing decisions under guidelines: offense severity and prior record. Offense severity is the guidelines' scale developed by the PCS, ranging from 1 indicating the least serious offenses (e.g, retail theft misdemeanor) to 10 indicating the most serious offenses (e.g., third-degree murder). The analyses will also control for offense type. Fifteen dummy variables will be used to indicate types of offenses. By measuring both offense severity and offense types, these analyses will treat offense variables in a much more rigorous way than do most other studies. The measures of offense severity and offense type are not redundant, since the severity measure can vary within the offense types[3] in these data, and since the failure to adequately capture within-offense variation in severity is a frequent problem in prior sentencing research (Stolzenberg and D'Alessio 1994, p. 308).

Prior record is measured by the guidelines' weighted seven-point scale capturing both the number and severity of an offender's past convictions. All prior felonies, as well as prior misdemeanors punishable by at least one year's incarceration, are included. Any and all prior misdemeanors can total no more than two points on the prior record score,[4] while prior felonies count one to three points each, depending on their severity. These measures of offense type/severity and prior record are more rigorous than those employed in the large majority of other sentencing studies (see reviews by Hagan and Bumiller 1983; Kleck 1985; Kramer and Steffensmeier 1993).

The case processing variables used in the analysis include mode of conviction, number of conviction charges, and court workload. Mode of conviction is measured by dummy variables indicating other guilty pleas (i.e., no contest pleas, "open" guilty pleas without a plea agreement), negotiated pleas (negotiated plea agreements with concessions such as charge reductions/drops or sentencing agreements), bench trials (trial by judge), and jury trials. Court caseload is calculated by dividing a court's average annual number of cases by its number of criminal court judges.

The defendant-related variables (age, race, and gender) are fairly straightforward. Defendant's race is a dummy variable coded zero for nonblacks and one for blacks. While it would be ideal to disaggregate Hispanic offenders in the analyses, very few of the county courts in the analyses include enough cases with Hispanic offenders to provide meaningful comparisons. Rather than create a combined black/Hispanic category, I include Hispanic defendants with nonblack defendants because their descriptive statistics on the independent and dependent variables are much more similar to nonblacks than to blacks. Defendant age is measured in years, and the analyses exclude juvenile offenders (those less than eighteen years old) in order to avoid confounding factors that influence juvenile sentencing with those that influence adult sentencing (see Frazier et al. 1992).

The county-level variables (discussed in the previous chapter) reflect measures found to influence sentencing in other studies

TABLE 3.1

Independent and Dependent Variables Used in Statistical Models

Independent Variables	Coding
Legally Prescribed	
Offense severity	1–10 scale (1=least severe)
Offense type	15 dummy variable for offense categories
Prior record score	0–6 scale of prior convictions weighted by severity
Case Processing	
Mode of conviction	
type of guilty plea	0 = other guilty plea (reference category); 1 = negotiated plea
type of trial	1 = bench trial; 1 = jury trial
Number of conviction charges	0 = single charge; 1 = multiple charges
Court caseload	mean annual number of sentencing cases / number of judges
Defendant Characteristics	
race	0 = nonblack; 1 = black
gender	0 = male; 1 = female
age	years (includes only defendants 18 or over)
Court Context and County Demographic Variables	
court size	0 = small courts (reference category); 1 = medium courts; 1 = large courts
% urban	percent of county population residing in urban areas (U.S. Census)
% black	percent of county population made up of blacks (U.S. Census)
% Republican	percent of county voters registered as Republicans (Statistical Abstracts of Pennsylvania)
Index crime rate	county Uniform Crime Report Index crime rate
Incarceration	0 = nonincarceration; 1 = county jail or state prison
State imprisonment	0 = nonincarceration and county jail; 1 = state prison
Dispositional departure below guidelines	0 = nondeparture; 1 = departure (includes only guideline cells that recommend incarceration)

TABLE 3.1 (continued)

Independent Variables	Coding
Incarceration length	minimum length in months
Durational departures from guidelines	
departure below	guideline mimimum— actual minimum/ guideline minimum (includes only guideline cells where departure below is possible)
departure above	actual minimum—guideline midpoint/ guideline midpoint

TABLE 3.2

Number of Pennsylvania Counties by Court Community Size

	Number of Courts	Proportion of Total Cases
Small Courts (7 judges or fewer)	51	27%
Medium Courts (8–15 judges)	14	39%
Large Courts (16 judges or more)	2	34%

(see Myers and Talarico 1987; Nardulli et al. 1988). Table 3.1 lists these variables and the sources from which they were collected.

Sentencing cases for 1985–87 are matched with the 1980s county-level variables, while cases for 1989–91 are matched with 1990s county variables.

Also included in the county-level factors are dummy variables indicating court community size. The county courts and their size classifications are listed in Table 3.2.

I base these size categorizations on the number of judges in each county's court and the number of cases accounted for by each size category. In deciding where to draw the divisions between each size category, I relied on frequency distributions of sentencing cases by number of judges per county. Roughly 27 percent of cases were sentenced in courts with seven or fewer judges, 39 percent of the cases were from courts with between eight and fifteen judges, and 34 percent of the cases were from courts with sixteen or more judges. To obtain roughly proportionate numbers of sentencing cases per size category, I therefore categorized courts with seven or fewer judges as small, courts with between eight and fifteen judges as medium, and courts with over sixteen judges as large. In all, fifty-one county courts are in the small category, fourteen in the medium category, and two in the large category.

The analyses will focus on three dispositional sentencing outcomes (whether the defendant is incarcerated, and in what type of facility) and three durational outcomes, or those involving the length of sentences. Dispositional outcomes include overall incarceration decisions (nonincarceration versus county jail or state prison), state imprisonment decisions (non-incarceration and county jail vs. state prison), and dispositional departures below guidelines. Durational sentencing outcomes include incarceration length, and durational departures above and below the guidelines. In addition to including state prison sentences in the overall incarceration measure, I also analyze state prison decisions separately for two reasons. First, state prison sentences are popularly seen as *qualitatively* more severe than jail sentences, since state imprisonment is potentially more stigmatizing, and since inmates face greater risks of violence and sexual victimization at the hands of other inmates and are more likely to be more isolated from their communities, families, and friends (see Schmid and Jones 1990). Second, in Pennsylvania, state prison inmates cannot be paroled before they serve their minimum sentences (i.e., no "good time"), and are released at the discretion of the state parole board. In fact state inmates serve on average 133 percent of their minimum sentences (Steffensmeier 1992). On the other hand, county jail inmates are released at the discretion of local courts, and many counties (including Metro and Rich, discussed later) have programs of early release based on "good time." Thus, state prison sentences are potentially *quantitatively* more severe, since they usually represent greater amounts of incarceration time actually served.

The dispositional and durational guideline departure variables require some explanation. A dispositional departure from the guidelines occurs when a defendant receives a nonincarceration sentence when the guidelines call for a period of incarceration. Thus, dispositional departure is a special type of departure below the guidelines, a more lenient sentence than called for by guideline ranges. Unlike other guideline systems, such as those in Minnesota, in Pennsylvania only dispositional departures below guidelines are possible, since the guidelines always allow courts the option of incarceration (see Appendix A). Dispositional departure is measured as follows:

1) Guidelines cells that recommend a non-incarceration minimum sentence are omitted since dispositional departures are impossible in these cells, and only cells that recommend an incarceration minimum are retained. The four guideline cells below offense severity level 3 that recommend short periods of incarceration are also omitted due to insufficient numbers of dispositional departure cases per offense type.

2) A dichotomous variable is coded 0 if an incarceration sentence is given, and 1 if a non-incarceration sentence is given.

In other words, a dispositional departure is measured as any non-incarceration sentence given in the guideline cells that recommend a minimum period of incarceration.

Durational departures, or incarceration sentences given by a court that deviate from the guidelines' recommended lengths, may be either above or below the guidelines. Durational departure below refers to the proportion by which the minimum period of incarceration given a defendant deviates from the guideline standard range minimum. The minimum of the guideline range is used for two reasons. First, it is most representative of the prescriptive sentence intended as a standard norm under the guidelines (see Kramer and Scirica 1986). Second, if some other point of the guideline range is used—the midpoint for example—sentences that are congruent with the recommended minimum would be inappropriately classified as departures. Thus, the standard range minimum seems to be the most representative figure of guidelines recommendations, and the best baseline against which to measure variation in durational departures below guidelines.

I measure durational departure below by selecting only those cases where a departure below is possible (as with dispositional departure), and selecting only cases where the minimum given is below the guideline range minimum. I then subtract the actual minimum sentence from the applicable guideline range minimum, and then divide by the range's minimum (guideline minimum – actual minimum/guideline minimum). This ratio (ranging from zero to one[5]) thus measures the proportion of the recommended minimum sentence by which the actual minimum sentence falls below the guideline standard.

Departures above guidelines, however, present a more complicated measurement problem. The upper limits of Pennsylvania's guideline ranges do not actually prescribe an absolute maximum sentence length, but only establish the maximum allowed length for a sentence minimum. In other words, the top boundary of the guideline range represents a "maximum minimum." By Pennsylvania law, minimum sentences cannot exceed one-half the statutory maximum for the offense. At the upper levels of the guideline matrix, the top of the ranges are at or close to this legal limit. Clearly, the standard range minimum is not an appropriate baseline for departures above, because many sentences that are above the minimum but still within the standard range would be inappropriately considered departures. However, because so few sentences exceed the standard range maximum statewide (since these are typically at or close to statutory limits), using this maximum as a baseline would not only include too few cases for a least-squares regression analysis, but would also be substantively meaningless. To partially solve these problems, I use the standard range midpoint as a baseline against which to measure departures above guidelines. This approach does inappropriately classify as departures some sentences that fall within the standard ranges but above the midpoint. However, it retains enough cases for meaningful analyses and establishes a general baseline against which to measure sentences that are more severe than a standard guidelines-based average.

Departures above guidelines are therefore measured as follows: I subtract the guideline range midpoint from the actual minimum given, and divide by the guideline range midpoint (actual minimum – guideline range midpoint / guideline range midpoint). This ratio results in positive values greater than zero, and represents the proportion of the guideline range midpoint by which a minimum sentence departs above that midpoint. In contrast to dispositional and durational departures below guidelines, departures above are possible in any guideline cell (see Appendix A). I therefore include all guideline cells in the analyses of durational departure above.

In the statewide and focus counties' statistical analyses, I model the sentencing outcome variables according to the predictors described above. The dispositional, dichotomous sentencing variables (overall incarceration decisions, state imprisonment decisions, and dispositional departures) will be modeled using logistic regression, while the continuous sentencing variables (incarceration length and durational departures) will be modeled using ordinary least-squares techniques. Although other techniques for modeling dichotomous dependent variables exist (e.g., least-squares linear probability models; discriminant function analysis), logistic regression is widely held to be the most appropriate procedure (Hanushek and Jackson 1977; Aldrich and Nelson 1984; Agresti and Finlay 1986). While results from least-squares regression with dichotomous dependent variables may be more easily interpreted, they tend to seriously underestimate individual coefficients and produce inaccurate standard errors, particularly when a dependent variable has a skewed distribution (Aldrich and Nelson 1984). Logistic regression is also more easily performed and interpreted than discriminant function analysis.

Some studies of sentencing decisions (e.g., Berk 1983; Peterson and Hagan 1984; Albonetti 1991) have suggested statistical corrections for sample selection bias when modeling incarceration lengths, since length decisions follow the initial decision to incarcerate.[6] I therefore include a correction for selection bias in the models of incarceration length, using the two-stage estimation procedure recommended by Berk (1983).

Statistical Data Limitations

An ideal statistical analysis of case processing and sentencing outcomes would include data on original charges (i.e., charges at arrest or arraignment stages) as well as conviction charges, plus other variables found to be important influences on sentencing in some prior studies. I had originally planned to combine the PCS sentencing data with an additional data set that would have provided the following variables not contained in the PCS data: (1) original offense charges, (2) bail and pretrial release information, and (3) type of defense counsel. Unfortunately however, these data exhibited many unresolvable problems that rendered them virtually useless for the purposes of this study.[7]

However, while not ideal, less is lost by not including the original charge data than would appear. First, as useful as it may be to analyze changes in charges, such an analysis would still be unable to indicate anything about other crucial aspects of the guilty plea process[8] (see Nardulli et al. 1988, p. 238). As noted above, this type of data says nothing of the circumstances or processes that produce changes in charges from arrest to conviction. Further, these data do not capture possible guilty plea concessions that do not involve charge reductions, but may be quite important under sentencing guidelines, such as explicit or implicit sentencing agreements, manipulation of guideline enhancements, or even negotiation over prior record scores (see Ulmer and Kramer 1996; Goodstein and Kramer 1989; Tonry and Coffee 1987; Miethe 1987).

Second, many if not most studies in the sentencing literature do not include data on original charges (e.g., Hagan et al. 1979; Uhlman and Walker 1980; Thomson and Zingraff 1981; Spohn et al. 1982; Zatz 1984; 1985; Moore and Miethe 1986; Myers 1987; Myers and Talarico 1987; Griswold 1987; Albonetti 1987; 1991; Spohn 1990; Bickle and Peterson 1991). On the other hand, studies such as Eisenstein and Jacob (1977), Bernstein et al. (1977a), and LaFree (1985) use only original charges in their analyses, rather than final conviction charges. While I would hardly argue that past limitations justify present ones, some evidence indicates that while the inability of this study to include original charge data is a flaw, it is not a crippling one. The handful of studies that do use data on both original and final charges generally show that final conviction charges are considerably more important for sentencing outcomes than original charges (e.g., Miethe and Moore 1985; 1986). In fact, Nardulli et al. (1988, pp. 238–40) and Miethe (1987) find that charge manipulations themselves have very little real effect on sentencing outcomes compared to other types of plea negotiation concessions (this, however, varied between counties). In any case, the PCS data include information on type of guilty plea (negotiated versus other), and this will provide at least a general indicator of guilty plea cases that entail plea concessions of various kinds.

In sum, reliance on the PCS data alone is not ideal, but it appears to be the most realistic strategy given constraints in obtaining other usable data. However, this reliance on the PCS data set for the statistical analyses makes triangulating it with the focus counties' ethnographic data all the more necessary.

Ethnographic Data

Analyses of court community contexts and case processing strategies under sentencing guidelines will rely on ethnographic data from the three focus counties. In other words, these data will be used to investigate the processual and contextual aspects of this study's central research questions. I was part of a four-person research team who collected these data from the spring of 1991 to the summer of 1993 in connection with a larger project sponsored by the Pennsylvania Commission on Sentencing. These data consist of semistructured interviews with judges, district attorneys, private/public defenders, and probation officers, along with field notes from observations of courtroom activities. The number of interviews per county is as follows:

1. *Metro County.* seven judges, seven prosecutors, seven public defenders, four private attorneys, and four probation officers (twenty-nine total interviews).

2. *Rich County.* six judges, five prosecutors, four defense attorneys (two of whom worked as public defenders as well as private attorneys), and four probation officers (nineteen total interviews).

3. *Southwest County.* three judges, two prosecutors, two public/private defense attorneys, four probation officers, and the court administrator in charge of processing the sentencing guidelines (twelve total interviews).

The interviews, which lasted from one-and-a-half to two hours, were tape-recorded[9] and transcribed in full. Although these interviews emphasized the role of sentencing guidelines in case processing, they also included focused and detailed discussions of general case processing organization and workgroup activities, relations between sponsoring agencies, and other relevant topics. While the initial interviews and observations in Rich County were very complete, I collected additional interviews in Metro and Southwest Counties to fill in gaps uncovered in analyzing these counties' initial interviews. Some of these additional interviews were follow-ups with individuals initially interviewed, while other individuals were interviewed for the first time. The specific focus and content of later interviews differed according to the strengths and weaknesses of the first wave of data for the two counties. Appendix B shows the central topics and concepts around which portions of the interviews relevant to this study focused, and examples of questions by which they were investigated in both rounds of interviews.

Analyses of the ethnographic materials follows the "constant comparative method" and coding procedures developed by Glaser and Strauss (1967), Strauss (1987), and Strauss and Corbin (1990) for the grounded theory approach to research. My ethnographic data were collected in a more structured, less open-ended, and less inductive way than is recommended for a true grounded theory study. As mentioned, the content of the interviews focused on fairly specific questions aimed at gathering information on key concepts of predetermined interest. Nevertheless, my analysis of these data followed the coding techniques appropriate for grounded theory, since these are suitable for any qualitative data (Strauss and Corbin 1990). While these coding and analysis procedures are presented here as discrete steps, they were (and should be) interrelated and continuous processes that were performed throughout the analysis (Strauss 1987).

"Open coding" focused on identifying interview and observation materials that represent core categories of analytical interest, such as court community political contexts, sponsoring agency power relations, case processing norms and strategies, and sentencing decisions. This was made easier by the fact that interview questions were specifically aimed at gaining information on these key conceptual issues, though subjects often wandered to other topics in the course of answering questions. Open coding thus consisted of reading and labeling blocks of transcribed text from each interview[10] with keywords denoting topics and their conceptual relevance, and then sorting them accordingly.

The "axial coding" then centered around sorting and classifying segments of interview and field data according to the conceptual properties and dimensions they represented, and relating these properties and dimensions to court community contextual features and contingencies, case processing strategies, and sentencing outcomes. This was the most important and detailed coding procedure involved, since it entailed rereading the sorted material several times, sometimes recategorizing them, and making further coding notes that compared various categories to one another.

Finally, my "selective coding" focused on integrating the various notes, within-county comparisons, and tentative propositions regarding the key concepts of interest, and comparing the focus counties with one another in terms of these issues. I then rechecked these against the data, and altered and refined them accordingly. The selective coding was basically a process of comparison and data reduction, organizing unwieldy masses of data and coding notes into a coherent whole for presentation. My strategy was to form a coherent set of stories about the various levels of court community political contexts, sponsoring agency organization and relations, the influence of these on workgroup strategies and norms, and the role of workgroup strategies in producing sentencing patterns in each county.

Ethnographic Data Limitations

Although the ethnographic portion of this research represents an improvement over many existing studies of case processing and sentencing under guidelines—which include only statistical data—there are important limitations. First, the study lacks direct longitudinal data necessary for a fully adequate examination of changes in court community contexts, sponsoring agency relations, and case-processing strategies before and after the implementation of guidelines.[11] For example, the lack of pre- and postguidelines data especially presents difficulties for examining changes in prosecutorial and judicial discretion due to guidelines, which is a longitudinal question. My analysis is limited to making inferences about issues of change over time, based on ethnographic data gathered roughly a decade after the Pennsylvania guidelines were implemented (1982). On the other hand, this study is an investigation of what court community arrangements, case-processing strategies, and sentencing outcomes are like under guidelines, and not a direct test of the impact of guidelines implementation.

Second, my selection of focus counties presents both limitations and advantages. While court community size is a variable in the statewide analysis, my selection of only one focus county from each size category provides a limited basis of comparison. In terms of any comparison and generalization about court community size itself, the analysis will be limited to comparing findings from the focus counties with those from the statewide analysis. An alternative sampling of counties would include three same-sized counties, as in the studies of Eisenstein and Jacob (1977), Nardulli et al. (1988), and Eisenstein et al. (1988). Focusing on three counties of the same size would enable a more in-depth comparison of court community structure and activities, as well as the role of sentencing guidelines, while factors associated with size are "controlled." On the other hand, very few studies compare counties of different sizes and attend to contextual factors that may vary with size, and a study that does so could fill a gap in the literature.

Having discussed the data sources, analytical strategies, and limitations of the study, I turn to the statewide statistical analysis of sentencing outcomes in the next chapter. Following the statewide analysis, a chapter each is devoted to analyses of the statistical and ethnographic data from the three focus counties.

4

Statewide Sentencing Outcomes

This chapter presents findings from the statewide sentencing analyses in two parts. First, I discuss the main-effects models of incarceration decisions, sentence lengths, and guidelines departures that form the backbone of the statewide analysis. Next, I examine models of curvilinear and interaction effects, specifically those involving the influence of prior record.

Main Effects Models

Appendix C lists descriptive statistics for the independent and dependent variables to be used in subsequent models.[1] For example, offenses cluster around the middle levels of severity, the majority of cases entail only one conviction charge, and the vast majority of cases are convicted through guilty pleas of some kind.[2] Appendix C also shows descriptive statistics for sentencing outcomes by offense category. These categories are specific enough to differentiate a wider range of offense types than is included in most sentencing studies, and yet broad enough to avoid redundancy with the offense severity variable, since the offense severity measure can vary within each offense category. Further, defendants are largely males between the ages of 20 and 36, and blacks are overrepresented. While blacks comprise about 12 percent of the state's population, they comprise 39 percent of trial court sentencing cases. In terms of the sentencing outcome variables, 63 percent of cases are sentenced to jail or prison incarceration,[3] while 37 percent of cases receive nonincarceration sentences such as probation, partial confinement, house arrest, work release, or intermediate punishments. Also, 14 percent of the cases in guideline cells where dispositional departure is possible result in such departures (dispositional departures make up about 6 percent of the total number of cases).

Sentencing entails two distinct decisions: the decision to incarcerate and the length of incarceration. Accordingly, I begin with several logistic models of incarceration decisions, including dispositional departures from guidelines. I then present OLS models of minimum sentence length—corrected for the kind of selection bias discussed in chapter 3—and move on to models of durational departures below and above guidelines.

Before discussing the specific findings, a few points are worth noting about interpreting these results. First, each of the analyses includes a very large number of cases—much larger than most sentencing studies. Even effects that are of little substantive importance may attain statistical significance, and very conservative standards for statistical tests must be used. I have therefore set the "critical value" for statistical significance at a very strict .005 except where otherwise indicated. Second, I follow the conventions described in Aldrich and Nelson (1984), Agresti and Finlay (1986), and Hanushek and Jackson (1977) in interpreting the logistic regression models of incarceration decisions and dispositional departures.[4] I use the percent of cases for which the model accurately predicts the value of the dependent variable (a test somewhat analogous to the R-squared statistic in OLS regression) to assess the "fit" between the model and the data. In judging the relative importance of the independent variables, I rely on size of the variables' odds ratios.[5] In judging the relative importance of variables in the OLS models of sentence length and durational departures, I rely on the variables' metric and standardized coefficients, and contributions to the model's R-squared value.

A third caveat concerns model specification in terms of the county-level aggregate characteristics and court community size. For example, county percent black population is strongly correlated with percent urban (.64), percent Republican (–.60), and index crime (.89). Percent urban is also strongly correlated with index crime (.69), while large court size is strongly correlated with index crime (.68), percent black (.72), percent Republican (–.60), and of course percent urban (.74). Of course, these strong correlations produced severe multicollinearity when all of the county variables were included together in preliminary models. Further, the county-level characteristics individually or collectively contributed little beyond the court size variable alone to the explanatory power or substantive interpretation of the various sentencing models. Therefore, in order to avoid the problems of multicollinearity and in the interests of parsimonious model specification, all subsequent models presented include only the court community size dummy variables.

However, correlations do give an interesting profile of aggregate case and county-level characteristics for courts of different sizes. They indicate, for example, that large courts tend to handle more severe offenses (.20), conduct more bench trials (.24), and have somewhat fewer negotiated pleas (–.17). Further, large court judges have somewhat smaller workloads (–.15), and large courts tend to handle more black defendants (.44). Small courts, on the other hand, tend to handle somewhat less serious offenses (–.13), have more negotiated pleas (.18) and fewer bench trials (–.14), handle fewer black defendants (–.37), and tend to be in areas with smaller black populations (–.49) and larger populations of young people (.40). Medium courts share many of the characteristics of small courts, except that medium courts tend to be located in more Republican-dominated counties (.40), and medium court judges tend to have somewhat larger workloads (.12).

Incarceration Decisions

The first model in Table 4.1 shows a logit model of overall incarceration decisions (county jail and state prison combined).

The model accurately predicts these incarceration outcomes in 76% of the cases. Prior record and offense severity—two legally prescribed variables—are the strongest predictors of incarceration. A one-point increase in prior record is associated with a 57 percent increase in the odds for incarceration, while a one-point increase in offense severity yields a 56 percent increase in incarceration odds. Since prior record and offense severity are continuous variables, their effects on the odds of incarceration are cumulative. For example, defendants with a prior record score of 1 would face odds of 1.57 to 1 for being incarcerated, while defendants with a score of 4 would face incarceration odds of 6.08 to 1.[6] Likewise, defendants with an offense severity score of 2 would face incarceration odds of 1.56 to 1, while those with a score of 5 would face incarceration odds of 9.2 to 1.

The offense categories also vary considerably in their effects on the odds of incarceration. Of the ten statistically significant offenses, five are associated with greater odds of incarceration, while five are associated with decreased odds, compared to the reference category (retail theft). Incarceration is most likely for rape/IDSI, robbery, drug felonies, and homicide, while it is least likely for forgery, weapons offenses, theft, criminal trespassing,

TABLE 4.1

Logit Models of Overall Incarceration, State Imprisonment, and Dispositional Departures: Odds Ratios (logits in parentheses)

Variable	Overall Incarceration	State Prison	Dispositional Departure
Constant **	— (−2.86)	— (−4.32)	— (1.49)
Year	1.02 (.017)	.994 (−.006)	1.02 (.02)
Homicide	1.48 (.39)	4.05 (1.4)	**
Kidnapping	1.58 (.46) *	4.22 (1.44)	**
Rape/IDSI	1.90 (.64)	3.78 (1.34)	.83 (−.19) *
Robbery	1.82 (.60)	2.83 (1.04)	.55 (−.60)
Aggravated assault	1.01 (.006) *	1.93 (.66)	1.65 (.50)
Simple assault	.97 (−.03) *	1.34 (.29)	**
Arson	.86 (−.15)	1.62 (.49)	1.21 (.19)
Weapons	.61 (−.49)	1.28 (.26)	2.63 (.97)
Burglary	1.07 (.07) *	1.61 (.48)	1.16 (.15)
Criminal trespassing	.86 (−.15)	1.49 (.40)	.90 (−.11) *
Theft	.72 (−.33)	1.49 (.40)	1.38 (.32)
Forgery	.57 (−.56)	1.28 (.25)	1.68 (.52)
Drug felonies	1.80 (.59)	1.97 (.68)	.81 (−.22)
Drug misdemeanors	1.32 (.28)	1.84 (.61)	**
Offense severity	1.56 (.445)	1.99 (.69)	.69 (−.38)
Prior record	1.57 (.45)	1.65 (.50)	.75 (−.29)
Multiple conviction charges	1.22 (.193)	1.15 (.14)	.82 (−.20)
Negotiated plea	.90 (−.103)	.87 (−.144)	1.10 (.10)
Bench trial	1.18 (.164)	1.42 (.35)	.77 (−.27)
Jury trial	2.81 (1.03)	4.26 (1.45)	.31 (−1.17)
Court workload	.999 (−.001)	.999 (−.001)	1.00 (.001) *
Race (black=1)	1.57 (.45)	1.25 (.22)	.63 (−.46)
Gender (female=1)	.53 (−.64)	.76 (−.27)	2.13 (.76)
Age	.98 (−.02)	.994 (−.002) *	1.02 (.02)
Medium court	.82 (−.20)	.78 (−.25)	1.11 (.10) *
Large court	.39 (−.94)	.80 (−.23)	1.64 (.49)
N =	166,247	166,247	70,421
Chi-square	54,396	62,115	6,184
(model accuracy)	(76%)	(85%)	(86.7%)

* Denotes coefficients not significant at .005 or less.
** Retail theft, other guilty pleas, and small courts are reference categories. In the dispositional departure model, homicide and kidnapping are omitted due to too few dispositional departure cases; simple assault and drug misdemeanors are omitted due to too few cases where dispositional departure is possible.

and arson. While kidnapping is not statistically significant due to its small number of cases, it too is associated with increased odds for incarceration. These offense-related odds for incarceration are also suggested in a general way by the incarceration rates per offense in Appendix C.

The final legally relevant variable, multiple conviction charges, is associated with slightly greater odds for incarceration (1.22). On the other hand, jury trial is second only to prior record and offense severity in the strength of its effect on incarceration odds. Net of the other variables in the model, those convicted by jury trial are 2.8 times more likely to be incarcerated compared to those in the reference category (other guilty pleas). Those convicted by bench trials also face slightly greater odds (1.18) of incarceration. On the other hand, the incarceration odds of those convicted through negotiated pleas are only 10 percent less (.90 to 1) than other guilty pleas. This suggests that those convicted by jury trials are at a considerable disadvantage in incarceration decisions. However, those with negotiated plea agreements enjoy only a slight advantage over the reference category, other guilty pleas (e.g., open pleas, no-contest pleas). The final case processing variable, court workload, appears to have little effect on incarceration decisions, which supports the conclusions of Heumann (1978) and others (Church 1979; Eisenstein and Jacob 1977; Meeker and Pontell 1985).

While their effects are not nearly as strong as prior record and jury trial, each of the defendant characteristics exert notable influence on incarceration outcomes. The strongest effect is gender; females face incarceration odds that are almost half those of males. Additionally, blacks face 57 percent greater odds (1.57) of incarceration compared to nonblacks, and a one-year increase in defendants' age yields a 2 percent decrease in incarceration odds. The effect of age appears trivial until one considers that, like prior record and offense severity, it is cumulative: a considerable difference exists between much older defendants and much younger ones (this analysis, however, oversimplifies the influence of age in sentencing, which is actually curvilinear—for a fuller treatment, see Steffensmeier, Kramer, and Ulmer 1995). A fifty-five–year-old defendant, for example, would be exactly half as likely to be incarcerated as a twenty-year-old. In sum, females, nonblacks, and much older defendants are less likely to be incarcerated, net of other factors.

Results from logistic regression models are sometimes more easily interpreted when odds ratios are converted to actual probability differences between groups being compared (see Lichter 1989). Therefore, the relative importance of the jury trial, gender, and race influences on incarceration decisions can be further illustrated by converting the odds ratios to probability differences in incarceration outcomes, net of the other factors in the model (see Aldrich and Nelson 1984; Lichter 1989).[7] The odds indicate a .48 net difference in the probability of incarceration between jury trials and other guilty pleas, a -.31 probability difference between men and women, a .22 difference between blacks and nonblacks, a .08 difference between bench trials and other guilty pleas, and only a -.06 difference between negotiated pleas and other pleas. In other words, those convicted by jury trial have a 48 percent greater probability of being incarcerated than those convicted by other guilty pleas, women have a 31 percent lesser probability of being incarcerated than men, blacks have a 22 percent greater probability of being incarcerated than non-blacks, and so forth.

Finally, compared to the small court reference category, defendants in the large courts have 61 percent lesser odds of incarceration. Medium courts show a much smaller decrease in incarceration odds (12 percent) relative to small courts. Converting these odds to probability differences shows a -.44 difference in defendant's probability of incarceration between large and small courts, and a -.10 difference between medium and small courts. Net of other factors, defendants in small court communities are noticeably more likely to be incarcerated, those in large courts are less likely, and the odds for defendants in medium-sized courts are in between these two extremes. As mentioned, the models shown in this chapter do not include the aggregate county demographic variables due to their collinearity with court size. However, models that included these variables indicated that counties with a higher percentage urban population were associated with moderately lower odds (.99) of incarceration, and counties with a higher percentage of Republican voters were associated with moderately higher incarceration odds (1.01).

The second model in Table 4.1 measures incarceration decisions in terms of whether defendants are sent to state prison versus county jail/probation. The strength of the relationships between several of the variables and prison decisions differs considerably from those in the first model. First, prior record and especially offense severity exert a stronger influence on the odds of going to prison. Most interesting, however, are the changes in the strength of extra-legal effects. The influence of negotiated pleas on state imprisonment odds is roughly the same as for overall incarceration. However, bench trials increase imprisonment odds to a greater extent compared to overall incarceration, and the effect of jury trial on imprisonment is much greater. Further, the state imprisonment odds associated with race, gender, and large court size are much smaller compared to their effect on overall incarceration. Converting to probability differences in imprisonment yields a .18 difference between bench trials and other guilty pleas, a .62 difference between jury trials and other pleas, a comparatively smaller .12 difference between blacks and nonblacks, a –.14 difference between men and women, and a –.12 difference between those sentenced in large and small courts. Models (not shown) that included the county demographic variables also indicated that defendants were moderately less likely to be sent to state prison in more urban counties (odds = .99), and in counties with higher black populations (odds = .97). In sum, while race, gender, and court size exert considerably less influence on state imprisonment, trials—especially jury trials—exert greater influence.

The first two models in Table 4.1 consider all incarceration decisions together, including cases in which defendants are given dispositional departures below the guidelines (e.g., a defendant is given probation or some other nonincarceration sentence instead of jail or prison). I examined a supplementary model (not shown in Table 4.1) of overall incarceration omitting the roughly 9,500 dispositional departure cases, that is, a model including only incarceration decisions that are in conformity with the guidelines' standard ranges. Since dispositional departures are a relatively small proportion of all incarceration decisions (about 6 percent), one would not expect much difference in results. There were, however, some small but interesting decreases in the size of the effects of jury trial, race, and gender.

Thus, the first two models in Table 4.1 demonstrate that while legally prescribed variables exert the strongest influences on incarceration decisions, factors such as conviction by jury trial, gender, race, age, and court size also affect whether defendants will be incarcerated. However, these extra-legal differences decrease slightly in models where dispositional departures are omitted, suggesting that such extra-legal factors may also affect dispositional departure decisions themselves. The third model in Table 4.1 therefore examines the various influences on the chances of receiving a dispositional departure; that is, receiving a nonincarceration sentence when the guidelines call for incarceration. Accordingly, the model *only* includes cases in those guideline cells where incarceration is recommended as a minimum sentence.

As with incarceration decisions in general, the strongest predictors of dispositional departures are offense severity and prior record, with several offense categories also exerting considerable influence. A one-point increase in offense severity results in a 31 percent decrease (.69) in the odds of receiving a dispositional departure, while a one-point increase in prior record score results in a 25 percent (.75) odds reduction. Again, the influence of these two variables can best be seen by considering their cumulative impacts. An offender with an offense severity score of 9 would have roughly 53 percent lesser odds (i.e., a 15.6 percent chance) of getting a dispositional departure compared to one with a score of 4. Similarly, someone with a prior record score of 6 would have 82 percent lesser odds of getting a dispositional departure (i.e., about an 18 percent chance) compared to someone with a score of 0.

Three offense categories are notable for their greater likelihood of dispositional departure. Weapons offenses are over two-and-a-half times more likely to result in dispositional departures, while forgeries and aggravated assaults have 68 percent and 65 percent greater odds of receiving them, respectively. On the other hand, robberies have 45 percent lesser odds of resulting in dispositional departures. These offense-related effects are consistent with those for the full model of incarceration decisions, as well as the descriptive statistics for offenses in Appendix C. The results for multiple conviction charges are also similar to those for general incarceration decisions; the odds of dispositional departure decrease 18 percent for those with multiple convictions.

The effects of modes of conviction on dispositional departures are a mirror image of their effects on the overall incarceration decision. Those convicted by jury trial are comparatively much less likely (69 percent) to get dispositional departures, while those convicted by bench trial fare somewhat better, with only a 23 percent decrease in dispositional departure odds. On the other hand, conviction by negotiated guilty plea is associated with only 10 percent greater dispositional departure odds compared to other guilty pleas. The odds-to-probability difference method indicates a net difference in dispositional departures of –.42 between jury trials and other pleas, a –.13 difference between bench trials and other pleas, and only a .05 difference between negotiated and other pleas. As with incarceration decisions, the measure of court workload makes almost no difference in dispositional departure odds.

As suspected, defendant characteristics also significantly influence dispositional departure chances, even while controlling for the legally prescribed factors. The strongest effect is again gender; the dispositional departure odds for females are more than twice those of males. In addition, blacks face odds that are only 63 percent those for nonblacks; that is, the dispositional departure odds for blacks are 37 percent less than those for non-blacks. In terms of probabilities of receiving dispositional departures, these odds translate into a −.23 black versus nonblack difference and a .36 female-male difference. Finally, age exerts an almost identical influence on dispositional departure decisions as for overall incarceration. A one-year increase in defendant's age is associated with a two-percent increase in the odds for receiving a dispositional departure. Again, this influence is most important in a cumulative sense—the dispositional departure odds for a fifty-year-old defendant would be roughly 81 percent greater than for a twenty-year-old. This finding contrasts with Blumstein et al.'s (1978) argument that older offenders are more likely to be incarcerated.[8] Court community size also exerts meaningful influence on dispositional departure odds. Defendants in large courts have 64 percent greater odds of getting dispositional departures compared to those in small courts. Further, models including the county demographic variables indicated that dispositional departures were moderately more common in more urban counties (odds = 1.01), and less common in more Republican counties (odds = .99).

Once the decision to incarcerate a defendant is made, what factors most influence the length of that incarceration? The next set of models takes up this question, and also examines the problem of selection bias in models of incarceration length.

Incarceration Length

Table 4.2 presents an OLS model of incarceration sentence length, corrected for selection bias due to the incarceration decision.[9]

According to Berk (1983), Peterson and Hagan (1984), and others (e.g., Spohn 1990), results for models of sentence length can be inaccurate when the factors that go into the selection of defendants for incarceration are not taken into account. Thus, models of incarceration length consider a group of defendants who have "exceeded a threshold on the selection criteria" for incarceration (Peterson and Hagan 1984, p. 60). Sentence length is therefore not only a linear function of the independent variables in the length model, but also a nonlinear function of the "hazard rate"

TABLE 4.2

OLS Models of Incarceration Length, Corrected for Selection Bias
(includes incarceration cases only)

Variable	b (Beta)	Contribution to R^2
Constant **	−41.0 (—)	—
Year	.40 (.044)	.001
Homicide	36.5 (.17)	—
Kidnapping	30.0 (.06)	—
Rape/IDSI	23.4 (.20)	—
Robbery	13.4 (.18)	—
Aggravated assault	7.1 (.07)	—
Simple assault	3.9 (.04)	—
Arson	4.4 (.05)	—
Weapons	−5.23 (−.033)	—
Burglary	2.34 (.045)	—
Criminal trespass	1.98 (.015)	—
Theft	−.13 (−.003) *	—
Forgery	−4.44 (−.04)	—
Drug felonies	11.9 (.134)	—
Drug misdemeanors	4.4 (.09)	—
Total offense R^2 contribution		.226
Offense severity	8.5 (.85)	.117
Prior record	5.8 (.67)	.112
Multiple charges	2.75 (.06)	.004
Negotiatied plea	−.62 (−.02)	.0002
Bench trial	2.1 (.03)	.001
Jury trial	14.6 (.17)	.025
Court workload	−.01 (−.06)	.0015
Race (black=1)	3.12 (.08)	.0042
Gender (female=1)	−6.6 (−.10)	.01
Age	−.09 (−.04)	.001
Medium court	−1.0 (−.02)	.0002
Large court	−7.1 (−.18)	.005
Correction factor	—	.041
N =		99,680
Adjusted R^2		.56

* Denotes coefficients not significant at .005 or less.
** Retail theft, other guilty pleas, and small courts are reference categories.

involving the impact of factors that go into the incarceration decision (Peterson and Hagan 1984). I corrected for this type of selection bias by first running a logistic model of incarceration decisions, and then saving the predicted incarceration values for the cases in the model. I then included these predicted values as an overall correction factor variable in the OLS model of length. This effectively controls for any selection bias stemming from a "threshold" or hazard effect for incarceration (this procedure is detailed in Berk 1983). The correction factor is moderately collinear with offense severity and prior record, since these are also heavily influential in incarceration decisions. The tolerance ratios for offense severity and prior record each drop to about .30, indicating that 30 percent of the variance explained by each of these variables is not shared with at least one other factor in the model (i.e., the correction factor). This multicollinearity indicates caution in assessing the coefficients and individual R-squared contributions of offense severity and prior record (Hanushek and Jackson 1977).

Nevertheless, these two variables' are still the strongest influences on sentence length by far. A one-point increase in offense severity yields about an eight-month increase in mean minimum incarceration length, while a one-point increase in prior record yields roughly a five-month increase in mean length. Several offenses are also notable for their effects on sentence length, and these are unaffected by multicollinearity. Homicide, kidnapping, rape/IDSI, and robbery all have the longest incarceration terms, while weapons offenses and forgeries have the shortest. Further, those with multiple conviction charges are incarcerated on average 2.75 months longer than those with single convictions. Together, these legally prescribed variables account for about 46 percent of the variance in incarceration length, or 83 percent of the model's explained variance.

Jury trial contributes two-and-a-half points to the R-squared value, and those convicted by jury trial are incarcerated on average 14.6 months longer than those convicted by other guilty pleas. While bench trial does not contribute much to the model's predictive power, bench trial convictions also result in incarceration terms that are an average of two months longer than other guilty pleas. On the other hand, negotiated guilty pleas are associated with incarceration terms that are only about half a month shorter than other guilty pleas. As with incarceration decisions, there is evidence of sizable differences in sentence length based on mode of conviction: those convicted by jury trials and (to a far lesser extent) bench trials tend to receive longer sentences, but those with negotiated guilty pleas fare only slightly better than other guilty pleas.

Gender is the fourth-strongest effect in the model, contributing one point to the R-squared value. While this predictive contribution appears small, gender's slope indicates that women receive sentences that are on average six-and-a-half months shorter than do men—a substantial difference. While race does not contribute as much as gender to the predictive power of the model, its slope also indicates meaningful differences. The mean minimum incarceration length for blacks is 3.12 months longer than for non-blacks. The effect for age is the weakest among the defendant characteristics. A one-month increase in age is associated with roughly a one-tenth of a month decrease in average sentence length. That is, a thirty-year age difference would translate into about a three-month difference in average sentence length (again, however, this analysis oversimplifies the relationship of age to sentencing, which Steffensmeier et al. [1995] found to be curvilinear).

Defendants in large courts also receive incarceration terms that tend to be about seven months shorter than those in small courts, while those in medium courts receive sentences that average one month shorter than small courts. This pattern also resembles the relationship of court size to incarceration decisions, where defendants in large courts were less likely to be incarcerated. Additionally, models including the county demographic variables showed that incarceration sentences were moderatly shorter in more urbanized counties (Beta = –.08), but were moderately longer in more Republican counties (Beta = .05) and in counties with higher UCR Index crime rates (Beta = .07).

I have already illustrated that one type of departure below, dispositional departure, is the site of important extra-legal sentencing differences. Is the same true with durational departures below and above guidelines? The first model in Table 4.3 includes only cases where a departure below occurs, and like the model for dispositional departure, includes only the guideline cells where departure below is possible.

The model predicts the size of durational departures below guidelines, proportionate to the guideline minimum recommendation for each case. Since dispositional departures are also departures below guidelines, the model also contains the roughly 9,500 dispositional departure cases. Compared to the analyses of incarceration length, the first model in Table 4.3 explains only a meager portion (16 percent) of the variance in durational departures below guidelines. Prior record is clearly the strongest influence on such departures—accounting for about 63 percent of the model's

TABLE 4.3

OLS Models of Durational Departures Below and Above Guidelines

	Below		Above	
Variable	b (Beta)	Contribution to R^2	b (Beta)	Contribution to R^2
Constant	1.17 (—)	—	-.68 (—)	—
Year	-.003 (-.02)	.0002	.017 (.026)	.0009
Homicide	-.01 (-.002) *	—	.305 (.002)	—
Kidnapping	-.001 (-.0001) *	—	.41 (.014) *	—
Rape/IDSI	-.006 (-.003) *	—	.03 (.003) *	—
Robbery	-.03 (-.02)	—	.64 (.14)	—
Aggravated assault	.06 (.05)	—	.49 (.07)	—
Simple assault	**	—	.98 (.12)	—
Arson	.023 (.02) *	—	.57 (.09)	—
Weapons	.054 (.03)	—	.44 (.035)	—
Burglary	.03 (.04)	—	.40 (.11)	—
Crim. trespassing	-.02 (-.01) *	—	-.03 (-.01) *	—
Theft	.043 (.044)	—	.18 (.05)	—
Forgery	.06 (.04)	—	.33 (.035)	—
Drug felonies	-.02 (-.02) *	—	.15 (.04)	—
Drug misdemeanors	**	—	.12 (.02) *	—
Total offense R^2 contribution		.027		.0053
Offense severity	-.053 (-.19)	.0144	-.11 (-.15)	.01
Prior record	-.05 (-.36)	.10	-.14 (-.21)	.038
Multiple convictions	-.02 (-.03)	.001	.05 (.02)	.0008
Negotiated plea	.02 (.031)	.001	.052 (.017)	.0008
Bench trial	-.014 (.01) *	.0001	.005 (.001) *	.0005
Jury trial	-.03 (-.014) *	.0002	.36 (.073)	.005
Court workload	-.001 (-.04)	.0006	.0005 (.04)	.0015
Race (black=1)	-.05 (-.075)	.0044	-.0003 (-.001)*	.0005
Gender (female=1)	.07 (.07)	.004	.18 (.03)	.0016
Age	.002 (.064)	.004	.01 (.04)	.0017
Medium court	-.001 (-.003) *	.0001	.20 (.06)	.002
Large court	-.01 (-.02) *	.0001	.14 (.05)	.001
N =		26,808		33,850
Adjusted R^2		.16		.073

* Denotes coefficients not significant at .005 or less.
** Simple assault and drug misdemeanors are omitted from departure below model—insufficient cases where departure below is possible.

explained variance by itself—while offense type and severity are the next strongest influences on these departures below guidelines. Not surprisingly, the model indicates that defendants with greater prior records and those convicted of more severe offenses tend to receive smaller durational departures below. Five offenses are significantly associated with larger durational departures below guidelines: aggravated assault, weapons offenses, forgeries, theft, and burglary. As indicated earlier, these offenses are also associated with greater odds for dispositional departures. Those with multiple convictions also tend to receive smaller departures below, but this variable contributes little to the model's explanatory power.

In contrast to incarceration decisions, dispositional departures, and incarceration length, mode of conviction appears to exert little influence on the size of durational departures below guidelines. Only the effect for negotiated plea is significant; those with negotiated pleas tend to receive slightly larger durational departures below than those with other guilty pleas. Negotiated plea, however, only contributes .001 to the model's R-squared value. While the defendant characteristics are not as influential as they are for the other sentencing outcomes, collectively they do contribute about .013 to R-squared, roughly equal to the contribution of offense severity. These effects indicate that blacks receive slightly smaller departures below than nonblacks, while women and older defendants receive larger ones. Court size also appears to make little difference in durational departures below guidelines (nor do the county demographic variables).

In contrast to the models for dispositional departure and durational departure below, the second model in Table 4.3 includes all guideline cells, since departures above are possible in any cell. The model also includes only cases where a sentence departs above the standard range midpoint by some amount. The explained variance (7.3 percent) in durational departure above is even poorer than for departure below. To the extent that any of the variables meaningfully influences the size of durational departures above, it is prior record, followed by offense severity and type. The negative effects of prior record and offense severity on the size of departures above guidelines, however, seems counterintuitive. Why would defendants with more extensive prior records and more severe offenses receive smaller departures above guidelines? The answer probably lies in the structure of the guidelines themselves. As noted in a previous chapter, both the width of guideline ranges and the length of their sentence recommendations increase sharply for high prior record/

offense severity cells. The midpoint of these ranges, against which departures above are measured, represent very severe sentence recommendations. In fact, the top of these ranges are at or near statutory limits (a minimum sentence cannot exceed one-half the statutory maximum for the convicted offense). Therefore, only rare and extremely harsh sentences would exceed the standard range midpoints by a large proportion at the upper guideline ranges. At lower prior record and offense severity levels, however, the sentence ranges are narrower and their midpoints represent shorter sentences. It would not be difficult for a sentence to exceed the midpoint of the range by a larger proportion at these levels. In sum, when the midpoint of the guideline range already recommends a relatively long sentence, departures above will be smaller in proportion to the midpoint. When the ranges recommend a relatively short sentence, departures above will be larger in proportion to the midpoint.

The only other factors that exert meaningful influence on the size of departures above are jury trial and medium court size. Those convicted by jury trial tend to receive moderately larger departures above compared to other guilty pleas, and jury trial's contribution to the model's explanatory power is roughly equal that of the combined contribution of offense type. The departures above for defendants in medium courts also tend to be larger than those for defendants in other courts, but this variable contributes less to R-squared than jury trial. It is also notable that race exerts no significant influence on departures above, and the influences of gender and age are very small.

Interaction Effects Models

So far, the analysis has concentrated on additive models of sentencing outcomes, but has not considered the possibility that the effects of some variables on sentencing may depend on the influence of other variables. This section examines statistical interactions influencing incarceration decisions and lengths. I first summarize the results for interactions involving race/trial convictions and gender/offense severity. I then consider interactions involving prior record by separately modeling cases involving defendants with serious vs. less-serious prior records.

Significant Interaction Terms

I first tested a number of interaction terms in models of the various sentencing outcomes discussed above, but only four were both statistically and substantively significant. Cross-product terms for race and trial conviction (combining both bench and jury trials)[10] were significant for incarceration and dispositional departure. For incarceration, the odds for the race*trial term are 1.18 (logit = .173), while the odds for the same term in a model of dispositional departure are .77 (logit = –.26). In this case, with an interaction between two dummy variables, the logistic interaction term's odds can be interpreted as the difference between blacks and nonblacks in the effect of trial conviction on the odds of incarceration or dispositional departure (see Aldrich and Nelson 1984). In other words, the incarceration odds for blacks convicted by bench or jury trials are 18 percent greater than those for similar nonblacks. Likewise, blacks convicted by trial face a 23 percent decrease in the odds for dispositional departures compared to nonblacks. That is, the dispositional departure odds among blacks convicted by trial are only 77 percent as great as those for nonblacks. Overall, these two interactions suggest that the "trial penalty" in terms of incarceration and dispositional departure decisions may be moderately greater for blacks.

Though the effects are smaller than for race and trial, gender also interacts with offense severity in terms of incarceration and dispositional departure. For incarceration, the odds for the gender*offense severity term are .95 (logit = –.05), while for dispositional departure the odds are 1.17 (logit = .157). In this case, with a logistic interaction term for a dummy and a continuous variable, the odds can be interpreted as the difference between genders in the impact of offense severity on the odds of incarceration or dispositional departure (Aldrich and Nelson 1984). Thus, offense severity has 5 percent less impact on the odds of incarceration for women than for men. While this interaction effect is modest, the effect for dispositional departure is more meaningful. The decrease in dispositional departure odds associated with offense severity is 17 percent smaller for women than men. These terms indicate that increases in offense severity have less impact on the incarceration and dispositional departure odds for women than for men.

Prior Record

Exploratory analyses also suggested a number of statistically significant prior record-related interaction effects. Since the prior record score is weighted to reflect the severity as well as the number of prior convictions, I can distinguish between those with a score composed of prior misdemeanors and/or less serious felonies, and those with a score that reflects at least one serious felony conviction. In determining prior record scores, any prior misdemeanors may total no more than two points, while felonies may count one to three points each, depending on their severity. For example, a prior record score of two may represent either a number of prior misdemeanors or two less serious felonies. To reach a score of three or greater, however, a defendant must have at least one prior serious felony conviction. Therefore, I separated the cases into two prior record levels: those with either less serious prior convictions or none at all (prior record score of two or less), and those with one or more serious prior felony convictions (prior record score of three or more). Table 4.4 shows logit models of incarceration decisions for defendants with serious versus less serious prior records.

Several key differences exist between these two models.[11] The size and direction of the odds for the offense categories differ between the two models, but they are not strictly comparable since some offenses are omitted in the second model due to insufficient cases. Most notably, the effect of the prior record score itself is much greater among those with less serious prior convictions than for those with serious ones. A one-point increase in prior record is associated with a doubling of the odds for incarceration among those with a prior record score of two or less, but only a 25 percent increase in incarceration odds for those who already have serious prior records. Prior record exerts a stronger influence among those with less serious records despite the greater range of variation in the prior record score among those with serious priors. This suggests a possible "threshold" effect for criminal history in terms of incarceration decisions. Among defendants without serious priors, the prior record score has the most impact on the likelihood of incarceration. Among those who have at least one prior serious felony to their discredit, additional prior record score points make much less difference. A similar, though not as dramatic, difference exists for offense severity and multiple convictions. Increases in offense severity and having multiple conviction charges exert more influence on incarceration odds among those with less serious prior records.

The effects for mode of conviction differ between the two models as well. A negotiated plea is associated with a 10 percent decrease in incarceration odds among those with less serious prior convictions, but has no significant influence among those with serious priors. Additionally, bench trials increase incarceration

TABLE 4.4

Logit Models of Overall Incarceration, Cases With Prior Record Scores of 2 or Less and 3 or Greater: Odds Ratios (logits in parentheses)

Variable	Prior Record ≤ 2	Prior Record ≥ 3
Constant **	— (–3.17)	— ( )
Year	1.02 (.018)	1.01 (.01)
Homicide	1.60 (.47)	**
Kidnapping	1.52 (.42)	**
Rape/IDSI	2.08 (.74)	**
Robbery	1.90 (.64)	2.27 (.82)
Aggravated assault	1.05 (.05) *	1.04 (.04) *
Simple assault	1.01 (.007) *	.89 (–.12) *
Arson	.89 (–.114)	.81 (–.21) *
Weapons	.62 (–.48)	.66 (–.41)
Burglary	1.11 (.10) *	1.13 (.12) *
Criminal trespassing	.77 (–.26)	1.45 (.37)
Theft	.72 (–.33)	.80 (–.23)
Forgery	.55 (–.59)	.72 (–.33)
Drug felonies	1.94 (.66)	1.25 (.22)
Drug misdemeanors	1.43 (.36)	1.04 (.04) *
Offense severity	1.58 (.46)	1.48 (.39)
Prior record	2.03 (.71)	1.25 (.22)
Multiple conviction charges	1.23 (.21)	1.13 (.12)
Negotiated plea	.90 (–.11)	.98 (–.02) *
Bench trial	1.14 (.13)	1.34 (.29)
Jury trial	2.80 (1.03)	3.42 (1.23)
Court workload	.999 (–.001) *	.999 (–.001) *
Race (black=1)	1.59 (.46)	1.43 (.36)
Gender (female=1)	.52 (–.654)	.68 (–.39)
Age	.99 (–.013)	.98 (–.024)
Medium court	.80 (–.23)	.95 (–.05) *
Large court	.37 (–1.01)	.57 (–.57)
N =	127,513	38,504
Chi-square	38,196	4,559
(model accuracy)	(80%)	(77%)

* Denotes coefficients not significant at .005 or less.
** Retail theft, other guilty pleas, and small courts are reference categories. Homicide, kidnapping, and rape/IDSI are omitted from the second model because all cases for these offenses at prior records of 3 or greater received incarceration.

odds among those with serious prior records to a greater extent than among those with less serious records. The biggest difference, however, concerns the effect of jury trial convictions. Those with less serious prior records who are convicted by jury trial are 2.8 times as likely to be incarcerated. Those with serious priors who are convicted by jury trial are 3.42 times as likely to be incarcerated. Thus, trials—especially jury trials—increase the likelihood of incarceration to a considerably greater extent among those with serious prior records than among those with less serious priors. In other words, the "trial penalty" seems to be greater for those with serious priors who go to trial—especially jury trial—and lose. On the other hand, negotiated pleas gain those with less serious records a moderate advantage compared to other guilty pleas, but this advantage effectively disappears for those with serious records.

Interestingly, gender and race effects *decrease* moderately among those with serious prior records. That is, gender and race differences in incarceration odds each become smaller among those with serious prior convictions. This suggests that the presence of one or more serious felony priors may present a moderate "equalizing" influence in terms of gender and race differences in incarceration chances. Relatedly, the effects of court size also decrease among those with serious prior records. While those sentenced in large courts are less likely to be incarcerated no matter what their prior record, the size of the incarceration odds associated with large court size decreases among those with serious records.

Table 4.5 presents similar models of dispositional departures broken out by prior record levels.

The prior record interactions for dispositional departure are almost identical to those for incarceration decisions in general. The only difference is that the effect of court size remains virtually the same for the two prior record groups. Once again, a threshold effect for prior record is evident. Each increase in prior record score produces a 42 percent drop in dispositional departure odds for those with less serious prior records, but only a 9 percent drop for those who already have serious records. The effect of increases in offense severity also decreases somewhat among those with serious records, as does the effect of multiple conviction charges.

The difference in effects for mode of conviction also exhibits a pattern similar to that for incarceration decisions. While negotiated pleas are associated with a 14 percent increase in dispositional

TABLE 4.5

Logit Models of Dispositional Departure, Cases With Prior Record Scores of 2 or Less and 3 or Greater: Odds Ratios (logits in parentheses)

Variable	Prior Record < 2	Prior Record > 3
Constant **	— (2.86)	— (–.90)
Year	.98 (–.124) *	1.002 (.002) *
Homicide	**	**
Kidnapping	**	**
Rape/IDSI	**	**
Robbery	.53 (–.63)	.47 (–.75)
Aggravated assault	1.58 (.46)	1.02 (.02) *
Simple assault	**	**
Arson	1.21 (.19)	.76 (–.28) *
Weapons	2.51 (.92)	2.00 (.69)
Burglary	1.15 (.14) *	.89 (–.12) *
Criminal trespassing	.90 (–.11) *	.78 (–.25) *
Theft	1.32 (.28)	1.41 (.34)
Forgery	1.95 (.67)	1.38 (.32)
Drug felonies	.73 (–.31)	.84 (–.18) *
Drug misdemeanors	**	**
Offense severity	.63 (–.46)	.67 (–.40)
Prior record	.58 (–.55)	.91 (–.10)
Multiple conviction charges	.80 (–.224)	.87 (–.135)
Negotiated plea	1.14 (.13)	1.01 (.01) *
Bench trial	.82 (–.20)	.63 (–.46)
Jury trial	.32 (–1.15)	.28 (–1.26)
Court workload	1.00 (.0002) *	.999 (–.001) *
Race (black=1)	.63 (–.46)	.67 (–.41)
Gender (female=1)	2.25 (.81)	1.52 (.42)
Age	1.02 (.02)	1.03 (.03)
Medium court	1.14 (.13) *	1.13 (.12) *
Large court	1.68 (.52)	1.63 (.49)
N =	43,416	27,005
Chi-square	4,329	1,307
(model accuracy)	(84%)	(91%)

* Denotes coefficients not significant at .005 or less.
** Retail theft, other guilty pleas, and small courts are reference categories. Simple assault and drug misdemeanors are omitted due to insufficient cases where dispositional departure is possible for these offenses. Homicide, kidnapping, and rape/IDSI are omitted due to insufficient dispositional departure cases.

departure odds among less serious prior record defendants, they have no effect among those with serious records. The effect of jury trial on dispositional departure is also greater among serious prior record defendants, though the difference is not nearly as strong as for the incarceration models. The effects for bench trial show the biggest differences: serious priors defendants convicted by bench trials have 37 percent lesser odds of receiving a dispositional departure, compared to an 18 percent decrease in the odds of these departures for less serious priors defendants.

The influence of race and gender once again decreases among serious priors defendants. For dispositional departures, the gender effect shows the biggest difference. Females with less serious priors are 2.25 times as likely to receive dispositional departures, while their counterparts with serious records are only 1.52 times as likely. The difference between race effects is much less noteworthy; only four points separate the race-related odds for the two prior record groups.

Therefore, the effects of several variables on incarceration decisions, including dispositional departures, depend on the prior record of defendants. Not only do the effects of offense severity and multiple convictions, mode of conviction, gender and race, and sometimes court size depend on the number/severity of defendants' prior convictions, but the influence of prior record itself shows a curvilinear pattern. Among defendants with less serious prior records, increases in prior record points are very damaging to the chances of getting a non-incarceration sentence. The serious prior records of the other group have already done most of their damage, however, and increases in prior record points have much less impact. To a lesser extent, the same pattern is observed with offense severity and multiple convictions.

Additional analyses (not shown) suggested no substantial prior record-related interaction effects for the durational departure variables. However, the pair of models in Table 4.6 shows prior record interactions for incarceration length.

The model for less serious prior record defendants explains about 8 percent less variance than the serious priors model. This difference may signify that sentence lengths for less serious defendants are less predictable due to greater exercise of discretion in these decisions, or it may simply result from the fact that prior record score is constrained to vary by only three points in the first model. This is supported by the fact that prior record's slope is slightly smaller for serious priors defendants (where prior record

TABLE 4.6

OLS Models of Incarceration Length, Prior Record Scores of 2 or Less and 3 or Greater (incarceration cases only)

Variable	Prior Record < 2 b (Beta) [cont. to R^2]	Prior Record > 3 b (Beta) [cont. to R^2]
Constant **	−46.4 (—) [—]	−11.8 (—) [—]
Year	.46 (.06) [.002]	.25 (.025) [.0008]
Homicide	36.6 (.22)	34.6 (.24)
Kidnapping	26.6 (.06)	23.8 (.04)
Rape/IDSI	23.7 (.25)	20.0 (.13)
Robbery	10.2 (.16)	17.1 (.21)
Aggravated assault	6.0 (.076)	7.3 (.06)
Simple assault	2.8 (.037)	5.4 (.04)
Arson	2.1 (.03)	7.4 (.08)
Weapons	−5.66 (−.044)	−3.7 (−.02)
Burglary	−.26 (−.01) *	6.02 (.11)
Criminal trespassing	−.21 (−.002) *	7.8 (.07)
Theft	−1.05 (−.025)	2.0 (.036)
Forgery	−5.6 (−.056)	−1.2 (−.01) *
Drug felonies	11.0 (.15)	9.8 (.096)
Drug misdemeanors	3.3 (.09)	1.9 (.03)
Total offense R^2 contribution	.294	.319
Offense severity	7.5 (.81) [.072]	10.2 (.75) [.108]
Prior record	6.3 (.31) [.026]	5.5 (.31) [.065]
Multiple conv. charges	2.9 (.08) [.006]	1.98 (.04) [.0015]
Negotiated plea	−.40 (−.012) [.0001] *	−.39 (−.01) [.0001]
Bench trial	2.0 (.03) [.0007]	2.9 (.034) [.001]
Jury trial	14.2 (.18) [.027]	15.3 (.18) [.025]
Court workload	−.007 (−.054) [.0015] *	−.012 (−.062) [.002]
Race (black=1)	3.1 (.092) [.005]	2.65 (.06) [.003]
Gender (female=1)	−6.1 (−.12) [.01]	−4.9 (−.05) [.003]
Age	−.066 (−.033) [.001]	−.19 (−.07) [.004]
Medium court	−1.36 (−.036) [.0006]	.28 (.005) [.0001]*
Large court	−7.4 (−.22) [.007]	−4.5 (−.102) [.002]
correction factor	43.6 (.60) [.02]	81.8 (.40) [.02]
N =	66,975	32,494
Adjusted R^2	.481	.562

* Denotes coefficients not significant at .005 or less.
** Retail theft, other guilty pleas, and small courts are reference categories.

can vary by four points), but its contribution to R-squared is about five points larger. In any case, a curvilinear effect for prior record is much less evident for length: the slopes for prior record differ by only eight-tenths of a month.

The slopes for multiple convictions also differ, but only by a month. On the other hand, offense severity exerts a considerably greater effect—and contributes more to the explained variance—among serious priors defendants. Each increase in offense severity produces a 10.2 month increase in sentence length for serious priors defendants, but only a 7.5 month increase for those with less serious priors. This result differs from the earlier incarceration/ dispositional departure models, where the effect of offense severity decreased among serious priors defendants.

The interaction effects on length involving prior record and mode of conviction, gender, and court size are similar to those for incarceration. The slopes of conviction by jury and bench trial are each about one month greater for serious priors defendants, while negotiated plea exerts no significant influence in either model. The gender effect again decreases among serious priors defendants. The length differences attributable to court size also become narrower among serious priors defendants: the slope for large court size drops by about three months, and medium court size becomes insignificant. The slopes for race, however, do not differ substantially between the two prior record groups.[12]

Summary

Together, these analyses suggest a broad picture of sentencing patterns under Pennsylvania's guidelines. First, the analyses indicate several consistent influences on the decision to incarcerate under a variety of conditions. The most important influences on incarceration decisions are type and severity of offense and prior record, the two factors that are supposed to be the primary determinants of sentences under the guidelines. These relationships are strongest when dispositional departures are removed from consideration, but hold even when courts are given full discretion over whether to incarcerate and when courts dispositionally depart from guidelines. On the other hand, extralegal factors such as jury trial, gender, race, and (to a lesser extent) age also exert consistent influences on incarceration decisions that cannot be ignored. That is, defendants convicted by jury trial, males, and blacks are consistently more likely to be incarcerated, even controlling for the other factors in the models. In addition, the odds of incarceration also vary according to court community size—large courts are consistently less likely to incarcerate defendants than small or medium courts.

As with incarceration, the primary predictors of incarceration length are also legally prescribed. Legally prescribed variables—especially prior record—are also the best predictors of the size of durational departures, to the extent that these are predictable at all. Overall, the low predictive value of the durational departure models suggests that decisions regarding the size of durational departures apparently are either much more indeterminate and unpredictable than sentence length decisions, or are influenced by factors not measurable by these statistical data, or both.

Also similar to the incarceration analyses, jury trial, gender, race, and large court size are associated with important differences in sentence length. The length models suggest that those convicted by jury trial and blacks are sentenced to comparatively longer incarceration terms, while women and defendants in large courts are sentenced to comparatively shorter terms. In addition, while the degree of extralegal influence is much less for durational than for dispositional departures, they do have noticeable effects. Race, gender, and age influence the size of durational departures below to a modest extent, while jury trial and medium court size influence departures above.

Several interaction effects are apparent in addition to these main effects. First, blacks convicted by bench and jury trials are moderately more likely to be incarcerated, and less likely to receive dispositional departures, compared to white trial defendants. Also, increases in offense severity have slightly less impact on women's chances of incarceration and dispositional departure; that is, women's chances of getting nonincarceration sentences, especially dispositional departures, are hurt less by the severity of their offenses.

Further, the effects of several factors on various sentencing outcomes differ according to prior record score levels. Most interestingly, if a defendant already has a serious prior record (a prior record score of three or more) additional increases in the prior record score have comparatively less impact on whether they are incarcerated or receive a dispositional departure. This curvilinear effect is also present for sentence length, but it is far less strong. The negative impacts of offense severity and multiple convictions on the likelihood of avoiding incarceration or getting a dispositional departure also decrease moderately for those with serious priors. For sentence length, however, the effect of multiple convictions also decreases for the serious priors group, but the effect of offense severity becomes stronger.

Trials, especially jury trials, consistently carry a greater penalty among defendants with serious priors in terms of incarceration, dispositional departure, and sentence lengths. Further, negotiated pleas offer serious priors defendants no sentencing advantages over other guilty pleas. While age has a greater negative influence on sentence length for the serious priors group, serious prior convictions seem to have a moderate "equalizing" effect on the gender and race differences in terms of incarceration, dispositional departure, and length.

This chapter, then, has presented a detailed picture of statewide sentencing outcomes under the guidelines, and the relative influence of legally prescribed and extralegal factors.[13] But what insight can we gain into the kinds of processes behind these sentencing outcomes, and into the contextual influences on these processes? The next three chapters analyze sentencing outcomes, court community contexts, and case processing strategies in the three focus counties; Metro (large), Rich (medium), and Southwest (small).

5

Metro County

With a population of nearly one-and-a-half million, Metro County encompassed one of the major metropolises in the state. Once an economically depressed area that relied on heavy industry, Metro County had experienced something of an economic and civic rebound. The area's average unemployment rate for 1990 and 1991 was about 4 percent, slightly below the state average. While the county's black population was smaller than the state average (about 11 percent), it was also home to large and vibrant ethnic communities.[1] The county had long been a Democratic party stronghold, with 68 percent of its voters registered as Democrats (see also Levin 1977).

In order to illuminate patterns in sentencing outcomes in Metro's large urban court community, I present statistical analyses similar to those in the previous chapter. I then turn to the ethnographic data to discuss the court community's political and organizational contexts, workgroup members' case processing strategies, and the relationship of these factors to the sentencing outcomes evident in the statistical analysis.

Statistical Analysis of Conviction and Sentencing Outcomes

Appendix C shows descriptive statistics for the 26,077 cases used in the Metro County analyses. Most of the variables' descriptive profiles are similar to those in the statewide analysis, though the range of variation in offense severity and prior record is slightly larger. While overall incarceration decisions are split nearly 50-50, more than 20 percent of cases in the cells where dispositional departures are possible result in such departures. Further, 23 percent of all sentences in Metro County were either durational or dispositional departures below guidelines, while 14 percent of all sentences depart above the midpoint of the standard guideline

TABLE 5.1

Modes of Conviction by Offense Severity: Metro County
(cell percentages by row)

	Modes of Conviction				
Offense Severity	Other guilty pleas	Negotiated pleas	Bench trials	Jury trials	Total
1	2,864% 71%	9330% 23%	226% 6%	370% 1%	4,060
2	1,554 67%	464 20%	262 11.3%	36 1.5%	2,316
3	2,145 78.5%	402 14.7%	162 6%	23 1%	2,732
4	887 67%	318 24%	99 7.5%	16 1%	1,320
5	6,181 76%	1,406 17%	429 5.3%	113 1.4%	8,129
6	2,248 63.4%	862 24.3%	240 6.8%	194 5.5%	3,544
7	1,781 57.5%	842 27.2%	294 9.5%	183 5.9%	3,100
8	145 48%	80 27%	41 13.6%	35 11.6%	301
9	209 39%	110 21%	100 18.6%	119 22%	538
10	25 45%	5 9%	11 20%	14 25%	55
Total	18,039 69%	5,422 21%	1,864 7%	770 3%	26,095

Chi-squared = 1,958   df = 27 $p<.0001$

ranges. Clearly, then, Metro County court actors are not reluctant to sentence outside the guidelines, and are more apt to sentence below them than above them.

Table 5.1 shows a crosstabulation of mode of conviction by offense severity, which exhibits an interesting pattern.

In Metro County, the vast majority of cases were disposed through "other" guilty pleas that, according to the interview data, consist overwhelmingly of open pleas (guilty pleas to original charges without a negotiated agreement between counsel). Only 21 percent of cases were disposed through negotiated plea agreements. On the other hand, Metro County court experienced more trials (just over 10 percent) than the statewide average (6 percent). Most of these trials were bench trials. However, the proportion of open pleas declined steadily with offense severity, while the proportions of negotiated pleas, bench trials, and jury trials increased. As I discuss later, the ethnographic data show that this pattern in convictions reflects an important feature of actors' case-processing strategies.

Table 5.2 shows models of overall incarceration decisions, state prison decisions, and dispositional departures in Metro County.

The models are quite similar to those in the statewide analyses, but show some notable differences. Once again, the strongest influences on these sentencing outcomes were the legally prescribed ones that are supposed to be the primary sentencing considerations under guidelines. Those convicted by bench and especially jury trials as well as blacks were considerably more likely to be incarcerated (the first model) and less likely to receive dispositional departures (the third model). The size of these effects are roughly similar to the statewide analyses.

On the other hand, the effects for negotiated pleas and gender differed from the statewide analysis. While negotiated pleas were much less frequent than open pleas in Metro County, they brought decreased odds for incarceration and greater odds for dispositional departures compared to the rest of the state.[2] These odds indicate a –.16 probability difference in incarceration favoring negotiated pleas over open pleas, and a .26 difference in the probability of dispositional departures. The gender effect, however, is smaller than in the statewide analysis. The incarceration odds for females were 31 percent less than those for males, (compared to about 50 percent less statewide) and the dispositional departure odds for females are only 61 percent greater than those for males

TABLE 5.2

Logit Models of Overall Incarceration, State Imprisonment, and
Dispositional Departures: Metro County
Odds Ratios (logits in parentheses)

Variable	Overall Incarceration	State Prison	Dispositional Departure
Constant **	— (–3.9)	— (–1.31)	— (–3.33)
Year	1.005 (.005) *	.92 (–.087)	1.05 (.04)
Homicide	2.13 (.756)	3.39 (1.22)	**
Kidnapping	.51 (–.69) *	2.33 (.85)	**
Rape/IDSI	2.55 (.94)	4.9 (1.59)	.39 (–.93)
Robbery	1.71 (.53)	3.0 (1.10)	.62 (–.485)
Aggravated assault	1.23 (.20) *	1.89 (.64)	1.06 (.057) *
Simple assault	1.18 (.17) *	1.37 (.318)	**
Arson	1.03 (.033) *	2.42 (.88)	.90 (–.106) *
Weapons	.86 (–.15) *	.56 (–.57)	2.07 (.726)
Burglary	.96 (–.04) *	2.18 (.78)	1.32 (.276)
Criminal trespassing	.97 (–.03) *	1.94 (.66)	.50 (–.70) *
Theft	.72 (–.33)	1.96 (.67)	1.55 (.44)
Forgery	.63 (–.47)	1.51 (.41)	1.58 (.457)
Drug felonies	1.59 (.46)	1.86 (.625)	1.08 (.08) *
Drug misdemeanors	1.14 (.13) *	1.79 (.58)	**
Offense severity	1.85 (.61)	2.14 (.76)	.73 (–.314)
Prior record	1.61 (.48)	1.68 (.52)	.79 (–.234)
Multiple conviction charges	1.08 (.076) *	.85 (–.16)	.78 (–.247)
Negotiated plea	.73 (–.31)	.61 (–.50)	1.73 (.54)
Bench trial	1.60 (.47)	1.49 (.40)	.51 (–.67)
Jury trial	2.85 (1.04)	3.96 (1.38)	.33 (–1.11)
Race (black=1)	1.65 (.49)	1.32 (.28)	.64 (–.45)
Gender (female=1)	.69 (–.37)	.80 (–.22)	1.61 (.478)
Age	.99 (–.01)	.99 (–.01)	1.01 (.01)
N =	26,077	26,077	11,351
Chi-square	11,231	11,222	1,057
(model accuracy)	(85%)	(84%)	(79%)

* Denotes coefficients not significant at .005 or less.
** Retail theft and other guilty pleas are reference categories. In the dispositional departure model, homicide and kidnapping are omitted due to too few dispositional departure cases; simple assault and drug misdemeanors are omitted due to too few cases where dispositional departure is possible.

(compared to more than two-to-one odds for females statewide). This amounts to a –.18 female-male probability difference for incarceration and a .24 probability difference for dispositional departure.

However, the second model in Table 5.2—the state prison model—differs from Metro's overall incarceration model in important respects. First, in terms of mode of conviction, negotiated pleas protected defendants from imprisonment to a moderately greater extent than from overall incarceration, and the imprisonment odds associated with bench trials were smaller than were the odds for incarceration. On the other hand, jury trials increased the odds of imprisonment to a much greater extent than they did for overall incarceration. Conversion of these odds ratios to probability differences indicates a –.24 difference in the probability of state imprisonment between negotiated and other guilty pleas, a .19 imprisonment probability difference between bench trials and other pleas, and a .60 imprisonment probability difference between jury trials and other pleas. Second, as in the statewide analysis, the effects of race and gender were weaker for imprisonment than for overall incarceration. The imprisonment odds for Metro County blacks were 32 percent higher compared to nonblacks, and the odds for women were only 20 percent less than those for men. The odds convert to a .14 black-nonblack difference in the probability of state imprisonment and a –.12 female-male imprisonment probability difference.

Table 5.3 presents Metro County's incarceration length model (as with the length models in chapter 4, it is corrected for selection bias and includes only incarceration cases).

The model explains nearly 60 percent of the variance in minimum incarceration lengths. It is again similar to the statewide analysis in that offense type/severity and prior record are the strongest determinants of sentence lengths. While defendants convicted by trial, blacks, and males tended to receive longer incarceration terms, the size of these effects differed from the rest of the state. Sentences in bench trials in Metro County were about 2.5 months longer than statewide sentences in bench trials, but sentences in Metro jury trials were 3.5 months shorter. As with incarceration decisions, negotiated pleas (though less frequent than open pleas) brought a much greater sentence length advantage over open pleas than in the statewide analysis. The Metro County race influence on sentence length was 1.7 months greater than that for the rest of the state, while the gender effect was shorter by about three months.

TABLE 5.3

OLS Models of Incarceration Length, Corrected for Selection Bias: Metro County (incarceration cases only)

Variable	b (Beta)	Contribution to R^2
Constant **	−25.2 (—)	—
Year	−.03 (−.003)	.0001
Homicide	36.4 (.136)	—
Kidnapping	20.1 (.045)	—
Rape/IDSI	26.9 (.21)	—
Robbery	16.6 (.235)	—
Aggravated assault	12.3 (.09)	—
Simple assault	4.7 (.045)	—
Arson	9.5 (.096)	—
Weapons	−4.37 (−.034)	—
Burglary	−.35 (−.01) *	—
Criminal trespass	4.7 (.025)	—
Theft	−.15 (−.003) *	—
Forgery	−2.7 (−.02)	—
Drug felonies	17.5 (.20)	—
Drug misdemeanors	2.5 (.05)	—
total offense R^2 contrib.		.218
Offense severity	12.1 (.86)	.142
Prior record	7.65 (.62)	.134
Multiple charges	.85 (.02)	.0005
Negotiatied plea	−3.8 (−.076)	.005
Bench trial	4.5 (.06)	.0038
Jury trial	12.1 (.13)	.015
Race (black=1)	4.8 (.11)	.01
Gender (female=1)	−3.2 (−.048)	.0022
Age	−.14 (−.06)	.003
Correction factor	63.8 (.67)	.056
N =		12,769
Adjusted R^2		.59

* Denotes coefficients not significant at .005 or less.
** Retail theft and other guilty pleas are reference categories.

As in the statewide analysis, the influence of mode of conviction, race, gender, and prior record itself on overall incarceration and dispositional departure differed for defendants with serious and less serious prior records (models not shown). First, increases in prior record score increased overall incarceration odds by 2.27 among those with less serious prior records, and decreased the odds of dispositional departure by 40 percent (odds=.60). Among those with serious priors, additional increases in prior record score only increased incarceration odds by 28 percent (odds=1.28), and decreased dispositional departure odds by 20 percent (odds=.80).

Second, negotiated pleas benefited defendants with serious priors to a greater extent than those with less serious priors. Negotiated pleas decreased the odds of incarceration by 43 percent (odds=.57) for serious priors defendants but only by 14 percent (odds=.86) for those with less serious prior records, and increased the dispositional departure odds by 62 percent (odds=1.62) for those with serious priors, but only by a nonsignificant 18 percent for less serious priors defendants. On the other hand, while jury trials increased the incarceration odds for less serious priors defendants by 2.86 and decreased dispositional departure odds by 61 percent (odds=.39), incarceration odds increased for serious priors defendants by 3.56 and dispositional departure odds decreased by 72 percent (odds=.28). Thus, jury trials hampered serious priors defendants' chances of getting a nonincarceration sentence to a much greater extent than among those with less serious priors.

Third, as in the statewide models, gender differences in overall incarceration decisions decreased among serious priors defendants (dispositional departure models showed no substantial difference in race and gender effects between the two groups of defendants). The incarceration odds for women with less serious priors were .67, or 33 percent less than for men, but among those with serious priors, women's odds were .86, or 14 percent less than those of men. However, unlike the statewide models, race differences became more pronounced among those with serious priors. Blacks' incarceration odds among less serious priors defendants were 1.53, or 53 percent greater than those for nonblacks (less than the statewide prior record interaction effect), but for those with serious priors were 1.83, or 83 percent greater than those of nonblacks.

I also tested models of durational departure below and above guidelines, but these explained little variance and did not differ substantially from the statewide models. Therefore, they are omitted here. These statistical analyses of Metro County's sentencing patterns laid the groundwork for the ethnographic analysis, which explores the contexts, organizational arrangements, and interaction strategies that lie behind the sentencing outcomes.

Ethnographic Analysis

Political Contexts and Sponsoring Agency Organization

The county's violent crime rate for the late 1980s and early 1990s was the second highest in the state, ensuring heavy caseloads for the county trial court. According to interviews, however, news media paid little attention to court case processing and sentencing except in sensational, high-profile cases. Apparently, routine court matters could not compete with the city's many other social, political, and sports happenings for media attention, and the conviction and sentencing of thousands of ordinary felonies and misdemeanors largely escaped the notice of the public.

Not surprisingly, the large criminal bench in Metro County (roughly twenty-five judges who regularly handled criminal cases) had long been dominated by judges closely aligned with the Democratic party. In fact, only one of the criminal court judges was a Republican. Most judges had been either public or private defense attorneys, or had worked in private practice in other areas of law. The bench's level of judicial experience varied considerably—while three judges had more than twenty years' experience on the bench, most had three to five years of judicial experience, and a few had come to the bench within the previous two years.

The judges did not specialize in terms of criminal case types, but were instead assigned a mixed caseload. The cases came in from the lower district justice courts to the trial court clerk's office, and were then screened by a District Attorney's office committee. After case screening, the administrative judge maintained an individual calendar system and assigned cases to judges according to two criteria he called "complexity" and "equality."

Complexity referred to the amount of courtroom time a case was likely to consume; that is, whether a case would likely be resolved by a quick guilty plea or whether it had problematic features that demanded more time to resolve. By equality, the administrative judge meant the fair allocation of a mix of difficult and more routine cases to judges, ensuring that high-profile cases were spread around to different judges. In fact, he tried to make sure that judges who were up for election or retention got more high-profile cases, which offered the opportunity for a judge to garner favorable media attention (a strategy which could, of course, backfire if the case resulted in critical media attention).

Nardulli et al. (1988) and Flemming et al. (1992) state that "judge shopping," or routing cases into the courtrooms of particular judges who will be more likely to give a particular sentence, is less likely under individual than master calendar systems. Metro County's individual calendar system exemplified this proposition. Assistant District Attorneys and defenders interviewed in Metro County indicated that judge shopping was nearly impossible. The administrative judge had almost total control over case assignment, and other workgroup members had almost no opportunity to influence case assignment. Once assigned, the case stayed with a particular judge throughout pretrial, conviction, and sentencing stages.

The only limited possibility of judge shopping occurred when a judge formally rejected a plea agreement. The prosecution and defense could then get another judge to accept the plea agreement, but if and only if they could find a judge with both the docket space and the inclination to do so. Overall, this relative inability to judge-shop added to the sentencing influence and overall power of judges; once a case was assigned to a judge, counsel were generally stuck with him or her (cf., Eisenstein et al. 1988, pp. 111–12, 237).

The current chief DA in Metro County was also a Democrat and was first elected to this position fifteen years before the collection of the interview data. The large district attorney's staff of assistant district attorneys (ADAs) were organized into teams that specialized in handling different types of offenses. This staff had a high turnover, and therefore, most ADAs were young and inexperienced. The ideological tone of the DA's office, which stemmed largely from the chief DA himself, was described by judges and defense attorneys as "liberal" and "practical." Interviews with ADAs and team supervisors indicated a belief in rehabilitation as an important—though not overriding—sentencing goal, a willingness to sacrifice punitiveness for moving cases quickly, and a belief that tough sentencing practices alone could not solve the city's crime problems. To control the inexperienced ADA trial court teams, the office had instituted a policy of formal and centralized supervision of case processing. The DA's office had also assumed control over compiling and calculating the guidelines for criminal history and offense severity information. This information went largely uncontested by other court actors.

Finally, the Public Defenders' office was also centrally coordinated. The roughly fifty members of the PD staff were all part-time, and members worked in private practices on the side. In general, the PD's office employed more individuals with longer experience practicing in the court community than did the DA's office. The PD's office also experienced less personnel turnover, with attorneys reportedly staying in the office for an average of two to three years, and then typically moving on to a fully private practice.

Unlike ADAs, PDs worked individually and without much supervision. This arrangement was partly the result of the organizational and personal style of the chief public defender, which was described as "laid back" and "laissez faire." It was also partly due to the fact that most of the public defenders had enough trial court experience to warrant less supervision. Also, unlike the ADAs, PDs did not specialize, but rather handled a mixed caseload of various kinds of offenses. Newly hired PDs received very little organized training from the office or informal socialization from their peers. One PD explains the office's organization this way: "We are really on our own. No one reviews our cases, even for homicides. When you first come on, there's nobody who tells you what to expect or what to do. Mostly you just learn what you're doing by doing it." While the PD's office handled most of the court's cases, Metro County had a sizable and experienced private defense bar. The administrative judge (the most senior member of the bench) reported that about twenty-five fully private attorneys were "regulars" in the trial court.

In this political and organizational context, what role did the guidelines play in the distribution of case processing discretion between court-sponsoring agencies? Levin's (1977) research in this same county, as well as some of the interviews for this study, indicated that before implementating the guidelines, Metro County judges had exercised enormous discretion in sentencing. As will be seen later, the guidelines certainly had not removed judges' sentencing discretion. On the other hand, they did appear to foster more uniformity and predictability in judges' sentences. Judges had come to accept and rely upon the guidelines as a convenient tool for easier decision making. This was especially true of the roughly ten judges who had come on the bench within the last five years. The following quote exemplifies the general embracement of guidelines among Metro County's newer judges: "The guidelines give me a lot of discretion and they give me some guidance. That is what they are supposed to do. It makes me feel a little more secure. When I was running for judge, I was thinking about how tough it would be to be a judge. When do you say 1 to 2? When do you say 5 to 10? The guidelines offer me something that helps me." Judges' acceptance and use of the guidelines also allowed ADAs and defenders to predict sentencing outcomes with reduced uncertainty. As an ADA team leader described: "You walk into a lot of judges' courtrooms and the judge will almost always sentence in the mitigated range. Other judges will hit the standard range every time . . . We also might have a new judge who doesn't really have a good feel for sentencing. You at least know that there is some benchmark that they can use."

The structure of the guidelines also formalized the range of potential items on the plea agenda that ADAs and the defense bar could use in plea negotiations. Under guidelines, several plea concessions were theoretically possible: (1) charge reductions or drops that reduced offense severity levels; (2) agreements for specific standard, mitigated range, or departure sentences; or more rarely, (3) agreements not to seek aggravating sentence enhancements specified by the guidelines (e.g., deadly weapon enhancements, aggravating factors for drug trafficking). Each of these were used at one time or another, with sentencing agreements being the most common. According to the hydraulic displacement of discretion argument, one would expect that this structuring of sentencing outcomes and formalization of plea agendas would have given ADAs more discretionary leverage in plea negotiations—especially those focusing on charge reductions—and greater ability to influence sentencing. One would expect this influence to be even further augmented given the DA's office's control over the processing of guidelines information and sentencing calculations.

However, these potential advantages did not seem to translate into greater plea bargaining leverage and sentencing influence for individual ADAs. The structuring of case processing around the use of guidelines also increased the ability of the team supervisors to control the activities of the many inexperienced ADAs, and to ensure greater uniformity in case processing decisions. As the chief assistant DA (who oversaw the team supervisors) explained:

> "The guidelines have been an aid to us. We are a pretty large office and we have a fairly good turnover. We hire a lot of people that have no criminal experience. There was a time when there were such differences of opinion as to what kind of sentence should be offered on a case. Now the guidelines give assistants a place to work from. It does make it easier to control things and make sure there is consistency."

This quote also suggests that before guidelines, judges' individualistic and widely varying sentencing practices and the heavy turnover in DA's personnel largely prevented the development of a strong system of informal going rates (cf., Eisenstein and Jacob, 1977, pp. 61-62). A longtime PD also indicates the lack of any informal sentencing norms that were not based on the guidelines: "There's very little sense of rules of thumb, other than the guidelines. There never were, actually."

Under guidelines, however, the DA's office had developed formal policies that expected ADAs to produce convictions resulting in guideline range sentences. Further, according to office policy, negotiated charge reductions and departures below guidelines (whether or not they've resulted from a plea bargain) had to be reviewed and approved by team supervisors. Thus, several people interviewed indicated that real plea bargaining discretion and authority lay with team supervisors, and not individual ADAs (especially inexperienced ones). Because of these office policies, ADAs had considerable discretion in unilateral charging decisions, but very little plea negotiating discretion.

Workgroup Strategies and Sentencing Guidelines

The contextual features noted above—such as the judges' political dominance, the case assignment system, the DA's office organization, the relative stability of the PD's office personnel compared to the DA's office, and the distribution of sentencing discretion under the guidelines—shaped the case processing strategies of workgroup members.

Judges' sentencing practices. Metro County judges traditionally preferred defendant-oriented, individualized sentencing, and were prone to leniency (cf., Levin 1977). The data indicate a continued orientation toward the particular situation and characteristics of individual defendants. When asked about their goals in sentencing, the judges' responses centered around dominant themes of rehabilitative potential and opportunity on one hand, and blameworthiness or desert of punishment on the other. The following quotes from two of the judges illustrate this:

> Every case is so different . . . People who steal like four or five dollars' worth of stuff from the grocery store, or are charged with possession of marijuana with intent to deliver—one or two months in jail doesn't do that person any good. It will make you lose your job and your place in society. I wouldn't give anybody a month or two in jail. But it's different if it's

violence, what I deem senseless violence. 'They were sleeping, why did you go upstairs and hit them in the head? There was no reason to do that.' I always consider the nature of the offense, the defendant's prior record, their character and attitude in general. It is just everything put together.

I see a retail thief, depending on what they are stealing, I had someone in here one time who stole 'Preparation H!' How are you going to bang someone for stealing a bunch of Preparation H? Or steak or bread for the kids? On the other hand, I had one occasion where I gave someone the maximum sentence, it was a very nasty rape, knifing thing. I put him away as long as I could.

Like most counties around the state (Steffensmeier 1992), Metro County jail resources were strained beyond capacity. In fact, Metro County was the first county in the state to be placed under a superior court order to reduce jail populations. To relieve crowding, jail inmates were often "farmed out" to neighboring counties. Further, less serious offenders were sometimes simply released from the jail before serving their minimum terms through the county's "good time" policy in order to make room for more serious offenders (as mentioned in chapter 3, the Pennsylvania state prison system had no early release program, but many county jails had their own "good time" programs allowing early release). The jail crowding situation often became a factor in sentencing decisions as well. As one public defender stated: "On some cases, judges are reluctant to put people in overcrowded jails—when it is only county time called for. The DA and the defense are both aware that the judge may be hesitant to put him in jail for a couple months. The judge can use jail overcrowding to go outside the guidelines." A judge described how he took jail capacity into account this way: "A retail theft or marijuana possession or something, I'm not going to put that person in jail. I say, 'Look, you might deserve to be there, but I don't have the space to waste on you.'" Members of the DA's office disliked the fact that jail capacity was taken into account in sentencing, but felt there was little they could do about it. As the head of the team supervisors said:

We do not ever take (jail capacity) into consideration as a factor, but judges do. They will usually do it in the guise of saying this thing that they don't want the guy to go to jail. What they really mean is that there are other people who should be in jail as opposed to this person. I don't think it is our position to deal with it and I don't think it should be the judges' either. It is not their fault that the jails are overcrowded. I think all of us are kind of surprised that they take it into account.

The guidelines provided specific mechanisms by which judges could reward what they called "deserving" defendants with lenient sentences, and also avoid exacerbating the correctional crowding problem. The most prominent example was a guilty plea discount based on the guidelines' mitigated sentence ranges. Many judges had informally established, through repeated sentencing decisions over time, a reward in the form of mitigated range sentences for defendants who pled guilty. In fact, this mitigated range discount was often given even in open plea cases, where the defendant pled guilty without a negotiated agreement. Metro County statistical data indicate that while mitigated range sentences were given in 50 percent of negotiated plea cases, 31 percent of open plea cases also received mitigated range sentences. Thus, both interview and statistical data show that while negotiated pleas provided a distinct advantage, they were not always necessary for a defendant to receive a plea reward. As one ADA remarked: "I've yet to see a judge in this county go beyond the mitigated range for a first- or second-time offender who pleads guilty."

Arguably, this practice penalized defendants convicted by trial. However, many of the judges felt that a plea of guilty indicated defendant "remorse" and cooperation with the court, and defined the plea discount as a necessity for rewarding such defendants (cf., Brereton and Casper 1984). The following quote is typical of many Metro County judges' interpretations of this plea discount:

> People who plead guilty always argue that remorse is a mitigating factor, and one cannot deny that. They are saying 'I am sorry, I did it.' I consider that a mitigating factor. If you don't plead guilty and go to trial, then there is the absence of a mitigating factor. Sure enough after a trial at the time of sentencing he will be remorseful. He might have taken the stand and said he didn't do it, now he is remorseful. I ask what he is remorseful about. He will say that he hates to be in this situation. I say that I am sure you do, and maybe I don't want to

be in this position either. You could look at it as a penalty but there is no other way of doing it. You have to give people credit for pleading guilty and expressing remorse. It is that simple. I choose not to call it a sentencing penalty.

Some experienced public defenders, however, agreed that judges reward guilty pleas, but argued that judges also may penalize trials, especially what they consider "frivolous" ones. As one PD stated: "In cases where it is obvious you are not going to win, they make it plain that if you go to trial you are not going to be very happy."

On the other hand, judges sometimes used the guidelines to give defendants breaks in bench trials. According to both DAs and defenders, the guidelines facilitated a practice that might be called "bench trial charge reduction." An ADA explains this practice: "Sometimes at a bench trial, you'll see the judge sitting there flipping through the guidelines, looking for a sentence range that fits with what he wants to give (the defendant). Then, he'll find the defendant guilty of a lesser charge that fits with a lesser guidelines range sentence that he wants to give him . . . They are the judge. They can do whatever the hell they want."

A judge also described the bench trial process: "Bench trials are very common here. What we often have is a situation where the assistant DA has to charge something higher than he wants in order to please his supervisor or the police. Then it will go to a bench trial and be reduced. That way the assistant looks good for his office and the defense is happy too."

In other words, the bench trial provided an opportunity for the judge to alter the charge to fit with a sentence he/she preferred to give. For example, I witnessed a fifteen-minute bench trial in which the judge reduced a felony auto theft charge to a misdemeanor charge involving unlawful use of property, and then sentenced the defendant to probation.

Thus, while the guidelines increased the uniformity and predictability of judges' sentences in general, they still used their ample discretion within the guidelines to mete out leniency for some defendants and greater punishment for others. Further, judges sometimes manipulated charges in bench trials, and in doing so used the guidelines as a reference to determine the sentencing consequences of different charges.

ADAs' case processing strategies. Because of the DA's close supervision policy and judges' frequent use of guideline ranges as mechanisms for leniency, ADAs learned to "play it safe" in charging decisions. Indeed, while ADAs and their supervisors held that guidelines generally facilitated charging decisions and enhanced the predictability of sentencing outcomes, their most salient complaints about sentencing under guidelines involved judicial discretion. Several of those interviewed wished that judges were more constrained from departing below guidelines, that the prospects for successful DA appeals of departures below guidelines were greater, and that the power of judges to alter charges in bench trials would be eliminated. Overall, Metro County DAs believed that the guidelines did not go far enough in limiting judicial discretion and power. This attitude further suggests the dominance of the bench in Metro County's court community.

Nonetheless, ADAs came to rely heavily on the guideline sentence recommendations as a baseline for charging decisions so they could obtain guilty pleas that resulted in sentences somewhere in the guideline ranges, and thus avoid scrutiny from team supervisors. Inexperienced ADAs became adept at using the guidelines matrix in charging decisions quite early in their on-the-job socialization. ADAs made case-by-case initial charging decisions on the basis of the following factors: (1) case evidence strength (the weaker the evidence, the less severe the charges), (2) the trial judges' reputations and preferences, (3) defense counsels' probable strategies, and (4) factors involving what they referred to as the defendant's "character." These factors included the seriousness of behavior related to the offense, the defendant's education, employment history, the age and seriousness of criminal history, and family status.

The ADAs then played "a numbers game" with the guidelines to select a charge that fit with a sentence range that would most likely induce a guilty plea from the defendant. Thus, while ADAs manipulated charges with guideline sentences in mind, they tended to do so *unilaterally*, without negotiation with defenders. One ADA described the guidelines' influence on his charging decisions and how he maximized the probability of a easy guilty plea to a guideline sentence: "You have to learn the judges and how to play with the different counting of crimes. You just have to be a little more creative in charging, to charge the right things and say the right things." Another ADA described a similar process: "I bring out this little gray book (guidelines manual) and I open it up and I say that I can convict the defendant of this crime and he has this prior record so this number you put on the chart here and this number over here and this is what he is going to get. More and more, the longer I have been here, the guidelines have become a crutch. I don't have to worry about anything."

The degree of negotiation with defenders concerning guilty plea agreement terms varied according to the negotiating discretion allowed by the team supervisor, which in turn generally depended on the experience of the ADA. Because ADAs were usually allowed little negotiating discretion, actual plea bargaining was comparatively infrequent in Metro County, as the statistics in Table 5.1 suggest. When ADAs did engage in plea negotiations, the negotiations were typically initiated by defenders, and this most often occurred with more serious cases. ADAs were more likely to negotiate plea agreements under certain conditions. First, ADAs were open to negotiation when case evidence was weak, and the ADA would rather make a concession than risk a trial. Second, ADAs would negotiate when the DA's office wanted the defendant as a cooperating witness in another case (especially in drug-related cases).

These conditions, in turn, varied by types of offenses and the policies of the offense-specialized teams' supervisors. For example, the strength of evidence typically varied by offense type. The supervisor of the sexual assault team indicated that his ADAs engaged in plea negotiations (with frequent charge reductions) more often because evidence in such cases was typically weak (e.g., reluctance of victims to testify in court, indefinite physical evidence, lack of witnesses). On the other hand, the supervisor of the drug team said that his ADAs seldom engaged in plea negotiations, unless they wanted to turn the defendant into an informant. The legislature's enactment of stiff mandatory sentences and special (and tougher) guideline ranges for drug felonies significantly raised the stakes involved in drug felony convictions for all concerned. Thus, if the team supervisor felt a case's evidence merited a felony charge, he/she would "prosecute to the fullest." If a potential drug felony case had evidence problems, they unilaterally dropped the case or reduced it to a misdemeanor unless they wanted the defendant's cooperation as an informant.

Overall, ADAs liked to avoid negotiation over charge reductions, because supervisors had to approve such agreements beforehand. Even so, one experienced PD reported that more experienced ADAs sometimes would agree to drop the most severe charge and then inform their supervisors later, and that both charge drops and sentence recommendations could sometimes be bargained. Usually, however, ADAs preferred to agree to make sentence recommendations, especially in cases involving more severe offenses. With or without a charge drop, sentence recommendations were often not very specific, as an ADA team leader described: "We'll agree to a sentence in the standard or mitigated range. As long as it's somewhere in the guidelines, we're happy." A PD also described the typical bargained sentence agreement: "They will say. 'the guidelines are such-and-such, and the mitigated range is such-and-such, and we'll leave it to the court's discretion.'"

ADAs also generally disliked negotiating explicit plea agreements for departures below guidelines, though they would do so on occasion. Such departures were more often the result of implicit sentencing agreements—ADAs would state that they did not object to a departure during the sentence hearing after a plea, a tactic known as "standing silent." The defender was then free to argue for a departure at the sentencing hearing while the ADA stood silent, and the judge was free to depart without risking any prosecutorial protest. A judge explained such implicit sentencing agreements for departures below guidelines:

> The DA will say that they are not agreeing with a departure, but they will not object to it. I love that. What does that mean? Is it a deal or isn't it? You have the right to object and you say that you are not going to object, therefore you are giving up something and they are giving up something. Therefore it is a deal.

This strategy of standing silent allowed the ADA to obtain a guilty plea conviction, while also avoiding the need for supervisors' approval of formally agreeing to a departure or charge reduction.

ADAs reportedly found either implicit or negotiated sentencing agreements for departures preferable to explicit plea bargains involving charge reductions. The difference between the two strategies hinged on the ADA's degree of accountability to the team supervisor. The need for prior supervisor approval made negotiated charge reductions less attractive to ADAs as concessions. Team supervisors also reviewed departure cases with ADAs, but the issue was usually whether to appeal the departure (which seldom occurred). ADAs were generally held less accountable for departure decisions, which were formally the judge's domain and beyond the ADA's control. In fact, team supervisors typically voiced the opinion that they would like to use the appeal process as a check on judicial discretion, but their appeals had been unsuccessful. As one team supervisor explained,

> The threat of appeals might constrain the judges a little, but I don't think they realize that we haven't been as successful as we'd like to be. . . . We've done a few appeals. We lost them all. The judge was always defended. [The appellate court] upholds the judges' reasons, whether we feel that they are valid or not. Now it just doesn't seem productive to keep hammering away at it. . . . We haven't really done an appeal in two years.

Defender strategies. Like ADAs, defenders formulated more or less unilateral, case-by-case strategies according to probable sentencing outcomes within the guideline matrix. One PD said: "My first move is to find out from the DA what the (guideline) numbers are, and then decide where to go from there." In fact, routine cases were seen by the PD and the ADA the day the case was scheduled for court, leaving little time for elaborate negotiations. Another PD described the way routine, less serious cases were handled: "On less serious cases, the general practice is to wait until the day the case appears on the trial list and then try to figure out what to do."

Because of the relatively lenient sentencing practices among judges and the lack of plea bargaining discretion among ADAs, an open plea with the possibility of a mitigated range plea reward from the judge (or even a departure below guidelines) was often an attractive strategy for defenders in routine cases. As one PD described, "There are a lot of open pleas, a lot of 'leave it to the judge' ideas. Because a lot of them are former defense attorneys, and we know pretty well the way they're thinking. So it's better to leave it to the judge. Plus, the guidelines make it more predictable."

In more severe cases (especially those involving drug-trafficking and other charges that carry mandatory sentences), defenders sometimes tried to negotiate an agreement, but would also sometimes opt for a bench trial in hopes of a "bench trial charge reduction." As one PD extensively described the uses of bench trials:

> Again, it's the personality of the bench. Certain judges you're never afraid to take a bench trial to, because you know you'll come out all right. You just go in and make your case and

they give you a decision right then. The DAs rarely make a stink about it. . . . Another time is when you think that once a judge gets a look at the victim, he's going to have a different reaction. Like if you have a simple assault and a resisting arrest, you can show that the assault was on the officer and he just charged the resisting arrest to get back at the guy. Or if it's from a suburban township, the DA might want to charge something less but the police won't let him because they've got a hard-on for the guy. Things like that are when a bench trial is useful.

The guidelines played a definite role of uncertainty reduction in these strategic decisions: "In some cases, the guidelines help you know if there is just nothing to gain from a plea, where there is just nothing to lose by going to trial. So you go to trial and maybe you will get lucky and get away with nothing. For example, it is hard to get someone to plead guilty to five years and not even put up a struggle."

After both open pleas and bench trials, defenders argued for leniency before the judge at the sentencing hearing, and their success depended on their ability to predict sentencing outcomes based on the sentencing guidelines, and their knowledge of various judges' preferences and attitudes. As one PD explained:

As you gain experience, you learn there is a whole list of types of cases that you know will more than likely be probation, no matter what. I could spend a lot of time listing them and I wouldn't hit them all. And your knowledge of this is pretty much based on the guidelines, although the more serious the case, the less clear the picture becomes, since the guideline ranges get wider for more serious cases. We also understand what will fly and what won't in certain judges' courtrooms. Like, there is a judge who really cares a great deal about auto theft. Where some judges will give probation, this guy will give six months or some amount of time . . . always consistent with the guidelines but still a little out of line with some of the other judges.

Thus, the bench and defense bar had greater membership stability, shared greater familiarity, and more ideological congruence than did the DA's office (see also Ulmer 1995). These factors, along with heavy reliance on guidelines to provide greater certainty of outcomes, sometimes made open plea and bench trial strategies as attractive as plea negotiations.

Given the constrained discretion of most ADAs, the sentencing practices of the judges, and the lack of time for elaborate bargaining, defenders would approach ADAs for plea negotiations only in cases that "really merit the effort" (e.g., cases with clear mitigating circumstances, weak prosecution evidence, or unduly severe charges): "On more serious cases or ones with problems, I will talk with the DA about the case and about any possible deals we can reach. Try to have it hammered out before the day of the trial. You know that it will be a little tougher to negotiate, but you don't want to have to deal with it under pressure, with a judge breathing down your neck to hurry up." When such cases occurred, defenders typically sought such guidelines-based concessions as general agreements for mitigated or bottom-standard range sentences, agreements for departures, the dropping of aggravating guidelines enhancements, county jail rather than state prison, or charge reductions. Charge reductions were less frequent and were often sought in clear cases of police overcharging or when a case involved a charge that carried a mandatory sentence. As one PD said, "Whenever there is a mandatory, I'm always asking for something, otherwise you might as well go to trial." On the other hand, both defenders and the ADAs in the drug unit indicated that mandatory drug charges were seldom successfully bargained down. If the prosecutors had sufficient evidence, they went forward with the mandatory charge.

The success with which defenders could extract such concessions largely depended on their experience and skill, the negotiating discretion allowed the ADA by the team supervisor (which varied by ADA experience), and the supervisor's attitudes toward the case. Indeed, experienced defenders sometimes went directly to DA team supervisors to initiate plea negotiations. As another PD described:

> The (DA) assistants don't have discretion. Your supervisors have the sole discretion. It is only the experienced ADA who has the freedom to go with the facts of the case and make a reasonable decision. So because they have such a young staff, you can't really work deals with them. You are dealing with a supervisor. And there are some of those supervisors who are just unbelievable. If it happens to be one of those that is a real hard-liner, you have nothing to work with. You might as well go to trial.

An experienced private defense attorney concurred, saying:

> I have cases where I think a departure below is appropriate. I go to the DA's office, above the trial assistant to the supervisor. I tell him that if I am able to get the judge to depart below based on these facts, will you agree not to object or appeal? Then I present it to the judge. I don't do it often, but I will when I have a case that merits it.

Although guidelines made much more extensive prior record information available to workgroup members than was the case before guidelines (see Kramer and Steffensmeier 1993), those interviewed indicated that prior record scores were almost never the subject of negotiation or even dispute. In fact, when I asked one PD if she ever bargained over prior record scores, she replied, "You can bargain over prior record? Quick, tell me how!" She and others indicated that convictions that were ten years old or more once posed a particular problem in that they inflated the defendant's prior record score and put him/her in a more severe sentence range than deserved. However, another PD stated that the DA's office had recently begun unilaterally excluding prior convictions that were older than ten years (except for violent and sex offenses) from prior record scores.

In sum, it appears that defenders more often directed their efforts at securing leniency for defendants toward judges rather than toward negotiation with DAs. These defender strategies in response to judicial practices and DA office policies explains the large proportions of open pleas for less serious offenses and offenders, and increases in negotiated pleas and trials at more severe offense and criminal history score levels. On the other hand, interviews with both defenders and ADAs indicated that a defendant with an extensive prior record was already at a severe disadvantage in terms of securing "breaks" in return for pleading guilty, and thus defenders often felt they had little to lose by pursuing a bench or jury trial. This is one thing the PD quoted earlier meant when she said that the guidelines' ranking of offense severity and prior record helped her decide when ". . . there is just nothing to be gained from a plea . . . nothing to lose by going to trial."

As mentioned, the guidelines' structuring of plea agendas and the DA's office's control over guidelines information and processing presented the potential for a great deal of prosecutorial power.

However, the above discussion suggests that two factors in Metro County checked ADAs' ability to take advantage of the potential to wield a great deal of plea bargaining leverage and sentencing discretion. First, the "personality of the bench" was such that judges used their ample discretion under guidelines to reward guilty pleas even in the absence of plea agreements, and fashioned sentences to individual defendants as they saw fit. Second, the DA's office's formal policies emphasizing centralized control largely restricted most ADAs' discretion to unilateral charge manipulations.

Sentencing Outcomes

The discussion of the organizational and interactional contours of case processing in Metro County allows some explanation of the statistical sentencing differences concerning modes of conviction, race, and gender. These extralegal influences apparently stemmed from the local context of judge-dominated individualized sentencing and the ways all the workgroup members used the guidelines within this context—not just prosecutors.

Regarding sentence differences by mode of conviction, I noted that many judges established the guidelines mitigated range as a routine reward for "deserving" defendants who pled guilty, often even in cases where there was no negotiated plea agreement. Therefore, the disparity in incarceration decisions between those who plead guilty and those convicted by trial—especially jury trial—largely flowed from these routine plea rewards. The interview data suggest that those convicted by jury trial did not get the mitigated range plea reward or any chance of leniency following a bench trial, and statistical data bear this out. An additional logistic model (not shown) predicting standard versus mitigated range sentences indicates that, controlling for the usual other factors, the odds of receiving a sentence in the guidelines mitigated range for those convicted by jury trials were about 60 percent less than for those who pleaded guilty. The jury trial defendant was therefore more likely to receive a sentence at or above the standard range minimum unless the defender could successfully persuade the judge to grant a lighter sentence at the sentencing hearing. As the interaction effect with prior record shows, this was especially true among those with serious priors. Likewise, dispositional departures below guidelines most often resulted from situations in which ADAs stood silent in the face of arguments by defense counsel at sentencing hearings, and this helps explain the disparity in departures concerning pleas and trials. Obviously, defendants convicted by trial—especially jury trial—missed the possibility for implicit or explicit agreements for departures.

On the other hand, the statistical analyses clearly show that negotiated pleas brought significant sentencing advantages in Metro County, especially for overall incarceration decisions and dispositional departures. Negotiated pleas were especially beneficial for those with serious priors. How does this finding square with the interview data? As the quotes above indicate, defenders certainly preferred negotiated agreements (especially sentence agreements). The problem was that negotiated pleas were more difficult to achieve because of the lack of negotiating discretion allotted to the young ADAs. Routine, less serious cases were often not worth the effort involved, but defenders would initiate negotiations on more serious cases, when the sentencing stakes were higher (see Table 5.1).

A similar situation characterized dispositional departures. Defenders preferred negotiated sentencing agreements in which the prosecutor explicitly agreed to a departure below guidelines, since judges very rarely rejected such agreements. Since ADAs usually were not given the leeway to negotiate explicit agreements for such departures, defenders usually had to settle for the next best possibility—the open plea with the expectation that the prosecutor would stand silent. In fact, 63 percent of dispositional departures involved open pleas. In sum, while negotiated agreements were ideal for improving chances for leniency, the open plea was the next best—and most common—defense strategy.

Bench trials were an intermediary strategy between negotiated pleas and jury trials, much like the judge-mediated "slow pleas" described by Mather (1973) and Eisenstein and Jacob (1977). On one hand, bench trials were risky for defendants because the advantages of an open or negotiated guilty plea were foregone. On the other hand, bench trials offered the chance of a charge reduction by the judge. The statistical models do not reflect this important possibility, since only conviction charges are included.

Apart from the possibilities for guilty plea rewards that trial defendants lost out on, a further reason for the plea/trial sentence differences became evident in the interviews. While bench trials were sometimes used to present mitigating characteristics of offenses and unfavorable characteristics of victims, both judges and defense attorneys noted that trials—especially jury trials—also risked disclosure of "ugly facts" about cases and defendants that defense counsel could otherwise hide in guilty plea hearings (cf.,

Flemming et al. 1992, ch. 5). The disclosure of such negative facts made it less likely that judges would respond favorably to defense arguments for leniency, as one judge stated:

> You might learn details during the trial that you would not learn at a guilty plea. Hearing that an eight-year-old may be traumatized is not the same as seeing her get up on the stand and sob and cry and fall apart. I had a case of an elderly couple that was robbed. Her husband got up to testify and his wife just collapsed in the courtroom. We had to call an ambulance. Knowing that this robbery had so traumatized these two had an effect on me.

A private defense attorney articulated a similar interpretation:

> Sure, there's a plea discount, but the trial penalty that you have to worry about is that the judge is going to learn too much when you go to trial that he wouldn't otherwise, because you can present a much better sentencing case if the judge doesn't learn all the ugly facts.

The race differences in Metro County were especially prominent for county jail incarceration decisions and dispositional departures. Some interviews indicated that race differences may have been partly due to differential charging and sentencing of black and white cocaine offenders. While white cocaine offenders were most often charged with possessing or dealing the drug in its powder form, the possession and dealing of crack cocaine was an overwhelmingly black-dominated offense. Crack defendants, in turn, were more at risk for charges carrying mandatory drug sentences. Even when mandatory sentences did not apply, several defenders and ADAs indicated that judges viewed crack possession and selling as much more serious offenses, and sentenced crack offenders more harshly than powder cocaine offenders. In other words, judges considered the selling or use of cocaine in its crack form as an aggravating sentence factor. The broad "drug felony" and "drug misdemeanor" categories available in the statistical data cannot capture this distinction between forms of cocaine.

Differences also likely stemmed from white defendants being more advantaged by the discretionary factors that persuaded judges to grant "breaks" at sentencing hearings. The success of defense arguments for probation and dispositional departures was heavily dependent on the judges' assessments of defendants' so-called "character" and risk of future crime. Interviews indicated that both judges and ADAs believed that factors such as the nature, age, and circumstances of prior convictions; participation in self-help programs; education; employment status; and family stability were all indicators of what they called a defendant's "character." To the extent that inner-city black defendants faced such social structural constraints as comparatively fewer educational opportunities, more job discrimination, and unstable family situations (see Massey 1993), the consideration of these kinds of "character" factors by prosecutors and judges in the sentencing process would potentially work to black defendants' disadvantage. A PD also described other factors as they were considered by judges in granting probation sentences, including dispositional departures: "Right off the bat, it would be what the defendant has done on their own to help themselves out. Get a job, put themselves in a drug or alcohol program without being ordered, or do something voluntary like that. All of it centers around the rehabilitation potential of the defendants." In addition, one judge stated that black defendants often could not afford to pay for the voluntary drug and alcohol treatment programs that could provide evidence of rehabilitative potential: "Your white defendants can afford treatment programs more often, when it's a situation where they have to pay. That's a shame, because this kind of thing can be used as an alternative to jail sometimes. Black defendants don't seem to have as much resources to stay out of trouble." As the interviews with the ADAs show, similar factors also influenced plea negotiations for sentencing agreements. To the extent that black defendants were less favorably viewed in terms of these so-called "character" factors, judges would be less likely persuaded toward leniency and ADAs would be less likely to negotiate attractive plea terms. This also illuminates the interaction effect between race and prior record in the Metro County data to some extent. Race differences in county jail incarceration and dispositional departure are well below statewide levels among those with less serious priors, but much greater than statewide among those with serious priors. Thus, when serious prior records combined with unfavorable status characteristics that could be correlated with race in the minds of court actors, race differences could become considerably more pronounced.

Further, some interviews suggested that the courtroom skill and experience of the defense attorney also contributed to a defendant's success in negotiating pleas and arguing for sentencing breaks. Some people interviewed stated that white defendants could often better afford more experienced and skillful private attorneys, and could thus obtain better plea agreements and lenient sentences more often than black defendants, though others disputed this proposition.[3] The following quote from a chief probation officer who worked closely with the court summarizes ways in which race could be associated with sentencing differences:

> Being black and a member of the black community, I'm sensitive to these things. I have seen many black people get convicted of things that, if they had a private attorney, they probably wouldn't have been convicted of. . . . get talked into pleading guilty to something they really don't understand. I am not saying that the PDs aren't effective, its just that a private attorney has more time and incentive to go in there and present a good case. . . . In cases where the judge could go outside the guidelines in favor of the defendant, I think a lot depends on this kind of thing, and whether the defendant is someone the judge may be sympathetic with. The way people look and present themselves can have an effect on the sentence they get. It isn't a perfect system.

Thus, race differences in Metro appeared to involve differential leniency for whites. It is arguable that Metro County's race differences stemmed less from direct, overt antiblack discrimination than from the combination of serious prior records with the consideration of intervening status and resource factors that sometimes disadvantaged black defendants. On the other hand, this distinction would hardly comfort a black defendant incarcerated for the same offense, and with the same prior record, as a white defendant who received probation.

Metro County women were, in general, sentenced more leniently than men, but these gender-based sentencing differences were considerably less than those in the rest of the state. In fact, among serious prior record defendants, gender differences were not even statistically significant. Two factors may help account for this. First, a comparatively greater proportion of the women defendants in Metro County were convicted of drug offenses: 17 percent of the county's drug felony defendants and nearly 20 percent of serious drug misdemeanor defendants were women, and many drug felonies carried mandatory incarceration terms. Thus, drug offenses tended to result in tougher mandatory sentences that allowed no judicial discretion to mitigate the sentence, and women defendants in Metro County were convicted of these proportionately more often than of other serious offenses.

Second, while Metro had a jail overcrowding problem, the county paradoxically had greater resources to accommodate women inmates compared to those of other counties. In fact, Metro County's jail had a large annex to house women offenders and could also farm them out to outlying counties (along with male offenders). Thus, there was less reluctance to sentence more serious women defendants to county jail time, especially those with serious prior records.

Despite these factors that tended to dampen gender differences in Metro County, a general pattern of differential leniency did appear to characterize the sentencing of women. That is, the same so-called character factors that advantaged whites over blacks also might advantage women defendants over men. For example, consider three factors noted above: offense circumstances, age and extensiveness of prior record, and family status. Previous research has found that women defendants are more likely to be involved in crime as an accomplice of a male, are more likely to have less serious criminal histories than indicated by the raw guideline prior record numbers, and are more likely to have dependent children (Steffensmeier and Allan 1991; Daly 1995). Thus, they would be more likely to be perceived by court actors as less blameworthy and better risks for rehabilitation (see Steffensmeier et al. 1993).

Summary

Three key features of Metro County's court community combined to shape the case processing strategies of courtroom workgroup members: (1) the judges' orientation towards individualized sentencing and tendency toward leniency; (2) the judges' routinized use of the array of guidelines sentencing factors to reward "deserving" defendants; and (3) the lack of plea negotiating discretion allocated to most ADAs. In turn, ADAs relied on unilateral charge manipulations to maximize the probability of guilty pleas, but were often less able to negotiate charge reductions or explicit agreements for guidelines departures. For their part, defenders usually relied on open pleas in less problematic cases in hopes of a routine plea reward from the judge, and usually only attempted to negotiate plea agreements in more serious and problematic cases. On the other hand, bench trials afforded the possibility of a reduction in charges by the judge.

These case processing arrangements resulted in wide differences between trial cases and guilty pleas in the chances for non-incarceration sentences (including dispositional departures) and to a lesser extent in sentence lengths. Further, judges' and ADAs' discretionary interpretations of the array of defendant characteristics lumped under the heading of "character" had the consequence of disadvantaging black defendants with serious priors, and to a lesser extent advantaging females with less serious priors over males.

Some further aspects of case processing under the guidelines in Metro County can be illuminated by a comparison to similar findings from a study of a non-guidelines court in the 1970s. Church (1976) found that a DA's office "ban" on charge bargaining, coupled with wide variation in judicial sentencing practices, led to an increase in trials and an increase in uncertainty in sentence-related guilty plea concessions. Without the structure of guidelines, sentence bargaining involved a highly problematic degree of uncertainty for prosecutors and defenders alike. Attorneys turned to "judge shopping" strategies to manage such uncertainty. That is, defenders brought more open pleas before judges with a reputation for leniency, and went to trial more often with judges who had a reputation for harsh sentencing.

The Metro County DA's office exercised a somewhat analogous degree of control over plea bargains involving charge reductions (though they certainly did not ban them). Negotiated guilty plea concessions (when they occurred) mostly revolved around guidelines-based sentencing agreements and implicit agreements allowing defense arguments for departures. Further, in routine cases, defenders often opted for open pleas before the judges, who exhibited a tendency toward rewarding guilty pleas of any kind. These are all similarities between Church's study and case processing in Metro County. The near impossibility of judge shopping, the lack of a strong tradition of locally developed going rates, and a relative lack of personal familiarity between ADAs and defenders (see also Ulmer 1995) also increased the potential for problematic levels of uncertainty in case processing.

However, sentencing guidelines served as a set of ready-made and externally legitimated going rates that mitigated all of these uncertainty factors. The guidelines provided Metro County ADAs with a mechanism for reducing the uncertainty of sentencing outcomes through unilateral charge manipulations, and provided judges with explicit sentencing factors (e.g., mitigated ranges, departures) to reward guilty pleas. For defenders, open pleas carried less uncertainty because of judges' guidelines-based plea rewards, and negotiated pleas also usually involved guideline sentencing factors.

Therefore, by serving as ready-made, conveniently codified going rates, the guidelines were used to reduce uncertainty in the sentencing process. Without the guidelines, Metro County case processing would have probably more closely resembled the jurisdiction studied by Church, or the Baltimore court studied by Eisenstein and Jacob (1977). But what role do guidelines play in a county with strong local going rates, and one where prosecutors rather than judges are more dominant? The next chapter, which focuses on suburban Rich County, provides an example.

6

Rich County

With a population of about 700,000, Rich County encompasses affluent suburbs on the rim of a large metropolis and was studied extensively by Eisenstein and associates in the early 1980s (Flemming et al. 1993; Eisenstein et al. 1988). Flemming et al. (1993) reported that Rich County was dominated by its Republican party, and that the court was dominated by its conservative judges. These judges were oriented less toward the needs of offenders than toward maintaining smooth and efficient case processing and protecting the safety and property of the community's residential areas and exclusive shopping districts. Although Flemming et al. (1993) reported some divisions and conflicts among the Rich County bench, Nardulli et al. (1988) described the county as a classic example of a consensus-oriented court community with a strong tradition of local going rates.

Rich County's court presents important similarities and contrasts with Metro County. My analysis proceeds as before, beginning with the statistical data to illustrate sentencing outcomes and moving to the ethnographic data to illuminate contexts and case processing arrangements.

Statistical Analysis

Appendix C presents Rich County's descriptive statistics for the cases used in the analyses. The average offense seriousness was slightly less, and defendants tended to have less serious prior records, than was the case in Metro County. Rich County's court processed fewer black defendants (46.5 percent) than Metro, but blacks were still greatly overrepresented in that they made up less than 6 percent of Rich County's population. A considerably smaller proportion of Rich County's sentences were dispositional departures (4.5 percent of all sentences) and durational departures below

TABLE 6.1

Modes of Conviction by Offense Severity: Rich County
(cell percentages by row)

	Modes of Conviction				
Offense Severity	Other guilty pleas	Negotiated pleas	Bench trials	Jury trials	Total
1	85 6.3%	1,248 91.7%	19 1.4%	9 .66%	1,361
2	123 7%	1,623 91.5%	18 1.0%	9 .5%	1,773
3	192 8.5%	2,041 90.2%	11 .5%	19 .8%	2,263
4	76 13%	498 85.4%	6 1%	3 .5%	583
5	535 15.7%	2,824 82.8%	24 .7%	29 .8%	3,412
6	413 25.8%	1,140 71.3%	17 1.0%	30 1.9%	1,600
7	289 30%	616 64%	15 1.6%	42 4.3%	962
8	17 28%	33 54%	4 6.6%	7 11.5%	61
9	40 32%	47 37.6%	10 8%	28 22.4%	125
10	4 29%	9 64.3%	0 —	1 7.2%	14
Total	1,774 14.6%	10,079 82.9%	124 1%	177 1.5%	12,154

Chi-squared = 1,222   df = 27   p<.0001

guidelines (9 percent of all sentences) as compared to Metro County. On the other hand, 19 percent of Rich County's sentences were durational departures above the guideline range midpoint, a greater proportion than in Metro County.

Interestingly, Rich County's conviction patterns were very different from Metro County's, as Table 6.1 indicates.

Rich County's convictions were dominated by negotiated guilty pleas, but the proportion of open pleas increased with offense severity. Very few trials occurred in Rich County; only 2.5 percent of the cases resulted in conviction by bench or jury trial. Trials occurred in notable proportions only for the most serious offenses (offense severity of eight or more).

Table 6.2 presents logit models of overall incarceration, state prison, and dispositional departure decisions.

As usual, offense type/severity and prior record were the most influential factors in these sentencing decisions: those convicted of more serious offenses and those with more extensive and severe prior convictions were more likely to be incarcerated (especially in state prison), and less likely to receive dispositional departures. Those with multiple conviction charges were also more likely to be incarcerated and less likely to get dispositional departures.

Mode of conviction produced vast differences in each of these dispositional decisions. In contrast to Metro County,[1] negotiated guilty pleas did not provide much benefit over open guilty pleas for defendants in terms of incarceration and were actually associated with decreased odds for dispositional departures. When these odds are converted to probability differences, negotiated pleas yielded only a −.04 lesser probability of overall incarceration, and were associated with a −.34 decrease in the probability of dispositional departure. However, negotiated pleas did significantly protect defendants from going to state prison—defendants with negotiated pleas faced 40 percent reduced odds for prison sentences, which converts to a −.24 probability difference. Jury trials drastically increased the odds for incarceration—especially state prison—and the chances of receiving a dispositional departure for those convicted by jury trial were very small. Converting the odds associated with jury trial into probabilities shows that those convicted by jury trial in Rich County faced a 58 percent (.58) greater probability of incarceration compared to open pleas, a 59 percent (.59) greater probability of going to state prison, and had an 89 percent (−.89) lesser probability of getting dispositional departures. Bench trials

TABLE 6.2

Logit Models of Overall Incarceration, State Imprisonment, and
Dispositional Departures: Rich County
Odds Ratios (logits in parentheses)

Variable	Overall Incarceration	State Prison	Dispositional Departure
Constant **	— (–8.1)	— (–11.8)	— (13.33)
Year	1.07 (.064)	1.05 (.05)	.86 (–.15)
Homicide	1.64 (.49) *	3.35 (1.21)	**
Kidnapping	.41 (–.91) *	3.03 (1.11)	**
Rape/IDSI	1.94 (.66)	2.04 (.714)	.65 (–.437) *
Robbery	2.29 (.83)	3.25 (1.18)	.88 (–.14) *
Aggravated assault	1.42 (.35)	.89 (–.12) *	1.04 (.04) *
Simple assault	.84 (–.18) *	.95 (–.05) *	**
Arson	.78 (–.244)	1.46 (.38)	1.63 (.49) *
Weapons	.59 (–.52)	.88 (–.124) *	2.13 (.755)
Burglary	1.30 (.26)	1.43 (.36)	1.31 (.273) *
Crim. trespassing	.88 (–.13) *	1.49 (.40) *	.38 (–.96)
Theft	.60 (–.51)	.94 (–.064) *	1.60 (.468)
Forgery	.56 (–.58)	.82 (–.194) *	1.60 (.47)
Drug felonies	1.66 (.50)	1.03 (.03) *	1.49 (.397)
Drug misdemeanors	1.32 (.28)	.86 (–.156) *	**
Offense severity	1.59 (.465)	2.37 (.864)	.83 (–.19)
Prior record	1.69 (.526)	1.95 (.667)	.81 (–.21)
Multiple conviction charges	1.38 (.323)	1.01 (.01) *	.69 (–.366)
Negotiated plea	.91 (–.095) *	.60 (–.512)	.50 (–.71)
Bench trial	1.55 (.44)	1.20 (.185) *	.12 (–2.12)
Jury trial	3.74 (1.32)	3.91 (1.36)	.06 (–2.91)
Race (black=1)	1.60 (.47)	1.70 (.53)	.56 (–.57)
Gender (female=1)	.49 (–.72)	.91 (–.10) *	2.01 (.70)
Age	.49 (–.72) *	1.002 (.002) *	1.002 (.003) *
N =	12,064	12,064	3,772
Chi-square	4,562	5,370	278
(model accuracy)	(83%)	(90%)	(86%)

* Denotes coefficients not significant at .005 or less.
** Retail theft and other guilty pleas are reference categories. In the dispositional departure model, homicide and kidnapping are omitted due to too few dispositional departure cases; simple assault and drug misdemeanors are omitted due to too few cases where dispositional departure is possible.

also sharply decreased dispositional departure odds, but only modestly increased incarceration and imprisonment odds.

The incarceration odds for race, which convert to a .23 probability difference between blacks and nonblacks, were roughly the same as in Metro County. Unlike Metro County and the rest of the state, however, race differences were greater for state prison decisions in Rich County. The imprisonment odds for blacks were 70 percent greater than for nonblacks, which converts to a 26 percent (.26) greater probability of imprisonment for blacks compared to nonblacks. Blacks' dispositional departure odds were also 44 percent less than nonblacks (a -.28 probability difference), and this effect was greater than in Metro County. The influence of gender on incarceration and dispositional departure was much stronger than in Metro County, and was more similar to the statewide results. On the other hand, gender was not a significant influence in state prison decisions.

Like the other medium-sized counties in the statewide analysis (see endnote 13, chapter 4), a yearly trend toward increased incarceration and state imprisonment, and toward decreased dispositional departures was evident in Rich County. Each sentencing year was associated with slightly increased odds for incarceration (7 percent) and imprisonment (5 percent), and decreased odds (14 percent) for dispositional departure. In other words, Rich County sentences became significantly more severe over time.

Table 6.3 models incarceration lengths in Rich County.

Offense type/severity, prior record, and multiple convictions accounted for .437—or 81 percent—of the model's R-squared of .543. Thus, the legally prescribed variables, especially offense type and severity, again emerged as the strongest predictors of incarceration lengths. Negotiated guilty pleas presented almost no advantage in terms of length (unlike in Metro County), while bench and especially jury trials resulted in considerably longer sentences. Jury trials were associated with 13.4 months longer mean incarceration lengths, while bench trials yielded about a seven-month mean increase in length. These trial effects—especially for bench trial—were also greater than in Metro County.

Race was associated with about the same degree of difference in length as in Metro County, with blacks receiving incarcerations that were on average 4.6 months longer than nonblacks. As with the dispositional sentencing decisions, the influence of gender on length was much greater than in Metro County, and

TABLE 6.3

OLS Models of Incarceration Length, Corrected for Selection Bias: Rich County (incarceration cases only)

Variable	b (Beta)	Contribution to R^2
Constant **	–68.4 (—)	—
Year	.69 (.03)	.005
Homicide	32.1 (.12)	—
Kidnapping	26.8 (.047)	—
Rape/IDSI	25.1 (.184)	—
Robbery	17.0 (.256)	—
Aggravated assault	6.2 (.06)	—
Simple assault	2.3 (.023) *	—
Arson	.53 (.006) *	—
Weapons	–7.94 (–.06)	—
Burglary	5.4 (.124)	—
Criminal trespassing	–.28 (–.002) *	—
Theft	–3.8 (–.09) *	—
Forgery	–5.4 (–.06)	—
Drug felonies	9.2 (.11)	—
Drug misdemeanors	4.2 (.10)	—
total offense R^2 contrib.ution		.157
Offense severity	8.4 (.82)	.137
Prior record	6.9 (.79)	.138
Multiple conviction charges	3.4 (.078)	.0005
Negotiatied plea	–.15 (–.004) *	.005
Bench trial	7.1 (.05)	.0038
Jury trial	13.4 (.125)	.015
Race (black=1)	4.6 (.14)	.01
Gender (female=1)	–6.7 (–.12)	.0022
Age	–.02 (–.01) *	.003
Correction factor	54.1 (.62)	.059
N =		5,936
Adjusted R^2		.543

* Denotes coefficients not significant at .005 or less.
** Retail theft and other guilty pleas are reference categories.

more comparable to the rest of the state. Women in Rich County received incarcerations that were on average 6.7 months shorter compared to men. Also similar to table 6.2, Rich County exhibited a yearly trend toward longer incarceration terms. Each year was associated with an increase of about two-thirds of a month in mean sentence lengths.

Separate incarceration, imprisonment, dispositional departure, and length models for less serious versus serious prior records (not shown) revealed a curvilinear effect similar to that in the statewide and Metro County analyses. Increases in prior record scores more than doubled the odds for incarceration (odds=2.33) and imprisonment (odds=2.45), and cut the dispositional departure odds by over half (odds=.47), among less serious priors defendants. Among defendants with serious priors, however, additional increases in prior record score only increased the odds for incarceration by 36 percent (odds=1.36), the odds for imprisonment by 62 percent (odds=1.62), and decreased the odds for dispositional departure by 25 percent (odds=.75). However, in contrast to Metro, prior record did not interact with race, gender, or mode of conviction. That is, the differences conditioned by race, gender, and mode of conviction in Rich's main effects model were almost identical between defendants with serious and those with less serious prior records.

As with Metro County, the results for durational departure below and above guidelines are also very similar to the statewide models in terms of effects and explained variance, and are not shown here. The only substantial difference for Rich County is that women received comparatively larger departures below guidelines, while jury trials were associated with comparatively larger departures above guidelines.

Thus, Rich County was similar to Metro in that legally prescribed variables were the most important factors in all sentencing decisions. However, both counties exhibited important extralegal differences conditioned by mode of conviction, race, and gender. The similarities stop there. Negotiated pleas were the dominant mode of conviction in Rich, but these only benefited defendants in terms of state prison decisions, and were actually associated with decreased dispositional departure chances. The incarceration and dispositional departure differences associated with trials, especially jury trials, dwarf those of Metro County. Further, Rich contrasts with Metro County and the rest of the state in that race became more influential for state prison decisions rather than less, and blacks in Rich County were even less likely to receive dispositional departures compared to Metro County and the statewide model. Finally, while the gender differences in Rich County are comparable to those in the statewide analyses, they are considerably larger than those in Metro County. The ethnographic analysis probes some sources of these Rich County sentencing patterns, and the organizational contexts and case processing strategies that are associated with them.

Ethnographic Analysis

Political and Organizational Context

The data here generally concur with previous characterizations of the Rich County context (see Nardulli et al. 1988; Eisenstein et al. 1988; Flemming et al. 1992), with some exceptions. The Rich County Republican Party remained dominant on the political landscape, and the court exhibited a local legal culture that was heavily colored by the views of influential Republican party figures in the court community. On the other hand, the interview data indicate that the DA's office, and not the bench, had become the center of both political and organizational power in Rich's court community. Also, the moderate conflict among members of the bench noted by Flemming et al. (1992) was not evident in the data here.

Bench organization. Six judges sat in criminal court, and one of those dealt with miscellaneous case procedural issues. The remaining five accepted guilty pleas, handled the relatively infrequent trials, and conducted sentencing hearings. Rich contrasted with Metro and Southwest in that its court assigned cases according to a master calendar, in which cases were prioritized on a master docket and then were assigned to different courtrooms for different stages of processing. For example, a case might be assigned to one judge's courtroom for indictment or pretrial motion hearings, and another judge's courtroom for the guilty plea hearing or trial, and sentencing. This differs from the individual calendar systems of Metro (and, as will be seen later, Southwest), in which cases were assigned to individual judges who handled cases through all stages of processing, and counsel were more or less "stuck" with whatever judge was assigned to the case. Under Rich's "list system," as court members called their master calendar, cases were scheduled by the court clerk's office on a four-week "trial cycle." One judge served as the "list judge" (a rotating position) who assigned cases to the other four judges' courtrooms at the beginning of each week. Each Monday morning, all prosecutors, defense attorneys, and defendants would crowd into the list judge's courtroom for the "calling of the list." The list judge conducted this as a speedy, no-nonsense affair, rapidly calling cases, asking attorneys about the status of the cases, and assigning them to courtrooms for the week. Prosecutors and defenders replied with short answers, such as "That's a plea bargain," "That'll be an open plea," or "Defense requests a continuance for further discussions." When defendants had not obtained counsel (which occurred on three occasions I observed), the judge revoked their bail, ordered bailiffs to handcuff the defendants and lead them to the holding cells in the court's basement, each time saying some variation of, "You've had plenty of time to call the public defenders or get an attorney. You're playing with this court!"

The master calendar system used before the one currently in place allowed widespread judge shopping, in which prosecutors and defenders routed pleas to one judge or another as a routine part of plea negotiations. As one long-time defense attorney explained: "Oh, I liked the judge shopping. I was very good at it. I was able to get my case where I wanted it, sometimes. Now the system's changed, and it's harder to do, at least for a defense attorney."

A public defender described how the new, current system came about: "First of all, what was happening before was that the DA's office were pulling the final list before the judges even got to see it. They knew the order of cases that was coming up. The AOPC (Administrative Office of Pennsylvania Courts) finally got wind of this and ordained that the court should be running the list, not the DA's office. The DA's office finally agreed to a new system." According to members of both the DA's office and the defense bar, the new system still allowed ample room for judge shopping by prosecutors. According to a defense attorney: "These lists are still modified by the DA's office and then coming to the judge. The case that the DAs have already decided is the one to be heard first or later is the one that gets assigned at the calling of the list. Secondly, the other cases that are on standby, who keeps track of these and when they move up? The DA's office does!"

Judge shopping was important to prosecutors not because the judges' sentencing practices were widely varied; in fact, the judges' sentencing practices were quite similar. Rather, two other factors were behind the DA's attempts at judge shopping. First, by influencing case assignment, the DA's office could delay cases with evidence problems or those that took extra time for plea negotiations. Second, the practice allowed individual ADAs to take advantage of the biggest difference in judges' styles—the propensity to become informally involved in plea negotiations.

Though two judges stated emphatically that they never got involved in plea negotiations (which is forbidden by the Pennsylvania judicial code), the others indicated a willingness to play an informal mediating role when necessary. For their part, counsel on both sides appreciated these judges' mediation in troublesome plea negotiation cases or open pleas. Such informal judicial involvement not only reduced sentencing uncertainty, but also fostered a sense of consensus and "teamwork." As one judge described:

> With an eye to knowing how overburdened everybody is, I might call up the lawyers and say, "Hey, what's the problem with this case that you fellows can't resolve? It looks like a garden variety residential burglary" or whatever. "Why shouldn't it be a sentence in the standard range?" They'll say, "Well, here are the mitigating factors that have to be considered." I'll say, "What do the guidelines say? How do you feel about a sentence in the mitigated range? If you think that's appropriate, that's okay." Then I'll signal a sentence at the top of the mitigated range, then everybody feels better about it and everyone knows what's going to happen.

The chief DA, like other prosecutors and defenders, expressed a preference for those judges who get involved in plea negotiations: "Some judges are sticklers for the law, but others who are more practical will get involved. They'll bring everybody in and say 'What are you asking, and what are you asking,' and we'll get it done. I think the rule that they can't get involved is ridiculous."

DA's office organization. The DA's office assigned sixteen ADAs to the trial court, and the chief DA and his assistant chief organized the trial court assistants into four teams of four assistants each. One team handled a mixed caseload, one specialized in rape and sexual assault cases, and two specialized in drug cases. Overall, the DA's office was less specialized and centralized than in Metro County. While the three specialized teams primarily focused on their own types of cases, they also shared a varied mixture of other cases with the general caseload team. In the words of one team leader, "Everybody pulls their fair share."

Assistants were assigned about three cases a day and given wide latitude in negotiating plea agreements (cf., LaFree 1985). As the chief DA described: "I think it is very important that they have discretion. They have a heavy burden, and have to make a lot of big decisions. If you can't trust your assistants, you better get rid of them. I was given that discretion a long time ago when I was an assistant, and I thought it was a tremendous vote of confidence, and I want to give that to them."

A newer ADA concurred, saying, "We're pretty much islands to ourselves. If we screw up we sink alone." The DA's office did, however, train new assistants to balance toughness with restraint in the interest of courthouse collegiality. The office preferred to hire new attorneys who were zealous advocates of law, order, and toughness on crime, but their socialization into the court community at the hands of experienced members tempered this with local norms of "practicality" and cooperativeness. As the chief DA stated:

> We tell them our philosophy and where their parameters are. I don't like what I call the "Top Gun syndrome," where somebody offers twelve months on a case worth six months just to get the defendant to trial so he can knock his brains out. I don't like "hatchet people," who just go out and try to hurt people. For the most part, I don't think we have that. Another thing I don't go in for is judge-bashing. We have very good judges here, and they help us out."

Defense bar organization. The other key actors in the process were the public defenders and private attorneys. The PD's office employed thirty attorneys, four of them full time. The others maintained private practices on the side, and handled criminal cases in these as well. The PDs did not specialize in terms of caseload, and the court administrative office estimated that the PDs handled about half of the trial court cases. Most of the remainder were handled by about eight or ten private attorneys who were "court regulars." Many of these private attorneys, in turn, were former members of the PD's or DA's offices.

The characteristics of the defense bar appeared to resemble the descriptions of Flemming et al. (1992). The interviews here indicated that a defense attorney's reputation for "professionalism," cooperativeness, and "integrity" were crucial to their ability to negotiate guilty pleas. Members of the PD's office and private attorneys were also involved in Republican party politics, and public defenders often needed political approval or sponsorship to obtain their jobs.

The PDs worked with almost no internal supervision, and most of their training consisted of informal socialization at the hands of experienced members, through which they learned the local informal plea bargaining and sentencing norms. An experienced public defender described this process: "A new person is pretty much responsible for finding out how things work on his own. What he does is go to a more experienced person and say, 'I've been offered this, what do you think?' I did that a lot. Now they come to me."

The training of new PDs was not only performed by PD office members, however, but also by members of the DA's office and the bench. The clearest example of this was the "practicum" for new PDs, which was organized by the DA's office and some of the judges. This example further illustrates the interorganizational ties within the court community as well as the leadership of the DA's office. A judge enthusiastically described this practicum and its importance:

> The Chief DA and I had a discussion about some of the young defense counsel who were not as experienced as they should be. We decided to hold a practicum for them. We're going to get the Chief and his best assistants, and the best defense lawyers around. We're going to have demonstration cases with lots of question and answer, so the new defense attorneys know what they should be doing. There's so much cooperation here, I think it's terrific!

Court community relations. The political environment established an organizational context in which those with career ambitions were susceptible to pressures to cooperate with court community elites, on whom they might depend for future political or professional favors. As implied earlier, the public defenders had strong ties to the DA's office, in that the DA's and PD's offices often exchanged personnel. As one judge observed: "A lot of them (ADAs and PDs) go back and forth between agencies." For example, the current chief DA was not only a former ADA, but also a former PD and private defense attorney. Further, the current chief PD (a position appointed by the county commissioners) was a former ADA. In fact, many if not most longtime members of the court community either had worked in the DA's office, or hoped to do so in the future. Thus, defense attorneys hoping to gain access to career advancement through the DA's office did well to avoid alienating its influential members. A story often told by court community members provides an extreme example. According to court community lore, a member of the Rich County PD's office was once fired for refusing to change his party affiliation from Democrat to Republican.

The exchange of personnel and importance of political and personal patronage extended to DA's office and bench relations as well. For example, the DA's office had served as an important stepping stone to the Rich County bench. Of the six judges who sat on the criminal bench, two previously worked as ADAs, and three had previously served as chief district attorney. In a particularly clear example, the current president judge had been chief DA for many years, and had hired the current chief DA as an assistant. Another judge and former chief assistant DA had hired the current chief PD as an ADA. From the Rich County bench, one could in turn hope to be appointed to a federal judgeship, as several Rich County judges had been over the years. Thus, in order to gain access to opportunities for career advancement, actors from each sponsoring agency did well to conform to the court community's strong informal norms of collegiality, and avoid "rocking the boat." The comment of one defense attorney is illustrative: "I always work with an eye to my reputation. Individual reputations are very important, in that they allow you to work things out well with others. If you cause trouble, people will hold it against you."

On the other hand, overly zealous ADAs also risked future penalties by alienating experienced members of the defense bar, especially if they wanted to enter private practice later. In the words of an experienced private attorney: "Some of these kids will come out of the DA's office and have no exposure to defense law. They call me up and ask what to do. If its someone who gave me a hard time before, occasionally I'll ask the little snot, 'You gave me such a hard time before, and now you're asking me for help?'"

The picture of Rich County thus is one of great workgroup and court community stability and familiarity, the roots of which extend beyond the courthouse to politics, career, and personal relations. As a further example of the stability in the court community, one judge complained about "high turnover" in the PD's and DA's office, by which he meant that "some people just stay for about four years, and then leave." Rich County's idea of high turnover would be considered high stability in the Metro County DA's office. As a final illustration of court community familiarity, three members of the DA's office were related (a husband, a wife, and the husband's father). A defense attorney indicated the importance of familiarity and cordial relations with judges and prosecutors:

> I know almost all the judges, and some are even close personal friends. You may appear in front of a judge that you're especially friendly with, and that judge is going to give you a break sometimes. It's not generally for the client, it's for the lawyer . . . But there was another defense lawyer around here that went out of business practicing criminal law because he was such a miserable cur. He found himself going to trial on every case because he could never get a deal with anybody because he was such a rotten person. He just didn't play the game very well.

Efficiency and "professionalism" were standards to which all members of the court community were held. In Rich County, this professionalism appeared to mean resolving cases with a minimum of conflict and effort for all involved, or as Flemming et al. (1992) called it, "getting along by (mostly) going along." An ADA elaborates the importance of workgroup stability and members' reputations for efficient case resolution: "You know the defense attorney. He knows you. So you get a lot of pleas just because the defense attorney knows you won't make a mistake."

The norms of cooperation and conflict minimization also influenced the court community's handling of news media attention. The local media reportedly were quite watchful for sentences that might be seen as too lenient by the public, and sought out aspects of the court's day-to-day operations that might be worthy of criticism. Media criticism of lenient sentences illustrates that the power of the DA's office and its advocacy of toughness on crime were lodged in the attitudes of the larger community, and also that the judges faced political consequences if they were seen as "soft on crime." On the other hand, court community members, especially the DA's office, seemed protective of the judges' public reputations. The chief DA describes one such case:

> They (media) did a story a couple weeks ago which was really unfair. They beat up a judge for not sentencing this guy to the state prison. In fact, I found out later the sentence was our fault, we inadvertently told the judge the guideline range was a year when it was actually three. But the press doesn't understand any of this. He just got beat up for no reason. I said so publicly too.

A defense attorney gave another example:

> The local paper can get after the judges. They don't accord them any slack at all, with sentences or other things. A few months back they did a story called "Lazy Judges," where they monitored the time that they started in the morning for a period of two weeks and then reported the average time as ten o'clock. That's not fair. It doesn't take into account that the DAs and defense might not be ready to go, or that the judge was in chambers talking to people. The judges are sensitive to it and I don't blame them.

The court community's level of cooperation and consensus was not just derived from self-interest and the need for political patronage, but also from a shared set of ideological beliefs about criminal justice and sentencing. Members of the DA's office and bench emphatically expressed beliefs in retribution and especially deterrence as the primary goals of sentencing, and Rich County court actors were oriented toward maintaining standards of tough sentencing. In fact, interviews indicated that the severity of sentences had been "ratcheting up" in recent years, which coincides with the yearly trend in the county's statistical data regarding increased use of incarceration and longer sentences (see Tables 6.2 and 6.3). The chief DA states: "We are getting harsher, this county has always been much harsher in its treatment of criminals. You can see it, we just react harsher. I think it is the climate of the public, and rightfully so."

These sentencing standards were especially directed toward a goal of deterring so-called criminal elements from the nearby metropolis from entering the county and preying on its residents and upscale shopping districts. A PD explains: "I think that Rich County has, especially the courts and the DA's office, has always considered themselves as being tough on crime. They see the city nearby as being lighter in sentencing, so it is up to Rich County to teach them all a lesson. The burglars and thieves that come out from the city are constantly getting sentences that they wouldn't dream of getting back home." An ADA concurred: "There is a reputation we like to uphold, where people say in the city, 'Don't go into Rich County to commit your crimes.' Sometimes people forget this, so we remind them."

Even a growing overcrowding problem in the county jail and state prisons did not dampen the ideological commitment of judges and prosecutors to tough sentences and heavy use of incarceration. Rich County finished construction of a larger county jail in 1986, which apparently fostered a belief that jail space was no longer a problem. The new jail soon filled beyond capacity, as the chief probation officer explained: "As soon as we got the new jail, people were going to jail more and getting longer sentences. The judges didn't think they had to consider that anymore, because they had a new jail."

The crowding of the jail presented a serious sentencing dilemma, but it was largely resolved in favor of continued reliance on tough sentencing standards, the backbone of which was county jail incarceration. A judge summarized his view of the problem of balancing jail resources with the court community's sentencing standards:

> I don't believe in extraneous considerations like jail populations. I don't think you should just bring in people and send them out just to get rid of the numbers and say, "Hey, we disposed of 1,000 cases this month." Well sure, everybody gets probation! That doesn't accomplish anything. There's no deterrence, no moral communication as to the wrongfulness of the conduct. You ask, "Is there pressure?" Yes, there is pressure, but I hope we can continue to resist it, so we don't compromise what we're all about.

Another judge put it more succinctly:

> "The situation with the jail doesn't influence me. While I'm sympathetic to the problem, it's not really within my purview to do anything about the overcrowding. I can't compromise what I think is right just because of the problems up there."

The court and the county jail administrators did work out two mechanisms to relieve overcrowding: increased use of weekend incarceration for offenders seen as less serious, and like Metro, a "good time" policy for discounting jail sentences. The county jail's "good time" policy, in which offenders could serve significantly shorter sentences contingent on good behavior, made the jail versus state prison sentencing decision even more important. County jail inmates could be released well before the expiration of the minimum sentence given by the judge, whereas state inmates, by law, had no possibility of early release (see chapter 3).

The "tough on crime" stance also strongly shaped the attitudes of members of the defense bar. A quote from one of the more experienced private defenders, who was also a former ADA and PD, sums up this set of attitudes well: "I put a lot of people away when I was in the DA's office, at high rates of conviction. And the personal side of me still believes in that. Sentences have gotten tougher, and professionally I don't like it but personally I do."

Given this organizational and ideological context, the DA's office was the logical center of court community power. As the quotes throughout this section imply, however, the leaders of the DA's office did not wield their influence in a dictatorial fashion. That is, the Rich County DA's office was not organized as what Flemming et al. (1992) called a "bureaucratic weapon." The chief DA was seen not as a tyrant but as a tough yet benevolent leader whose influence was based on efficiency, consistency, and collegiality. One judge summarized the prevailing views of the Chief DA and his office: "I have the highest respect for the guy. I just think he's an outstanding district attorney—very innovative, very courageous, very straight. I think we're all very fortunate to have a guy like him. He's very popular with everyone that works here, and he's struck a nerve with the people. He just does what he thinks is right, and it happens to sell politically."

In sum, the ADAs, public defenders, judges, and the private defense bar worked cooperatively to process cases and to uphold the Rich County values of "law and order," efficient case processing, and collegial professional relations. "Don't make anyone look bad," as one ADA put it, seemed to be a tacit rule throughout the court community. Perceived excesses in both prosecutorial zeal and defendant advocacy tended to ruffle feathers and incur potential future costs.

Courtroom Workgroup Strategies and Sentencing Guidelines

The combination of these interlocking organizational arrangements, shared ideologies, and stable and familiar professional and personal relations provided the basis for strong informal norms that shaped case processing and sentencing practices. Given the context described above, it is little wonder that adversarial tactics were minimized, and cooperative negotiations characterized case processing. The system heavily depended on modes of plea bargaining that minimized conflicts between the ADAs and defense bar.

The DA's office dominated case processing from the time cases came in from the lower courts to the time of sentencing. The ADAs initiated the guilty plea process by calling the defense attorneys and making plea offers (in contrast to Metro County, where defenders usually initiated any plea bargaining). In routine cases, the ADAs usually stuck to their original offers in a "take it or leave it" fashion. As one DA team leader stated: "I rarely change my original plea offer on a case. My team members follow my lead and do the same thing." Another ADA concurred, saying, "Mostly I give my best offer the first time. If you don't do this people won't take you seriously. If there's a trade off, it's usually a matter of you saying, 'Okay, if you stay quiet and cooperate we will agree to do this.'"

The power of the ADAs, even less experienced ones, in plea negotiations, was exemplified by another private defense attorney's observation that:

> You don't anger the assistant DA that's got the case. . . . You don't mind it when the ones that have more experience say 'This is what I'll give you, period.". . . But for some of them, they're practicing law their first year and I'm in my eighteenth year. It's a bit irritating to put up with some of their crap. But, if you anger them, then you're certainly not going to get a good deal. So, that's where personalities play a lot. You have to "kow-tow" to people who, ordinarily, I wouldn't let carry my briefcase."

Another defense attorney affirmed this view and noted, "I get along well with the DAs, because this is always in the best interests of my clients."

In cases with evidence problems or when a defendant cooperated with police (usually in drug cases), defenders could negotiate more concessions or convince the ADAs to back off a case. As one private attorney put it, "If they look at their case and they know it isn't a good one, they're going to come off it and be willing to negotiate a better deal." The degree of vigor with which an ADA prosecuted a case, in turn, mattered a great deal for sentencing, since it signaled to judges the DA's office's degree of concern about the case and defendant. The president judge summarized this type of situation:

> A lot of the difference in sentences depends on the degree of enthusiasm with which the DA goes after somebody in the pleas and at sentencings. Sometimes they go after somebody

like tigers. . . . Like recently, the DA argued for an aggravated sentence, and I didn't want to do it. But I was thinking, "Gee, he's arguing so vehemently, I have to do it.". . . Other times they just sit there like they don't mind what happens. When that happens you know something is up that they don't want to say in court, like they don't have enough evidence, or the guy is an informant for the police or something, and that's why they're giving the store away.

In general, the interviews indicate that sentence bargains were by far the most common plea offer. As one judge described: "Historically, the DA and the defense lawyer actually negotiate over a sentence. There's not so much plea bargaining in the sense of offense bargaining and then leaving the sentence up to the judge. The typical negotiated plea is a plea where the guy pleads to X, Y, or Z, and the negotiated sentence recommendation is something or other. That's been the tradition in this county"

Relatedly, an ADA team leader stated, "We generally don't bargain with the offense gravity score or the prior record score," while a PD said, "A majority of the DAs are willing to bargain time, but don't want to bargain charges." These sentence bargains often included agreements not to pursue guideline factors such as the deadly weapon enhancement, and especially agreements for county jail rather than prison incarceration.

Agreements to reduce charges occurred sometimes, but usually only in cases where a potential mandatory sentence was involved. Even in cases where the initial charge carried a mandatory minimum, the ADAs were reluctant to charge bargain except in cases where a drug defendant cooperated with police, or when a sex offender agreed to plead guilty and save the victim from testifying at trial. Other plea concessions were of a more symbolic nature, such as agreements to identify a defendant as a candidate for work release, or allowing a defendant to appear for custody at a later date.

Sentence agreements, in turn, depended on the perspective of the ADA and defender as to the going rate or "worth" of the offense. As one ADA stated: "I have a pretty good feel for what a particular crime is worth based on watching other district attorneys doing their stuff, especially the ones that have been there long. Other district attorneys come and ask you what a particular case is worth."

Rich County's court community thus exhibited very strong informal plea and sentencing norms. When asked, members of the DA's office could provide quite specific and detailed estimates of the probable plea agreements and sentences that would be associated with hypothetical charges and circumstances (the ADAs in Metro County had more difficulty providing such specific estimates—when presented with hypothetical examples, Metro ADAs would say things like, "Oh, that would probably be an open plea with a sentence somewhere in the mitigated range, it depends on the judge.") The chief DA best sums up the strength and importance of Rich County's going rates: "Call the case for what it is worth. A good prosecutor, a good defense attorney, if they sit down they can count a case within two months of what it should be. It's like selling cars! A 1972 Valiant is worth so much and nothing more. We try to give our people the proper balance, the proper experience, the proper attitude to evaluate a case properly." These going rates were based in consistent application of the informal norms and conventions established through past interaction (see Eisenstein et al. 1988). A private defense attorney illustrated the going rates and their basis in consistent application over time: "All I've ever asked for in plea bargaining is that there's consistency. I know that when I'm walking in, in a situation similar to somebody else, I'm not walking out with a worse deal than the other guy. If it's the best deal they'll give me, that's fine. As long as the next guy behind me doesn't get a better deal."

The guidelines provided additional, but secondary, sentencing boundaries. That is, the guidelines were used when they provided convenient information and benchmarks for negotiating sentences in less routine cases, but otherwise took a back seat to local sentencing standards. The guidelines, when originally proposed in 1981, were strongly denounced by influential Rich County court figures. In fact, they helped to successfully lobby for the rejection of the originally proposed set of guidelines as too lenient and restrictive. As the current president judge (a key figure in opposing the original guidelines) recalled:

> I had testified against the first set of guidelines. I thought they were incredibly weak in certain areas. I was the DA at the time, so when I say "weak" I mean that I thought they were too low. When the second guidelines came out, they were better, but I was still opposed to them. From a DA's perspective I didn't think we needed them. But once I took to the bench I found they weren't that bad. None of the disastrous things I imagined ever materialized. I found that we have pretty much unfettered discretion.

Rich County had maintained its strong plea bargaining traditions and informal norms under the guidelines. In the current context, the guidelines seemed to simultaneously facilitate and set boundaries around plea bargaining, and they did so without threatening the strong political and personal commitments among courtroom workgroup members. Two judges described the relative weight given to guidelines vs. local norms:

> What the guidelines are is a place to say, "Okay, where do we start?" You look at it and say, "That's not too bad," or "Well, that's not enough." But they're just a starting point. All in all, I don't think the guidelines have had much effect here.

> I just try and think about what the sentence should be and then look at the guideline to see if it fits my perception of the local legal community and a fair sentence given my 20-plus years as a DA and judge. I think what the guidelines are useful for is when a new DA or PD is in a tight spot, they can have some idea what to do without having to take time out to talk to all the other people in the office to see what the accumulated wisdom is.

Interviews suggested that ADAs consulted and used the guidelines to their advantage for more problematic types of cases and defendants, but simply relied on the informal going rates for more routine cases without consulting the guidelines. As a judge stated: "Generally, if it is presented as a plea agreement, we just go with it. After a trial or an open plea, you get presentence investigations and the guidelines are much more on the forefront of everyone's minds. When you are going through a volume situation, where there's a number of plea agreements, then the guidelines are not the first order of reference."

Further, judges reported that they often did not check on their own whether their sentences were within the guidelines, but simply trusted the prosecutors to ensure that sentences were appropriate. In fact, as Flemming et al. (1992) reported and as these interview data show, each judge rarely rejected plea agreements and almost always followed prosecutors' sentencing recommendations. A judge characterized routine sentencing hearings involving plea agreements: "The judge will accept the plea agreement and impose that sentence without calculating the guidelines independently, or even looking at the sheet the DA has prepared and hands up to the clerk. That's how it works in most cases."

On the other hand, the way prosecutors used the guidelines in the plea process fits somewhat with the hydraulic displacement characterization (see chapters 1 and 2). Guidelines were used as a "floor" by ADAs, and they were very unwilling to negotiate for sentences below the standard ranges of these guidelines. As one ADA stated:

> Often, you would have more trials (before guidelines) because the defense bar would continually seek probation on whatever crime had been committed. The guidelines mandate a certain number of months. As a result, there is only a certain degree that they (defenders) can negotiate. We can say "this is as far as we can go down. The negotiation has to stop here." If there wasn't that guideline, there would be more chance for trials, and you would waste more time negotiating.

Another ADA was even more enthusiastic about the advantages guidelines sometimes gave him:

> The guidelines can be a wonderful tool for us. They get us off the hook sometimes, you can say "Look, I can't get any lower than this, this is what the guidelines say." When I discovered that the sentencing guidelines existed, I thought, "Isn't this great? This is just what I need!" Once you learn how to work them, they work wonders in plea bargains.

Other defense attorneys indicated that "you can't go below the guideline minimums," and said that the guidelines give the ADAs the leverage and excuse to make "take it or leave it" plea offers. Additionally, the chief DA indicated that defense attorneys could use the guidelines as a mechanism for client control: "For some of the defense lawyers, it helps them with their clients. You can show them the guidelines and say, 'Look, this is the best you're going to get.'"

Sentence agreements in Rich did not automatically mean the bottom of the standard ranges. Rather, negotiated sentences could be anywhere between the bottom and midpoint of the standard ranges, and sometimes even above the midpoint (as will be seen, sentences at the top of the standard range and the aggravated range were usually reserved for trial defendants).

In light of these characterizations of how the guidelines were used (and *not* used) in Rich, it is interesting how the judges sometimes referred to the guidelines during sentencing hearings. Several times, in several judges' courtrooms, I heard judges and attorneys refer to the "mandatory guidelines" when pronouncing sentence in cases involving a sentence agreement. This type of statement, employed by judges and others when convenient, perhaps represented a rhetorical account indicating a lack of choice in selecting a sentence. In any case, these data indicate that the guidelines were secondary to local going rates, but that they could also be advantageously used by prosecutors to augment their power in sentence bargaining, and by judges to symbolically legitimize their ratification of bargained sentences.

In Metro County, the usual mode of conviction was the open plea, and when plea negotiations were attempted and an agreement could not be reached, the result was usually a bench trial. In Rich County, by contrast, the workhorse of routine case processing was the negotiated plea, and when an agreement could not be reached in more problematic cases, the result was usually an open plea. According to an ADA team leader: "In my negotiations I usually give an offer and if the defense attorney doesn't like it, then I say plead open and take your chances with the judge. That happens a lot of times when a case has something different about it and needs some thought or review, when it's hard to tell what it's worth." On the other hand, open pleas were a more hazardous strategy than negotiated pleas for defense attorneys, since the judge could give a sentence that was equal to or harsher than the one the prosecutor offered. As one ADA described: "Many times the defense attorneys don't like to do it (plead open) because the DA offer is more reasonable than what the court would give him on an open plea. I have an open plea scheduled for tomorrow. He couldn't take my offer. He will plead open and is hoping the judge will give him less than what I asked for. I doubt it, though."

As mentioned, the chief DA and his team leaders strongly discouraged assistants from negotiating agreements for departures below guidelines. One ADA states: "We generally don't recommend sentences in the mitigated range or below guidelines. If there is a case that the standard range seems harsh, we only offer an open plea." Thus, the most common circumstance in which plea negotiations failed in Rich County was when the defense pressed for a sentence below the guidelines' standard ranges (especially dispositional departures). In these situations, open pleas and the prosecutorial tactic of standing silent were interwoven workgroup strategies.

One defense attorney indicated that both judges and ADAs disliked departures below guidelines: "Prosecutors will not depart from the standard range, unless it is a drug case and there is cooperation between the defendant and undercover officers that they use. There is a certain political aspect [to departures], and I am not saying it is bad, I'm just saying it has to be recognized. If somebody is going to go outside the guidelines, the judges would prefer that the DAs would just plead them and let the judges go outside. Oftentimes neither one wants to make that step."

Even though neither judges nor prosecutors were comfortable with departures below guidelines, the DA's office deferred the responsibility to grant them to judges as a matter of informal policy. According to the chief DA:

> You have a defense attorney who wants probation, a departure. You feel you can't agree to that, but you want to give the defense the opportunity to sell his case to the judge. That might just be enough to make him plead guilty. So you say, "We will stand up and make no recommendation." Now the judge has complete freedom to do what he wants, and he knows nobody is going to go out in the hall and say the judge was lenient with this guy. If you don't make a recommendation, you can't very well complain. It takes all the heat off us. Judges don't like that, they want us to make the recommendation and take the responsibility. I laugh and say, "Hey, that's their damn job!"

Standing silent was a potent rhetorical tactic for DAs. That is, judges knew that the ADA's silence betokened tacit acceptance of downward departures or mitigated range sentences. If the DAs did not object to a departure below guidelines on a given case, they stood silent, and the judge would grant the departure. The DA's silence was an explicit trade-off in return for an open plea, and such cases typically involved cases with weaker evidence or drug defendants who cooperated with police. In this sense, then, many open pleas in Rich County were actually negotiated pleas. As one private defense attorney described: "It's [standing silent] definitely part of the bargaining process. They will agree to allow you to go right into the mitigated range or below, and they'll allow you to make whatever argument you want right to the court unchallenged." If prosecutors did object to downward departures, they argued for a sentence in the standard range. In the latter case, the sentence usually ended up being what the prosecutor recommended, and what he or she offered the defense in the first place. A private defense attorney described this situation: "I have a recent drug case that's an example: the DA's offer was at the upper end of the standard range, and I wanted mitigated. I simply couldn't allow my client to plead guilty to that. So what we did was we went open. But the DA asked for the standard range sentence in court, and the judge follows the guidelines and we're stuck. The DAs know this is going to happen, so they'll take a stance within the standard range and feel comfortable with it."

On the other hand, similar situations involving open pleas also occurred when the prosecution wanted a departure above the guidelines and the defense wanted a standard range sentence. As a DA team leader described:

> We might have cases where we will say to the defense attorney, "I understand what the guidelines are, but your guy has a prior record of 6, and that's only because the score only goes up to 6. If you stacked all these prior burglaries on top of each other he'd have a score of 18. Therefore I'm going to recommend a sentence in the top of the aggravated range." They'll plead open and I'll say to the judge, "Here is a burglar who is a recidivist of the first rank. He showed no remorse. He walks into the bedroom where the people are sleeping and scared the hell out of them. I ask the court to give 10 to 20 years for the following reason: the guy is a dirt bag. He is going to keep doing this no matter what, and we have to protect society from him." The judge says, "I agree with you, he is a dirt bag. He gets 10 to 20."

Finally, appeals of departure sentences by prosecutors or defenders were not used as a threat in Rich County, since such appeals would strain the court community norms of collegiality and cooperation and could potentially jeopardize the career ambitions of the attorney who filed the appeal. As one ADA stated: "I've never appealed a case. That would piss people off, and I don't like to piss people off." The chief DA expanded with an example of a case which illustrates the disruptiveness of appeals for court community relations:

> The only guideline appeal I know of. . . This one judge we have, he has been around the block a few times and he's

really good-hearted. He went way below the guidelines on a kid. The ADA handling the case went nuts. He really thought it was inappropriate. He went up to our appellate leader and, unknown to me, appealed him. Now the judge didn't do it to jam us, he was just trying to help out. He really thought the kid deserved a break and was trying to help us clear our criminal list, too. And we appealed the damn guy. I went and talked to him and came back and pulled the appeal.

Further, given the court community's degree of ideological consensus, very few sentencing situations had occasioned sufficient controversy for either defense attorneys or prosecutors to mobilize appeal efforts. As an example, the only guideline sentencing appeal case the president judge could remember was one which he himself asked the defense attorney to pursue because of a misinterpretation of the guidelines in that particular case.

Sentencing Outcomes

As in Metro County, guidelines provided a set of tools for inducing guilty pleas, but they were used in different ways, and with more pronounced results in terms of extralegal sentencing differences. Mode of conviction differences were much more pronounced in Rich than in Metro County, and there were several reasons for this. First, ADAs observed that almost all negotiated pleas fell within the lower end—though not always at the bottom of—the standard range. However, one noted that: "if they decide that they want to go to trial, then you are looking at the higher end of the standard range." Because of the width of the standard ranges, the difference between a sentence at the bottom versus the top of the range often meant the difference between incarceration or probation, or between county jail or state prison. As one ADA stated: "A lot of these ranges give us enormous leeway, like some of them are zero to twelve (months). That's hardly a limit at all." Another ADA expanded on this, saying: "If he goes to trial and gets convicted, he is probably going to get a sentence in the middle of the standard range or the upper part of the standard range. If he is being offered a sentence in the lower part of the standard range it is going to be in his or her [defense attorney's] best interest to suggest that the defendant plead guilty."

Unlike the routine plea discounts found in Metro County (and, as will be seen, Southwest County), the sentencing differences between guilty pleas and trials in Rich County seemed to represent a more genuine trial penalty. That is, conviction by trial risked significant additional punishment, and not merely missing out on a sentencing reward for pleading guilty. A major reason for this was that trials disrupted the cooperative and efficient case processing arrangements and caused inconvenience for everyone involved. As the assistant chief DA noted: "There is pressure [not to go to trial] in subtle ways. To try a case is all-consuming for both sides. You don't sleep, you are working on your opening, your closing. If it can be pled and justice done, that's always better. It's this human pressure that makes people reluctant to try cases." Another ADA noted that for both prosecutors and defenders, going to trial and losing risked embarrassment before one's colleagues throughout the court community: "People have a reluctance to go into court because they don't want to look like a fool in front of everyone if they lose."

The trial penalty seemed to also serve as a double punishment. Obviously, defendants who insisted on trials were punished with stiffer sentences, but defense attorneys who allowed cases to go to trial also risked a lack of cooperation in future cases for violating informal norms of cooperation. As one experienced private defense attorney described, "the DAs and judges can penalize you in this case, and the next one as well."

A plea hearing I observed provided an extreme but illustrative example of the strength of cooperative plea norms and the potential emotional reactions that the violation of them could produce. The defendant was supposed to plead open to a rape charge, but withdrew his guilty plea when the judge read the potential sentence he was facing. The ADA then stood up in open court and barked, "Don't worry, I'll get you, you son of a bitch, you're going away for a long time!" As the hearing concluded, the ADA hurried over to the PD and demanded an explanation. The PD apologized profusely and explained that she couldn't talk the defendant out of withdrawing the plea.

On the other hand, the statistical data show few sentencing differences between open and negotiated pleas, with the exception of state prison sentences. This pattern supports the earlier discussion of the role of open pleas and their sentencing consequences. While defenders resorted to open pleas when an attractive sentence agreement could not be reached, their chances of actually getting a more lenient sentence from the judge than the one the prosecutor offered were not at all assured. Negotiated agreements did, however, protect defendants to some extent from going to state prison. Whether a defendant was to receive a county jail or state prison sentence was a frequently negotiated plea concession.

Similarly, the finding that negotiated pleas were negatively related to dispositional departures is explained by the interview data presented earlier that the DA's office would not agree to departures, but instead agreed to stand silent (when it suited them), in return for an open plea. To the judge, the ADA's silence signified tacit acceptance of a departure below guidelines.

The statistics also indicate considerable gender differences for all sentencing decisions except state imprisonment, and significant race differences, especially in terms of imprisonment and dispositional departures. As implied earlier, one source of race differences might have involved Rich County court actors' views of the nearby large metropolis with its high crime rate and large black population. For example, recall the interview statements earlier that prosecutors and judges placed great importance on deterring individuals from the big city from "preying on" Rich County. To the extent that a greater proportion of offenders from the metropolitan area were black, this would account for some of the race differences.

However, the interview data suggest that the more important sources of these race differences were also more subtle. In Metro County, factors of so-called character and status exerted indirect influence on ADA's plea agreements and judges' bench trial and sentencing decisions, and these factors were sometimes linked to perceptions of black defendants. A similar but more pronounced process appeared to exist in Rich County, in which factors such as employment and job status, family stability and history, education, and even demeanor and physical appearance influenced judges' and DA's decisions about incarceration, sentence length, and especially state imprisonment. The following quotes from three judges illustrate the influence of these factors (emphasis added):

> You try to get a sense of whether the person really is likely to return, whether the person is the kind who can profit from probation, has a sense of remorse. . . . *I mean, it's everything you rely on in your experience and judgement in trying to size a person up.*

> You look at how far they went in school, their knowledge, their family background. How are they employed? When was the last time they did work? If ever? Are they on public assis-

tance? Who are they supporting? *You can get a good picture of someone in a few minutes.*

I look at if the person has maintained a stable lifestyle. Meaning job, family, spouse, that type of thing, which would be an indication that this is an aberration from their normal conduct. If going to jail would be extremely traumatic for them. *Some kinds of people, it just rolls off their back and doesn't affect them whatsoever.*

An ADA team leader described factors influencing sentence negotiations: "...The defendant's education, employment history, history of drug abuse, family background, everything like that." To the extent that low-income black defendants were perceived as having poorer employment histories and lower occupational prestige, lower education, and more unstable family backgrounds (see Feagin 1991; Feagin and Sikes 1994), they would be disadvantaged by the consideration of these factors in sentencing. The influence of these status factors, and their potential linkage to perceptions of race, also suggests why the race differences were larger for state imprisonment decisions. While jail sentences were used extensively for all kinds of defendants for expressive sentencing purposes, (e.g., communicating deterrence to the community), prison sentences were reserved for those deemed truly serious offenders. As the president judge stated: "Some of these kids are coming in, sold a $20 bag of cocaine or whatever, and its doesn't bother me a bit to say, 'Darn it, you need 16 or 17 months in jail to send a message back to the community.' But the state institution, I do have concerns. It's much harder time, more things can happen to you. It's for the really bad people." In addition, a private defense attorney described how demeanor and physical appearance came into play in decisions regarding jail vs. prison incarceration: "Somebody that's not physically large and can't fend for themselves, someone who's not mentally tough, they don't belong in the state system. The state system is pretty frightening. I mean, I've had clients that have gone in there and have been gang raped with a broomstick and things like that."

The status factors and their potential linkage to perceptions of race noted above may have mobilized attributions of offender dangerousness or blameworthiness (see Albonetti 1991; Farrell and Holmes 1991, p. 536). To the extent that low-income black defendants, especially those from the nearby big city, were stereotyped by the white, affluent Rich County court judges and prosecutors as physically and mentally tough or "hardened" compared to whites, they would be more likely to receive state prison sentences. Also, Pennsylvania's state prison population at the time was about 65 percent black (Steffensmeier 1992), and Rich County court actors may have been reluctant to sentence white offenders to prison for fear that they would be victimized by black inmates.

One plea/sentencing hearing I observed provides a particularly dramatic illustration of how these status factors could influence sentencing decisions. The thirty-eight-year-old white defendant entered an open guilty plea to a burglary charge. His PD asked for a mitigated range sentence while the ADA stood silent. The PD described how he had a history of sporadic heroin use, which he would finance by stealing. The attorney noted that whenever the defendant was off heroin, he had a good work record with his father's painting business, and pointed out the defendant's family sitting in court. The judge then delivered a withering moral lecture while the defendant broke down and sobbed. The judge concluded by noting that, "As far as I'm concerned, you're nothing but a thief, and I'm not sure but what that's all you'll ever be." Nevertheless, the judge gave a mitigated range sentence of six months' jail time, to be followed by enforced drug treatment, citing the defendant's work history and family support as the key reasons for the sentence.

On the other hand, the same status factors that seemed to work to the disadvantage of blacks may have advantaged women defendants in Rich County (see also Steffensmeier and Allan 1991; Daly 1995). This is particularly true for the family and children considerations noted above. A quote from a public defender illustrates the role of gender and common circumstances of women defendants:

> There are times when the facts really justify prison or jail, but the DA or judge might be reluctant to do it because of the person. I represent a young girl right now, 22 years old. She has two children, no husband. She got caught in a drug sting operation, and she's facing an awful lot of time in jail. I'm working like crazy to keep that from happening. It's a mistake to put a person like that in jail, because of the circumstances. What will happen to the kids?

Summary

Rich County's court reflected the conservative, law and order ideology of the larger community, and court community membership was highly stable, held together by relationships and commitments within and external to the courthouse. The DA's office dominated the court community, but did so mostly through cooperativeness, ideological consensus, and collegiality. Courtroom workgroups usually cooperated to maintain an efficient plea bargaining system and comparatively tough sentencing standards. Rich County also had a strong and well-entrenched tradition of going rates, and the guidelines were secondary to these.

Plea bargaining revolved mostly around agreements for lower and middle standard-range sentences. Charge bargaining came into play most typically when initial charges carried mandatory sentences, or when drug offenders cooperated with police. When agreements could not be reached (as when the defense wanted a departure below guidelines), defenders resorted to open pleas. Prosecutors would either agree to stand silent at open plea sentencings, or would argue (usually successfully) for a sentence more to their liking. Trials were seen as quite disruptive, reserved for the most problematic cases, and risked penalties for defendants and attorneys alike. Trial convictions greatly increased the chances of incarceration and the sentence lengths for defendants, and disrupted collegial and cooperative working and personal relations for defense attorneys.

Finally, Rich County's sentencing patterns exhibited greater race and gender differences than either of the other two focus counties. Arguably, the influence of race stemmed partly from the county's proximity to a large metropolis, partly from the consideration in sentencing of status factors that were linked to perceptions of race, such as employment and job status, family stability, education, appearance, and demeanor. Similar intervening factors conditioned gender differences, especially family and child considerations.

Overall, the Rich County example illustrates how prosecutors can use guidelines to their advantage within the context of a strong system of informal going rates based on organizational cooperation and ideological consensus. What role do guidelines play in a court community that not only lacks strong sentencing traditions, but is also riddled with ideological conflict between judges and prosecutors? Southwest County provides a picture of such a court community.

7

Southwest County

Southwest County encompassed a mostly rural population of about 100,000, with several small towns and one medium-sized city. As in Rich County, the political climate tended toward the conservative, especially on issues of criminal justice. Republicans accounted for 63 percent of the county's registered voters, and church-related organizations (mostly fundamentalist protestant and Roman Catholic) were active in local politics. Interestingly, Southwest's largest city did not dominate the political scene; in fact, it was not even the county seat. The results of the 1991 U.S. Senate special election illustrate the balance of electoral influence between the city and the small towns and rural areas. While the Democratic candidate won in the more politically moderate city, the Republican dominated in the surrounding areas, thus carrying the county. Southwest County provides a final context in which to examine court community arrangements, case processing strategies, and sentencing patterns under sentencing guidelines.

Statistical Analysis

Because of the comparatively smaller number of cases in the Southwest County analyses (1,335), two independent variables are coded in a different manner than the other two counties' analyses. Insufficient variation in offense types and severity prevent using the more specific offense categories in models simultaneously with the offense severity score. Therefore, I collapse the offense types into violent offenses (homicide, kidnapping, rape/IDSI, robbery, assaults, and weapons offenses), property offenses (burglary, thefts, arson, criminal trespassing, and forgery), and drug offenses (all drug felonies and misdemeanors). Since only seven bench trials appear in the Southwest County cases selected for analysis, I also collapse all trials into one category.

TABLE 7.1

Modes of Conviction by Offense Severity: Southwest County
(cell percentages by row)

	Modes of Conviction				
Offense Severity	Other guilty pleas	Negotiated pleas	Bench trials	Jury trials	Total
1	33 19.8%	129 77%	1 .6%	4 2.4%	167
2	73 26%	208 72%	3 1%	2 .7%	286
3	47 27%	118 67%	0 —	11 6%	176
4	16 16%	75 77%	1 1%	6 6%	98
5	102 25%	285 71%	1 .25%	15 3.7%	403
6	21 18.4%	89 78%	0 —	4 3.5%	114
7	5 8.3%	46 77%	0 —	9 15%	60
8	0 —	8 —	1 89%	0 11%	9 —
9	4 18%	13 59%	0 —	5 23%	22
10	0 —	0 —	0 —	3 100%	3
Total	301 22.5%	971 72.7%	7 .5%	5 4.2%	1,335

Chi-squared = 65.3   df = 27   p<.005

TABLE 7.2

Logit Models of Overall Incarceration and Dispositional Departures:
Southwest County
Odds Ratios (logits in parentheses)

Variable	Overall Incarceration	Dispositional Departure
Constant **	— (–10.9)	— (11.2)
Year	1.08 (.085) *	.92 (–.08) *
Violent offenses	2.64 (.97)	2.33 (.845)
Drug offenses	4.44 (1.49)	.55 (–.59)
Offense severity	1.96 (.67)	.45 (–.80)
Prior record	1.60 (.467)	.71 (–.35)
Multiple conviction charges	1.21 (.195) *	.65 (–.44) *
Negotiated plea	.97 (–.033) *	.72 (–.35) *
Trial	2.97 (1.09)	.19 (–1.65)
Race (black=1)	1.53 (.43) *	.70 (–.38) *
Gender (female=1)	.62 (–.477)	1.63 (.49) *
Age	.98 (–.022)	1.01 (.01) *
N =	1,335	414
Chi-square	635	36.9
(model accuracy)	(87%)	(86%)

* Denotes coefficients not significant at .05 or less.
** Retail theft and other guilty pleas are reference categories.

Appendix C shows Southwest's descriptive statistics. The most notable aspect of these figures is the very small numbers of trial cases and black defendants. Only sixty-three trials and only seventy-nine black defendants appear in the six years of data. Further, Appendix C, along with Table 7.1, indicate that Southwest's caseload comprised a comparatively less severe mix of offenses. Table 7.1 shows a crosstabulation of mode of conviction by offense severity, and like the other two counties, mode of conviction varied significantly by offense severity.

The majority of cases were negotiated guilty pleas, but as the discussion of the ethnographic data will point out, the proportion of open pleas for less serious offenses increased greatly between 1989 and 1991.

Table 7.2 shows logit models of overall incarceration decisions and dispositional departures, and Table 7.3 models sentence lengths.

TABLE 7.3

OLS Models of Incarceration Length, Corrected for Selection Bias: Southwest County (includes incarceration cases only)

Variable	b (Beta)	Contribution to R^2
Constant **	−116.2 (—)	—
Year	1.1 (.10)	.01
Violent offenses	11.7 (.26)	—
Drug offenses	7.3 (.214)	—
total offense R^2 contrib.		.24
Offense severity	9.1 (.81)	.129
Prior record	4.7 (.71)	.067
Multiple conviction charges	3.6 (.11)	.011
Negotiated plea	−3.6 (−.107)	.009
Trial	6.1 (.11)	.008
Race (black=1)	−2.5 (−.045) *	.002
Gender (female=1)	−7.2 (−.15)	.017
Age	−.06 (−.03) *	.001
Correction factor	38.0 (.64)	.029
N =		581
Adjusted R^2		.523

* Denotes coefficients not significant at .05 or less.
** Retail theft and other guilty pleas are reference categories.

In spite of the collapsed offense categories, the legally prescribed variables again dominated as predictors of incarceration and dispositional departures, and contributed most to the explained variance in incarceration length. Drug offenders were particularly likely to be jailed or imprisoned—with incarceration odds that were more than four times those of property offenders—and were less likely to receive dispositional departures. Drug offenses also resulted in incarcerations that were about seven months longer than property offenses. Violent offenses were also more likely than property offenses to result in incarceration and received considerably longer incarceration terms, but were paradoxically more likely to receive dispositional departures. The greater likelihood of dispositional departure for violent offenses is attributable to the inclusion of aggravated assaults and weapons offenses in the category. When these offense types are removed, violent offenders were considerably less likely than property offenders to receive such departures (analysis not shown). In addition, defendants with multiple conviction charges received moderately longer incarceration terms by 3.6 months.

The major extralegal influence on the three sentencing outcomes was mode of conviction. Incarceration odds for those convicted by trial were nearly three times those for other guilty pleas (a .50 probability difference), and 81 percent less for dispositional departure (a –.58 probability difference). Negotiated pleas offered little benefit over other (i.e., open) guilty pleas in terms of incarceration, and only a slight (and nonsignificant) benefit for dispositional departures. However, negotiated pleas did yield benefits in terms of incarceration length, resulting in incarceration terms that were 3.6 months less than defendants with open guilty pleas. The length effects for trial, while significant, were considerably smaller and added less to the model's predictive power compared to the other two counties and the statewide analysis.

Race does not attain statistical significance in the incarceration, dispositional departure, or length models. Since there were only seventy-nine black defendants in the data, the race effects should be viewed with caution. Substantively, blacks' incarceration odds were about 50 percent greater than those of nonblacks (a .21 probability difference), and 30 percent less for dispositional departure (a –.18 probability difference). These effects, while notable, were weaker than those in the other two counties and in the statewide analysis.[1] Further, blacks actually received incarceration lengths that were 2.5 months shorter than nonblacks. Gender was only significant for incarceration length; women received terms that were about seven months shorter than men's. Substantively, women's incarceration odds were 38 percent less than men (a –.24 probability difference), and dispositional departure odds were 63 percent greater (a .24 probability difference).

Unlike the statewide analyses and those of the previous two counties, Southwest's model for state imprisonment sentences did not differ substantially from that for overall incarceration, and is not presented here. Also, estimating separate models by prior record presented problems because insufficient numbers of serious prior record cases were left after simultaneously controlling for offense type/severity. Though not comparable to the findings for the other counties and the statewide analysis, simpler models including only offense severity, trial, race, and gender indicate no substantial differences between the factors affecting sentences for serious and less serious prior record defendants.[2]

In sum, Southwest County resembled the other two counties and the rest of the state in that offense type/severity and prior record were the major predictors of sentencing decisions, while mode of conviction and to a much lesser extent race and gender also conditioned important sentencing differences. On the other hand, Southwest differed from Metro County and resembled Rich County in that negotiated pleas offered little advantage over open pleas in terms of incarceration odds. They did, however, offer moderate benefits in terms of somewhat shorter sentence lengths. Finally, on the infrequent occasions when black defendants appeared in Southwest's courtrooms, race seemed to be less influential as a predictor of sentencing decisions than was true statewide or in Metro and Rich counties.

Ethnographic Analysis

The discussion of Southwest County's ethnographic data follows the same format as the previous counties, moving from local political and court community organizational contexts to workgroup case processing strategies, and concluding with sentencing outcomes. Since Southwest's court community had comparatively fewer members, I use pseudonyms to refer to key individuals for ease of presentation.

Political And Organizational Context

Not surprisingly, all three of the county's active judges (O'Connor, Hobbs, and Painter) were Republicans. The Republican dominance of the county was strong enough that one judge (O'Connor) changed parties after being appointed by the governor in order to retain his seat in the judicial election. O'Connor described the county's political climate this way: "When you talk about Southwest County, you're talking a real throwback . . . we're cresting a new century in a few years, and for Southwest it will be the 1800s, if that tells you anything. I mean, we're talking about some very conservative people, some who didn't like me because I'm Catholic, Irish, and a former Democrat. In that sense it amazes me that we even have a woman judge."

Each judge noted a necessity to appear "tough on crime" in order to win and retain a seat on the trial bench, and local news media were quick to dramatize high-profile cases in which defendants received lenient treatment. According to Judge Painter: "There is a real standard of sentencing that is expected by the community. Our media doesn't hesitate to editorialize about things if they see that sentences aren't to their satisfaction." The chief district attorney also described the amount of local media attention to court-related matters: "The court really generates news here. We have an in-house correspondent, who is responsible to the local newspaper, and he is a great contributor of page-one-type news. Sometimes there are two or three pages of sentencing in there, depending on what's going on. People like to see it." In fact, each judge had his/her own "horror stories" to tell about negative media publicity in high-profile cases. As will be discussed later, such negative media attention was often mobilized by the DA's office, and caused political problems for each of the judges.

The composition of the bench had been unstable in the previous three years due to retirements, judicial elections, and the long-term illness of the president judge. Thus, each of the three currently active judges was relatively new to the bench, and politically vulnerable. O'Connor was appointed in 1989, lost his first election in 1990, but was then reappointed four months later when another judge failed to win reelection (in Pennsylvania, the governor appoints people to fill vacancies on the bench, and the appointed judge must run for reelection one year later). O'Connor then won his second election campaign. Hobbs and Painter were also appointed in 1989 and won in the general election a year later.

The District Attorney's and Public Defender's offices were much smaller and less formally organized than those of the other two counties. The chief DA, also a Republican, had held his position for over eight years, while the chief PD had only occupied his position for less than a year. The chief DA employed one full-time assistant and five others part time, and these were relatively recent law school graduates. While the chief PD worked part time himself, his office employed one full-time assistant and four other part-timers. These assistants, like the assistant DAs, were relatively young and inexperienced at criminal work. Judge Hobbs characterizes the PD's office this way:

> They are very weak. None of them have much experience, including the chief, and he doesn't provide the others much leadership. Their full-time guy usually does a pretty good job with plea bargaining, but other than that . . . I sometimes question the competence of a couple of them. One had a trial in my court awhile ago and just botched it. She didn't like the sentence I gave her client and wanted to appeal. In private, I said "If you appeal, I'll have to go on the record about what a lousy job I think you did, and I don't want to do that." I guess we just have to give them time to learn.

All of the part-time PDs, including the Chief, also had private practices that encompassed criminal work. Thus, with the exception of a handful of other private attorneys in the county, the private and public defense bar were largely identical.

Judge O'Connor had spent the bulk of his career as a defense attorney, and later as chief Public Defender. By far, O'Connor had the most experience in criminal work. Most of Painter's career was spent in private practice doing primarily civil and family litigation. He then joined the PD's office and spent several years as an assistant before rising to chief public defender and then judge. Hobbs, on the other hand, had a more prosecution-oriented background. She worked for a brief time in private practice and joined the DA's office part-time in the mid-1980s. She then worked for the Southwest County jail on a project to develop techniques for prosecuting child-abuse cases. Although Hobbs was the acting president judge, O'Connor managed the criminal docket due to his extensive experience in criminal work.

Since the president judge was on long-term illness leave, the three active judges had to handle increased caseloads to compensate. This judicial personnel shortage was also aggravated by a statewide trend of much tougher enforcement of drug and drunken-driving laws, resulting in increased numbers of such cases in the trial courts. From 1989 to 1991 Southwest County's trial court experienced a 196 percent increase in total convictions, and a 186 percent increase in convictions for drug offenses. Thus, one of the key problems faced by the bench was the sharp increase in caseloads in the face of a reduced staff of judges.

As in Metro, O'Connor and his clerk assigned cases according to an individual calendar system. Given the shortage of judges and the increased caseloads, his primary administrative problem was to move cases quickly and avoid docket backlogs, which invited criticism in the local media. To improve efficiency, O'Connor instituted a case categorizing system (which bore a striking resemblance to Metro County's). He sorted cases as they came in from the lower courts according to their probable pleas, as indicated on standardized pretrial forms filled out by defendants. O'Connor assigned defendants who indicated that they wished to plead guilty at preliminary hearings to an accelerated plea list or "fast track," and assigned those who did not plead guilty at this stage to the trial list or "slow track." All three judges shared the criminal caseload, but O'Connor's caseload accounted for about two-thirds of the criminal docket since he handled all "fast track" guilty pleas in addition to many trial list cases. Hobbs and Painter both devoted roughly one day a week to criminal cases, and thus shared the remaining third of the criminal caseload.

The three judges coordinated their activities and schedules at informal weekly meetings, usually over breakfast or lunch. Each of the judges indicated that their relations were characterized by a solid consensus and a sense of "teamwork." Hobbs summed up the working consensus between the judges this way:

> We are all very different, but I would say the mix (of judges) we have now is an honest, real situation, where we can openly discuss, criticize, and share things. There is a real camaraderie. We all have our strengths . . . Judge O'Connor is more criminally oriented, Judge Painter is more civilly oriented, and I'm sort of a mix of both and we all have very different personalities. But it's nice because we can draw on each other's strengths and sort of help each other with our weaknesses.

This atmosphere of informality and familiarity extended to the courtroom. In Judge Hobbs's courtroom, for example, the procedures for handling the day's cases were often worked out by Hobbs asking the PD and assistant DA, "Do you people mind if we do it the way we did last week, have the pleas and sentencings all at once?" "Yeah, that would be good," the attorneys each replied. At the conclusion of these proceedings, Hobbs did not formally adjourn the court, leaving the bench instead with: "Don, Maryanne, Ted (the attorneys present), you all did a good job today, thanks. It's been a lovely morning!" Further, the judges, particularly Hobbs, often took up considerable courtroom time to deliver stern moral lectures or exhortations to defendants before pronouncing sentences.

Sponsoring Agency Relations

As will be seen, however, such informality and familiarity did not necessarily indicate a lack of conflict, particularly between the judges and the DA's office. The local political context and the court's caseload pressures heavily influenced judicial relations with the other key court community sponsoring agencies. First, the DA's office adopted an adversarial stance toward the judges and PD's office, and this conflict colored nearly every aspect of the court community's activities. This created special organizational and political problems for the judges. On one hand, the judges and

DAs were interdependent in that they had to jointly address the shared task of processing cases and avoiding backlogs. On the other hand, personal and ideological differences divided the bench and DA's office, and the differences were especially sharp between their two key players, Judge O'Connor and the Chief DA.

Given this situation, the balance of power and influence between judges and the DA's office was situationally contingent. Both had recourse to sanctions to use on each other, and the relative availability of these sanctions, and thus the balance of power between judges and DAs, varied by case circumstances and political contingencies. On one hand, the judges exerted their formal authority to influence the DA's office through their case dispositions and sentences. Judges also influenced the DA's office's case processing tactics through case scheduling and employed informal methods for encouraging speedy guilty pleas (discussed later).

On the other hand, the DA's office controlled important resources and sanctions with which to influence both the judges and PDs. As in any jurisdiction, prosecutors controlled charging discretion in trial court cases, and could potentially manipulate both the number and severity of charges—and thus sentencing outcomes—to their advantage in plea agreements. Second, prosecutors largely controlled the case information that came before the judges, and O'Connor noted that they were often less than cooperative in discovery processes with public defenders.

The most problematic aspect of the judges' relations with the DA's office, however, was the DA's ability and willingness to mobilize political pressure on judges. The judges perceived a lack of consistency between the routine and less politically visible case processing practices of the prosecutors and their more public political posturing. Hobbs explained how prosecutors would posture in open court: "They send you double messages sometimes. They are inclined to make plea agreements where, if the judge gets the rap for it, that suits them just fine. They will come in chambers and say 'Look, we really don't want to pursue this person,' and then they come into court and say that they want you to throw the book at them. It looks good."

The DA's office especially used the news media as a forum for portraying judges as "soft on crime." Each judge identified several cases in which they had sentenced according to a plea agreement, and the chief district attorney complained in the media about the leniency of the sentence. O'Connor elaborates with two of his own examples:

There was a retail theft case involving a few dollars' worth of merchandise, and I kicked it out at the bench trial. The DA stood up in my courtroom and said that it was out of line. He muttered loudly the whole way out and then talked to the press and said the usual DA stuff. On the other hand, there was this terrible gang rape case. I gave the main defendant as harsh a sentence as I could within the guideline ranges without giving them a reason to appeal. The DA then stands up in court and says, 'I haven't asked for this too often but I am asking for a sentence that would be 24 to 48 years.' He knows that can't apply. He was just using it for a showcase, trying to maintain the appearance of the DA's office mounting up on their white chargers doing battle with all of the evildoers.

Such negative media attention, in turn, often hurt the judges politically. O'Connor lost his first reelection bid largely because of a political backlash mobilized by negative media attention, and in O'Connor's recent successful campaign (in which the chief assistant DA ran for O'Connor's seat), negative publicity also played a prominent role. Judge Painter described another of the more salient of these types of cases, which involved a sexual abuse case handled by Judge Hobbs:

> This case with Judge Hobbs—a teacher touched a girl's privates with her underwear on and Judge Hobbs gave him ninety days in jail according to a plea agreement—and she really got in hot water with the local media. That was one of her first cases, and they haven't ever forgotten it. That story is still circulating around the community. I still go out places and hear people critical of her for one call on one case. She's not going to shake that ten years from now. She's pretty bitter about it . . . I know Judge Hobbs would have loved to take that reporter aside and say, "Come in here, you dummy! That was a plea agreement, negotiated not by the assistant but by the DA himself!"

The chief DA, however, tells a different story of the case:

> In that sexual abuse case with the teacher, we asked for a substantial sentence and Judge Hobbs, who was new on the bench, gave the guy a ninety-day sentence. Ninety days was absurd. We expressed that publicly, and there was a lot of

adverse publicity for her, and it was around election time. We haven't had too much trouble getting child abuse sentences out of Judge Hobbs since then.

Both Hobbs and O'Connor identified another set of political circumstances as indicative of the chief DA's "immaturity" (according to Hobbs) and unwillingness to "be reasonable" (according to O'Connor). The DA's office petitioned the county commissioners for a pay raise and more overtime pay for attending lower court preliminary hearings. Given the recent statewide budget crunch and resulting cuts in county funding, the commissioners denied the request. Therefore, the chief DA discouraged his assistants from attending preliminary hearings in the lower courts. This policy shifted charging and plea negotiation discretion to police in cases settled by the lower courts and even in some cases bound over to the trial court as "fast track" pleas. Hobbs explains: "When the D.A.'s office got spurned by the commissioners to pay them more money and overtime, they said 'Okay, we're not going to preliminary hearings anymore.' When the D.A.'s office sent out the message that they weren't attending anymore, they gave complete (charging) authority to the police officers. Now, we're getting a lot more fast track pleas where the police have cut deals with defendants. That's pretty unprofessional and immature in my book."

Of the three judges, O'Connor's relations with the district attorney's office, the chief DA in particular, were the most hostile. While this conflict involved a number of issues, it hinged on a basic ideological difference regarding sentencing goals and standards. O'Connor espoused a general belief in offering defendants opportunities to rehabilitate themselves and tended toward leniency for nearly every type of defendant except those involved in violent crimes and drug trafficking. The chief DA believed that sentencing was for retribution and deterrence, and saw tough sentences as necessary for achieving these purposes. Each individual characterized the other as an obstacle to achieving desired sentencing goals.

Because O'Connor managed the criminal docket and handled two-thirds of the criminal caseload, this conflict permeated routine case processing activities. According to the chief DA, O'Connor emphasized moving cases quickly at the expense of giving defendants sufficiently stiff sentences, and thus favored the public defenders' office:

[O'Connor] says that we should be contacting the defense counsel and leading them by the hand through discovery, we should be going out and helping these defense counsels who aren't too industrious, or we should prepare a plea agreement on every case. He says, "You ought to plea bargain this away." I take a hard stance and say no. They can't force me to do that . . . I take great offense at the very term "plea bargaining.". . . I'll be damned if I am going to plea bargain cases away just to beat the numbers. I think that is kind of an attack on me.

O'Connor in turn summed up his feelings about the DA's office eloquently:

We have a DA's office here that hates the fact that we don't have summary executions. Don't bother them with the Constitution. And I'm not just saying that because I'm a former PD. If anything there is great joy in seeing some of these people I had to represent for years going away for long periods of time. But concepts like fairness and due process still exist. We've had a running feud ever since I came on the bench.

The judges and PDs were tightly coupled in a manner similar to judges and prosecutors. Because PDs had fewer ways to influence judges, however, power relations between judges and PDs were weighted in favor of judges. First, PDs lacked the discretion that prosecutors enjoyed in terms of charging decisions and information control. True, judges needed the PDs' cooperation in moving cases by generating guilty pleas, and as I will discuss later, judges often relied on the PDs to counterbalance prosecutorial excesses in guilty plea and sentencing processes. However, PDs were more vulnerable to judges' discretionary use of their formal authority in case disposition and sentencing. For example, Hobbs sometimes rejected plea agreements that she felt were too lenient. Further, the PDs' office lacked the personnel and resources to mount appeals of judges' sentences. Finally, given the "tough on crime" political climate, the PD's office had little access to news media, and had little ability to use the media as a tool for political purposes.

The judges saw little need to exercise their authority over PDs, however, because their relations with them were quite cooperative compared to the problems with the DA's office. Each of the judges indicated that they had very few disputes with individual PDs or the office in general. As implied earlier, the judges identified shortcomings with the PDs' skills, but viewed them with a more tolerant attitude. In fact, the judges generally felt that the PDs were adequate in plea negotiations, and they often wished the PDs would take a more adversarial stance toward the DA's office. Hobbs attributed this to inexperience and a lack of legal competence among the PDs: "The PDs are very weak. The chief PD now is young and not very forceful. Their assistants are inexperienced. The PDs are effective most of the time in plea negotiations, but in terms of trial litigation they are very weak."

In sum, the PD's office lacked the organizational resources, discretion, political opportunities, or motives to pose the problems for judges that the DA's office did. Further, the judges and PDs sometimes formed a subtle coalition in order to check what they perceived to be prosecutorial excesses. This alignment of judges and PDs was evident in their workgroup case processing strategies.

Case Processing Strategies

The workgroup strategies of the Southwest County judges were in large part individual and collective adaptations to increased caseload pressure on one hand, and their strained relations with the DA's office on the other.

"Last-minute plea" strategies. The judges preferred early plea agreements or open pleas, or else early—and more or less final—decisions to go to trial. Early "fast track" guilty pleas disposed cases quickly, while early decisions to go to trial enabled cases to be scheduled on the trial list without difficulty. None of the judges indicated a dislike for trials. O'Connor, with his heavy criminal caseloads, tolerated what he called "meaningful" trials. Hobbs and Painter, with their lighter criminal caseloads, enjoyed trials because they provided opportunities to "act like real judges."

Trial list cases involving more severe offenses, however, involved last-minute plea agreements that resembled what Mather (1973) called "slow pleas."[3] The frequency of last-minute pleas caused particular problems for the judges. In such cases, counsel delayed until just prior to the trial date, at which point they either finalized plea agreement terms or the defendant registered an open plea. When prosecutors had strong evidence in more serious cases, they were reluctant to negotiate guilty plea terms, especially charge reductions. Typically, prosecutors would only negotiate sentencing agreements within standard guideline ranges. According to the chief DA, "If we have the evidence to prove a charge, that charge must be pressed. If we have the evidence that says we have got the charges, our plea agreements amount to sentencing somewhere in the guidelines standard ranges. If the defense counsel wants something less than that then they have got to really convince me that the guy is worth it. Like, if they say the defendant is a little old lady who wrote some bad checks."

In strong prosecution cases, PDs would wait until the trial date approached to see if any plea concessions were forthcoming, and then would either accept the DA's plea agreement terms, go to trial if the terms were especially unattractive, or enter an open guilty plea. On the other hand, when prosecutors had weaker evidence and did not want to risk trials, defenders would also maintain a plea of not guilty until the prosecution offered to negotiate plea agreement terms. In the latter case, defenders would seek charge reductions or drops if the evidence was especially weak. As the full-time PD described: "Quite honestly, it is to our advantage to haggle up until the day of the trial, even though the judges agree that the DA's office shouldn't be doing this, that it should have been settled well beforehand. The longer the defendant waits the better deal he is getting, because then even better offers come from the DA's office. I won't recommend for someone to plead guilty right off the bat on a serious charge, even if they want to. I tell them to sit on it for awhile."

Thus, last-minute pleas resembled games of "chicken" in which prosecutors and defenders would each wait to see if the other would cave in, and this aggravated docket backlogs and created scheduling problems. Judge O'Connor described the usual course of these last-minute pleas and the conditions that fostered them: "We get the backlog cleared up and then the DA adopts the attitude of 'no-more-Mr.-Nice-Guy,' we are going to prosecute everything to the fullest. No concessions. Then we are right back building another backlog. Then, when the public defender won't plead, or the DA isn't prepared for trial, he'll be dealing the night before they pick the jury."

The judges thus faced a dilemma in terms of case processing: they had to move cases quickly to avoid backlogs, and the best method for doing so was to generate fast guilty pleas. However, the conflictual relations between judges and the DA's office, specifically their divergent sentencing goals and standards, prevented their arriving at a working consensus regarding routine guilty plea policies. Further, the DA's and PD's last-minute plea strategies hindered the quick resolution of more serious trial list cases, and yet judges were prohibited by law from overt involvement in guilty plea negotiations. To resolve this dilemma, the judges employed three interrelated strategies: case scheduling pressure, an alignment with PDs, and lenient sentences as a reward for guilty pleas.

Case scheduling pressure. In order to reduce inefficiencies and backlogs brought on by the frequent last-minute pleas, O'Connor exerted strong pressure on counsel to reach plea agreements quickly through his case scheduling. He handled all pre-trial hearings and fast-track guilty pleas one day a week and scheduled large numbers of cases for each available trial date in the expectation that the great majority of trial list cases would "fold" and a guilty plea would be forthcoming. "I put lots of cases on back-up for trial dates. When they start folding on the day of jury selection you've got nowhere to go unless you have people standing by." He then scheduled trial dates for trial list cases as quickly as possible, so that counsel had less time to delay plea negotiations: "I tell them (counsel) that they can come here two weeks from now and enter a guilty plea. I tell them if it is not entered then, I'll put the case back on the trial list and then you'll be right up close and personal soon. We'll pick twelve and we are going to go to trial on such-and-such a date. That way I force their hands. I even like to have people sentenced right after they enter their guilty pleas, because even that delay can lead people to change their minds."

Alignment with public defenders: plea rewards. The second strategy for judges was a subtle alignment with PDs, an alignment facilitated by the sentencing guidelines. As noted earlier, sentencing guidelines could potentially restrict the sentencing discretion of judges, and therefore increase the power of prosecutors to exert disproportionate sentencing influence through charge bargaining (Tonry and Coffee 1987; Savelsberg 1992). However, such an effect was not apparent in Southwest County, where the influence of sentencing guidelines appeared to be quite the opposite.

As mentioned, the DA's office strongly disliked charge bargaining, and instead preferred to base plea negotiations around sentencing issues. The judges' use of the guidelines, however, constrained the DAs from obtaining sentences that they deemed severe enough. The guidelines provided a set of sentencing norms that the judges, especially O'Connor, used to legitimize comparatively more lenient sentences as a reward for guilty pleas. By doing so, the guidelines facilitated an alignment between the judges and PDs based on a tacit understanding regarding guilty plea rewards, especially for fast open pleas. In open pleas, the defense counsel would plead guilty to the original charges without a plea agreement with the prosecutor, thus bypassing the time-consuming process of haggling. The judges induced PDs to plead open more frequently by means of lenient sentences within the guidelines ranges or even sentences that departed below the guidelines. Indeed, the proportion of open pleas more than tripled during the time since O'Connor, Hobbs, and Painter came on the bench, from 11 percent of total convictions in 1989 to 34 percent in 1991. The judges especially used this open plea reward for certain property offenses with which prosecutors and defenders had problems in negotiating plea agreements in the past, such as retail theft, check forgery, and welfare fraud. Judge O'Connor explained his strategy of coaxing PDs to register open pleas:

> The PDs had the attitude that a case can never come to the court with an open plea. Everything had to be a plea agreement. I say, make it an open plea. They can just trust that I will do what the guidelines require, or else go below them. I keep telling people—I told the one attorney today that I did three felony retail thefts last week and all of them got probation. Hint, hint, hint—do an open plea. I send messages without sending messages, and stay out of the gray area of actually getting involved in plea agreements. Now I don't do that on homicides or rapes, but some of these cases are really nonsense, and I don't want to hear it. These people (PDs) ought to have figured out by now that I'm not going to put anyone in jail for retail theft or welfare fraud or bad checks, no matter what their prior record is.

Judge Painter concurred, saying:

> I think you get your best chance to send a message by your own sentence when you're in an open plea situation. If you think about it, that's how you send a message to your PD and your DA. If they see you doing something other than what they thought, then they know what the court is going to do, and that's going to change your plea process. If it's some-

thing more lenient, the PD is going to think, "Hey, I can get that." I think we send our best message by redirecting and setting our own standard by open pleas.

Two of the PDs explained how the sentencing guidelines and the judges' willingness to reward open pleas came to benefit them and disadvantage the DA's office:

> Now, if you feel you know what the judge is going to do and if you know what the guidelines are, you can go in and plead open. I go in and argue and pray, and sure enough it usually falls my way.

> This court just keeps getting better and better for us. If it wasn't for the guidelines, I think the DAs would be really out of control and they would be asking for outrageous sentences in some cases. I thank God that we have the guidelines, or the DAs would be arguing for longer periods of time in jail. Because these DAs, who have never been defense attorneys, are out of control. They have these hardened attitudes.

The chief DA also described how the guidelines and the tacit understandings between judges and PDs constrained his ability to control plea negotiations and obtain the types of severe sentences he would like:

> There are a lot of times where if we didn't have that sentencing guideline, I think we would be successful in getting the courts to impose a greater sentence. Not because I just like to have greater sentences, but because I think the defendant deserves a greater sentence. In that respect I think the guidelines hinder my negotiating a plea or getting a good sentence. Now the defense will go in with an open plea, they won't take the plea agreement. We ask for a substantial sentence and the court usually doesn't give it to us. We argue for a stronger or aggravated sentence, even though we know we can't get it.

Thus, Southwest's judges adopted a strategy similar to judges in an Illinois county court described by Flemming et al. (1992, ch. 5), where judges encouraged defenders to plead open through informal communications in order to circumvent the chief DA's policy restricting plea bargaining.

The guidelines also played two additional roles in the influence patterns within the courtroom workgroups, and both worked to the disadvantage of the DA's office and to the advantage of judges. First, the individual who processed the guidelines paperwork and compiled the defendants' prior record information became an important mediator between the workgroup members. Ironically, while this individual was housed in the DA's office, he unequivocally viewed his job as that of serving the judges' interests. He provided judges with sentencing information and helped to ensure efficient case flow by serving as an unofficial arbitrator of disputes between DAs and PDs in the guilty plea process. He described his role this way:

> People ask me who I work for, who is my boss, and I say that I really work for the judge. I am only helping the judge to prepare his sentence. I don't lean toward the DA's office, even though I am on his staff, but they have to put me somewhere, because I need access to the files and legal books. I try to be neutral between the DA and the defense counsel. In fact, I think the PD's office understands guidelines sentencing better than the DA...I tell the two sides that if they are going to argue about something, come and see me first, come and tell me their thoughts before they get to the judge. Sometimes that way I can help get things ironed out for the judge beforehand.

Because of his willingness to disagree with the DA's office on sentencing issues, both judges and PDs saw him as an important ally. As Judge Hobbs explained:

> The sentencing guidelines form is completely generated and controlled by the DA's office, but the man they have doing it is a real professional. There have been times when he disagrees with the DA's office, and so he's his own man, which you appreciate. If he feels that there is something unusual in a case, he will come over personally and say he just wants to warn you that this is the argument the DA is going to make and this is the argument the PD is going to make. He has such a reputation that even defense attorneys will call him for guidance.

On the other hand, the county probation office, which at one time exerted strong influence on sentencing through their presentence reports to judges, became largely decoupled from the sentencing process (cf., Hagan et al. 1979). In the judges' view, the sentencing guidelines mostly eliminated the need for presentence reports in guilty plea cases by providing adequate information on defendants' prior criminal records. More importantly, the judges felt that the probation officers were heavily influenced by the DA's office, and were thus of limited usefulness. Judge O'Connor explained: "Usually, I don't go along with probation's recommendations...I don't even ask for presentence reports except for trial cases. They see themselves as the arm of the court for the enforcement of everything. . . . They're very close with the DA's office. I would like to see them lean a little more toward the treatment side in helping these people instead of the hammer."

DA responses. The DA's office responded to the alignment of judges and PDs and their use of sentencing guidelines to legitimize lenient sentencing practices with three strategies: sentencing appeals, "standing silent" at sentencing hearings, and increased mobilization of negative media attention to judges. Sentencing appeals involved the only prosecutorial advantage that stemmed directly from the sentencing guidelines. Unlike the preguidelines era, when only defense attorneys could appeal sentences, the guidelines allowed prosecutors the right to appeal sentences that departed below guideline ranges and thus provided them with a potential sanction against the judges—especially O'Connor, whose sentences had been appealed the most. While the relative frequency with which the DA's office appealed O'Connor's sentences was in part due to the fact that he handled the most criminal cases and departed below the guidelines most often, he attributed the appeals to the ongoing conflicts between himself and the district attorney's office: "They love to appeal me. Its the biggest game in town to them. They never listen to me. They all think they know more law than I do. I'm just a judge, what do I know? Now, I ask the D.A. 'If I go outside the guidelines are you going to appeal?' I like to get them on the record on that."

None of the Southwest County prosecutors' appeals, however, were successful in overturning any of the judges' sentences. Thus, sentencing appeals by the DA's office were more of a symbolic protest than an effective mechanism for influencing sentencing decisions. Further, appeals consumed scarce time and resources for the DA's office, and were thus used sparingly and largely for political purposes in higher profile cases.

Like prosecutors in Metro and Rich counties, the Southwest DAs used a variation on the tactic of standing silent in sentencing hearings. The use of this tactic in Southwest, however, differed considerably in its use compared to the other two counties in that it was used mostly to allow the DA's office to disclaim responsibility for lenient sentences. Further, even though the DAs referred to the tactic as standing silent, it did not actually involve "silence" in the sense of making no sentence recommendations, which was what prosecutors in the two other counties meant by standing silent. Instead, the prosecutor would often argue for a more severe sentence of incarceration, but would then make a statement such as, "The Commonwealth will not object to probation," or a departure below the guidelines, or some other lenient sentence. This strategy served as an implicit substitute for a lenient sentence recommendation in open plea cases and had become increasingly used as an implicit concession in plea negotiations. Unlike a plea agreement involving an explicit sentencing concession, however, standing silent allowed the DA's office to disclaim responsibility for lenient sentences. By stating their preference for a more severe sentence at sentencing hearings, but at the same time stating that they would not object to whatever sentence the judge wanted to give, the prosecutors put the responsibility for a lenient sentence fully on the judge. This combination of recommending a sentence and yet capitulating to the judge's discretion thus allowed the DA's office to protest the sentence to the news media if the political need arose.

Relatedly, the DA's office responded with increased mobilization of negative media attention to judges and their "soft" sentences. This led to an even further polarization of the judges and DA's office. According to O'Connor: "Our relationship is more strained than ever. They [DAs] ask for tougher sentences in court even though they tell us they 'won't object' to probation. Now, in the news, its becoming more of a public plastering of everyone. And it's not just a matter of singling out one judge who's up for election anymore, it's just become a general-type thing."

Sentencing Outcomes

In Southwest, the most substantial extralegal sentencing difference concerned mode of conviction. As the statistical analyses indicate, the plea rewards, based on the alignment between judges and PDs, had very real consequences for incarceration decisions. As in Metro County, the judges did not interpret these sentencing practices as an explicit penalty for those convicted by trial. According to O'Connor: "You can't penalize people for exercising their constitutional right to a trial by jury. At the same time, I don't have to give him the benefit of a guilty plea that he refused. It is up to my discretion."

Painter concurred: "Yes, people who go to trial and people who plead get sentenced differently, but you've got to have some kind of reward to give people who plead. A guilty plea, the sooner the better, is an act of remorse, cooperation, which we reward with leniency. In fact, I wish Pennsylvania had something like the federal guidelines do, where they have a sentence reduction for pleading guilty."

The full-time PD, while cooperating with the judges' informal policy of rewards for open pleas and plea agreements, saw it as an explicit judicial strategy to move cases quickly: "The way things are in the court system, I usually prescribe to the client that the guilty plea can be better than going to trial and losing. You are penalized for going to trial. Not always, but in the majority of cases. I think that is the word the judges want to get out. If you move the court system along and get the people to understand that they are better off to plead guilty because it will help these judges in the long run."

Judge Hobbs also described a motive for denying defendants who insist on frivolous trials breaks at sentencing: "You're tempted to do it on occasion, if some people are really jerking around the system—we get a few of those. It's not really a penalty for the trial, it's more that they have abused the system. For those individuals who enter a plea and then withdraw it, or they have no real defense, they are just buying time."

On the other hand, the models show that while negotiated pleas offered little benefit for incarceration decisions and dispositional departures, they did offer a modest benefit in terms of incarceration length. This pattern probably reflects the DA's preference for bargaining sentence lengths rather than charge reductions.

Race appeared to be a less substantial factor in sentencing decisions in Southwest County, while the gender differences were similar in size to those in Metro County, and smaller than those of the rest of the state. One reason that gender had less influence than in the rest of the state may be that since 1989, Southwest County's jail had provided drug and alcohol treatment programs that were not available in many other counties, had a relatively well-managed and funded work release program, and even provided basic job training and education opportunities for select offenders after their release. Judges indicated that they sometimes sentenced women defendants to jail so that they could benefit from these programs, particularly when they had drug or alcohol problems.

The extralegal criteria that judges articulated for deciding whether to incarcerate or grant dispositional departures may have benefitted women defendants, and conditioned the comparatively modest gender differences that did exist. While Painter nearly always sentenced according to the bottom of the standard range because he felt he lacked adequate experience in sentencing, the other two judges indicated that they were most likely to impose probation (even if this entailed a dispositional departure) if defendants had stable family or job histories and responsibilities that would be disrupted by incarceration, or if they felt defendants would benefit from certain rehabilitative services that were not available in jail or prison. They also listed the following criteria for deciding upon incarceration: (1) if defendants had significantly serious criminal histories that were not captured by the prior record score, (2) if defendants' crimes exhibited particular violence or "cruelty," (3) if they felt defendants would be deterred, or afforded a chance at rehabilitation, through incarceration, or (4) if defendants failed to show remorse or exhibited "incorrigible" attitudes.

In line with the statistical findings, drug offenses were one of the few points of consensus among judges and the DA's office. In interviews, each of the three judges indicated that they viewed drug use and trafficking quite seriously, including marijuana. They indicated that their sentences for drug-selling offenses were aimed at deterring the spread of what Hobbs called "a big city drug problem" into the community, while their sentences for more simple drug use offenses were often intended to compel offenders to seek treatment. As O'Connor explained: "I think a lot of times the only way to get their [drug users'] attention and get them to admit they need help is to let them spend some time in the jail. Maybe that way they'll see that doing drugs has consequences—that they can wreck your life."

Summary

In Southwest County, a conservative public and active local news media expected a standard of tough sentencing. The DA's office in turn used the media to exert pressure on the judges and gain political advantage, which conditioned a polarization between the bench and DA's office. On the other hand, the court's caseload had increased beyond the capacity of the bench to easily handle, presenting the need to dispose of cases quickly through fast guilty pleas. Despite these heavy caseloads, the DA's office was reluctant to cooperate with the judges by offering lenient plea agreement concessions early on in more serious cases, conditioning protracted last-minute plea strategies that exacerbated court backlogs. The judges thus resorted to case scheduling pressure and an alignment with PDs that revolved around routine plea rewards, especially for open pleas. The sentencing guidelines aided these judicial strategies in that judges used them to legitimate more lenient sentences than the DA's office sought. The judges gained further advantages from the guideline administrator's role as an information provider and dispute mediator, and from the decoupling of the probation office from the sentencing process. While the DA's office responded with sentencing appeals and increased media pressure, they mostly responded to the judges' guidelines-based sentencing practices through the politically protective tactic of standing silent at sentencing hearings. On the other hand, their variation on standing silent allowed DAs to protest lenient sentences to the news media, further aggravating the polarization between the judges and the DA's office.

To an even greater extent than in Metro County, arrangements in Southwest illustrate a more complicated picture of the role of guidelines in case processing than prior literature paints. Like Metro County, Southwest indicates ways in which other workgroup members besides the prosecutor may be able to use guidelines to their advantage when court community contexts provide the means, motive, and opportunity. Not only were Southwest County's judges left with ample sentencing discretion under the guidelines, they could also align with PDs in using the guidelines as an authoritative set of standards that legitimized less severe sentences than those sought by the prosecutors.

The only potential advantages for the DA's office that stemmed directly from the guidelines were increased certainty regarding the sentencing consequences of charge reductions and the ability to appeal sentences. Since the chief DA disliked and discouraged charge reductions, and since the sentence appeals were largely a symbolic weapon, the guidelines were not a source of additional sentencing discretion and court community influence for DAs. Rather, their influence in the court system stemmed from the political pressure the DAs could mobilize against judges in the media and the larger community. In contrast to Rich County, members of the DA's office saw the guidelines as an unwanted constraint, while the judges and defense attorneys viewed them favorably as a check against prosecutorial power. In the next and final chapter, I summarize the statewide and focus county findings, compare and contrast the focus counties' contexts, organizational relations, case processing, and sentencing; develop propositions and directions for future research on courts, sentencing, and guidelines; and discuss this study's broader sociological implications.

8

Conclusion: Court Communities and Sentencing under Guidelines

This book has investigated sentencing outcomes, court community organizational relations, and case processing strategies under Pennsylvania's sentencing guidelines. The analysis began with an examination of sentencing patterns statewide for 1985–1987 and 1989–1991, and then focused on sentencing outcomes, organizational arrangements, and case processing in three county trial courts. This chapter draws together the various threads of these analyses by discussing the statewide results, comparing the contexts, case processing arrangements, and sentencing patterns in the three focus counties, and discussing sources of extralegal sentencing differences under guidelines. Below, I list twelve sensitizing propositions based on this analysis that can guide future research on court communities, sentencing, and sentencing guidelines. I then address some general possibilities and limitations of sentencing policies that seek to manage the dilemmas of formal and substantive rationality in law that are involved in the interplay between statewide policies and local court actors' discretion. Finally, I discuss some of the broader sociological implications of this study.

Statewide Sentencing under Guidelines

The various models of statewide sentencing presented a remarkably consistent picture. The results are summarized in detail at the end of chapter 4, so I will only recap them briefly here. Without exception, the legally prescribed factors of offense type, offense severity, and prior record are the most influential predictors of each dispositional and durational sentencing outcome, including departures from guidelines. These factors are also most influential in sentencing in the three focus counties. This finding is no surprise, since it is consistent with results reported throughout the sentencing literature, even those studies that do not rigorously measure legally prescribed factors.

On the other hand, mode of conviction, gender, race, and court size are associated with very important sentencing differences. In the statewide models, these factors are especially influential for overall incarceration and dispositional departure, but are less influential in state imprisonment decisions. Race, gender, court size, and especially jury trial also condition important differences in sentence lengths. These findings directly contradict arguments by Kleck (1985) and Wilbanks (1987) that race and perhaps other extralegal factors are unimportant once legally prescribed factors are adequately controlled. The findings also provide an important extension of the analyses by Kramer and Steffensmeier (1993) and Steffensmeier et al. (1993) by further specifying conditions under which race and gender differences emerge in incarceration decisions.

Some important curvilinear and interaction effects also appear in the statewide and three county models. The most important of these involve prior record. The influence of prior record on overall incarceration and dispositional departure is curvilinear: increases in prior record sharply increase the chances of incarceration and decrease the odds of dispositional departure among defendants with less serious priors, but not among those who already have serious prior records. This threshold effect of prior record for incarceration suggests that the guidelines provided a structured scheme for mobilizing typifications of offenders. The numerical prior record score is probably less important in sentencing decisions than how it is interpreted by sentencing decision makers in terms of a defendant's blameworthiness, risk of recidivism, or rehabilitation potential. Among defendants with less serious prior records, each increase in prior record score damages the chances of avoiding incarceration by making it more difficult for defense attorneys to argue that such defendants deserve leniency. On the other hand, defendants who have a prior felony are already likely to be seen as serious and dangerous criminals who should be incarcerated, and any additional points in the prior record score simply confirm that interpretation. As a public defender in Metro County said, "If your guy has a bad record, you're really stuck. It takes a lot of work to convince people that the guy deserves a break." The influence of mode of conviction, race, and gender on incarceration, dispositional departure, and sentence length also differ between those with serious and less serious priors. While trials are associated with greater incarceration chances and longer incarceration terms among defendants with more serious priors, the influence of race and gender on sentencing decreases among those with serious prior records.

These data point to the overall conclusion that the major determinants of sentencing under Pennsylvania's guidelines are legally prescribed ones, but case processing, defendant-related, and contextual factors such as trial convictions, race and gender (and to a lesser extent, age), and court size also exert influences that cannot be ignored or trivialized. From a sentencing policy perspective, the presence of these extralegal differences cuts to the heart of one of the major goals of sentencing guidelines—the reduction of unwarranted disparity. From a sociological perspective, these findings support labeling theory's long-standing contention that the characteristics of deviant acts and actors, the organizational characteristics of deviance-processing agencies, and the sociopolitical contexts in which these are all embedded influence the imposition of criminal punishments (see Schur 1980; Farrell and Swigert 1978). From the standpoint of either perspective, it is necessary to tease out the processes behind the statistics by connecting court community organizational contexts to workgroup interaction strategies, and interaction strategies to sentencing outcomes. This was the primary contribution of the three-county analysis.

Case Processing and Sentencing in Three Court Communities

As chapter 2 argues, the task of connecting the various institutional and interactional levels of analysis necessary to examine trial court sentencing practices under guidelines necessitates a conceptual approach that focuses on the interrelationships between contexts, interaction processes, and outcomes. I therefore combined the assumptions and analytical strategy of the social worlds/processual order approach with the substantive concepts and propositions of the court community framework to direct the analysis of qualitative data from three focus counties.

Table 8.1 compares the key features of the social worlds contexts discussed in the analyses of the three court communities.

First, the three court communities differed in terms of the degree of membership stability, or what symbolic interactionists Katovich and Couch (1992) call the robustness of shared pasts. While Metro County's DA's office exhibited high turnover, the personnel of the bench and defense bar were more experienced in

TABLE 8.1
Court Community Contextual Features by County

	Metro	Rich	Southwest
Size	Large, metropolitan	Medium, suburban	Small, rural
Membership stability/familiarity	unstable DA's office, greater stability and familiarity between bench defense bar	highly stable, exchange of personnel between sponsoring agencies	moderately stable, familiarity due to small numbers of participants
Dominant political party	Democrat	Republican	Republican
Dominant sentencing goals	rehabilitation and just desert	deterrence, just desert, and incapacitation	rehabilitation and just desert among judges, deterrence and desert with punitive emphasis among DAs
Media attention	light, attention limited to high-profile cases	sporadic and often critical	heavy and frequent criticism mobilized by the DA's office
Balance of power between sponsoring agencies	bench dominant	DA's office dominant	bench dominant, with significant challenges from DA's office
Docket system (is judge-shopping possible)	individual calendar (no)	master calendar (yes)	individual calendar (no)

TABLE 8.1 (continued)

	Metro Large, metropolitan	Rich Medium, suburban	Southwest Small, rural
Size			
DA organization style and type	conservator; efficient firm with sacrifice of punitiveness for moving cases quickly	conservator; reactive clan, maintaining norms of collegial relations and tough sentences	insurgent; proactive clan, heavy mobilization of political pressure on judges
Amount of plea negotiating discretion allowed ADAs	little for inexperienced ADAs, more for experienced ones	a great deal for all ADAs	moderate to little, assistants subject to chief's personal supervision, chief himself handles serious, high-profile cases
Character of sponsoring agency relations	competitive between DAs and defenders, collegial between bench and defenders	collegial between all sponsoring agencies	conflictive between DAs and bench, strategic coalition between bench and defenders
Basis of going rates	guideline-based	based on locally developed norms and traditions, guidelines are secondary	guidelines-based

dealing with each other because of their greater membership stability and familiarity. Rich County's court community exhibited the greatest membership stability, with extensive personal and professional ties between members of the DA's office, bench, and defense bar and frequent exchange of personnel between these sponsoring agencies. Southwest County's small number of court community participants allowed considerable familiarity despite the relatively young bench and defense bar.

The membership stability of the three courts influenced the character of relations between sponsoring agencies. Between the more stable and consensual bench and defense bar in Metro County, relations were quite collegial. The relations of both groups with the less stable rank-and-file membership of the DA's office was competitive, but not conflictual. Collegiality between all sponsoring agencies was the order of the day in Rich County, and this was based on the extensive personal and professional ties and ideological similarities between court community members. In Southwest County, the familiarity between members laid the basis for protracted conflict in and out of the courthouse between the DA's office and the bench. It also provided the basis for the defense bar's alliance with the bench, which was based on a developed trust that the judges would give them breaks for cooperation. Southwest County's situation thus supports Klingler's (1985) and Eisenstein et al.'s (1988) argument that workgroup stability and familiarity can provide the basis not only for cooperation and consensus, but for intense personal and professional conflict as well. These patterns therefore suggest the first proposition:

> *Proposition 1.* Court community membership stability and familiarity (shared pasts) can influence interorganizational relations between sponsoring agencies. The degree of membership stability and familiarity can provide the basis for either cooperation and consensus (as in Rich County), or conflict and coalition processes (as in Southwest County).

The three-county analysis also highlighted the importance of differences in dominant sentencing goals and ideologies, and the degree of consensus between sponsoring agencies regarding these goals. This suggests a second proposition:

> *Proposition 2.* The degree of interorganizational consensus between sponsoring agencies regarding ideological sentencing

goals is an important influence on sponsoring agency relations and sentencing practices.

Metro County's court community was dominated by Democrats, and even its DA's office was described as "liberal." The judges, many of whom were former defense attorneys, were the dominant sponsoring agency in the court community. They were oriented toward balancing just deserts or "blameworthiness" with the rehabilitative potential of defendants. Stiff, retributive sentences were reserved mostly for the most serious violent and drug trafficking offenses. Metro's orientation toward leniency and rehabilitation was further encouraged by a superior court-ordered mandate to reduce county jail populations. By contrast, Rich County was dominated by its Republican party, and the DA's office was the center of power. The court community—including many members of the defense bar—exhibited a strong consensus in favor of tougher sentencing standards that reflected an emphasis on deterrence, just deserts, and incapacitation goals. The bench and DA's office maintained their reliance on incarceration—particularly jail—as a mechanism for expressing deterrence and moral censure and for protecting the community from what they saw as dangerous predators, even in the face of a growing overcrowding problem in the local jails and the state prison system.

Southwest County points up the importance of ideological conflict in court communities, in this case between the bench and DA's office. Although court community members were predominantly Republican, the judge who handled most of the criminal caseload was a Republican in name only. All three judges emphasized a mixture of just deserts and rehabilitation goals in their sentencing. Even when they incarcerated offenders (especially drug users), it was often in hopes that they could have access to treatment, education, and work release programs available in the county. However, the chief DA set a tone in his office emphasizing "get tough" sentencing. He and his handful of assistants valued deterrence and the punitive dimensions of just deserts as primary sentencing goals. While the judges held the reins of court organizational control and sentencing discretion, the DA's office presented formidable political challenges.

The three counties contrasted markedly in the influence of news media attention and criticism. The media played a minor role at best in Metro County in that all but the most severe or sensational cases escaped media scrutiny. The only obvious influence of media attention was on the administrative judge's case assignment practices in that he was careful to make sure that each judge got his or her share of high-profile cases, while also making sure that judges facing election had adequate opportunities to gain favorable publicity through such cases. In Rich County, media attention was sporadic, but often critical. Other court community members, especially the chief DA and his top assistants, tried to protect and insulate judges from media criticism. The chief DA also forbade his assistants from "judge bashing," in the media or otherwise. Media played the most influential role in Southwest, the smallest court community. The chief DA and his assistants mobilized media attention to paint the bench as "soft on crime," putting each judge in political jeopardy at one time or another. These patterns suggest a third proposition:

Proposition 3. The threat of critical news media attention to sentencing is an important potential political danger, especially to judges (see also Altheide 1992). Negative media attention may be an external threat that fosters cohesion and mutual protectiveness among court community members, or may be mobilized as a political weapon by prosecutors' offices in interorganizational conflicts with the judges' bench.

The analysis also supports Nardulli et al.'s (1988) arguments regarding judge shopping and court case assignment practices. The only master calendar court, Rich County, was also the only court where judge shopping was possible to any significant degree. Rich County prosecutors, in cooperation with defense attorneys, routed nonroutine and more potentially problematic cases to judges who were more likely to get involved in the plea negotiation process. In Metro County, the administrative judge's control over case assignment and the individual judges' control over their own dockets augmented their dominance. Once a case was assigned to a judge's docket, counsel were stuck with him or her in most circumstances. Southwest also had an individual calendar system and a case assignment process that was remarkably similar to Metro's. With one judge handling two-thirds of the criminal caseload (to the supreme annoyance of the DA's office), judge shopping was largely irrelevant. Although the basis of comparison (three counties) is rather thin, the analysis suggests a fourth proposition:

Proposition 4. As Nardulli et al. (1988) argued, judge shopping is less likely in courts with individual calendar case assignment systems, and more likely under master calendar systems. Thus, individual calendar case assignment systems augment the power of judges in the court community.

One of the biggest contrasts between the three court contexts was in the organization and style of the DA's offices. Flemming et al. (1992) have adapted Ouchi's (1980) organizational typology of "efficient firms," "reactive clans," or "proactive clans" to prosecutor's offices. According to Flemming et al. (1992), efficient firms tend to be more bureaucratically organized and control their staffs through formal rules and policies, place great stress on efficiency, and are more flexible and accommodating in their dealings with judges and defense attorneys. Reactive clans tend to be less bureaucratic and rely on consensus, informal adjustment, and flexible, informal rules to govern their staffs and their relations with other sponsoring agencies. On the other hand, a clan-organized DA's office may be proactive, depending on whether the chief DA wants to challenge the status quo and has a taste for conflict with other court community agencies. Flemming et al. (1992, pp. 25–26) also add a distinction between "insurgent" and "conservator" prosecutorial styles: "Insurgents were most dissatisfied with the status quo and were prepared to do battle in order to change it . . . conservators accepted the status quo. Prosecutors who chose to be office conservators were most likely to perceive the status of their office as satisfactory."

The three counties studied in this book can be depicted according to these categorizations of organizational type and style as well. Metro's large, highly bureaucratic DA's office resembled an "efficient firm." The many inexperienced ADA's were given little plea negotiating discretion compared to the assistants in Rich, and the chief DA and his team leaders were usually willing to sacrifice punitiveness in the interest of moving cases quickly and maintaining as much adherence to the guideline ranges as possible. The Metro DA's office also most closely resembles the "conservator" style in that its leaders did not seem interested in mounting many significant challenges to bench dominance or judges' sentencing practices.

Rich County's dominant DA's office resembled a "reactive clan," and its leaders also adopted a conservator style. Control of ADAs was based on informal socialization into court community norms of pursuing tough sentencing standards through collegial negotiation. ADAs were given a great deal of discretion and trust—

as the chief DA said, "If you can't trust your assistants, you should probably get rid of them." Southwest's chief DA adopted an "insurgent" style, using media and political pressure as weapons against judges. He organized his small staff as a tightly-knit "proactive clan." Although the chief supervised his assistants through his personal leadership and handled a caseload of his own, the assistants had moderate plea negotiating discretion within the chief's limits (e.g., his strong dislike of charge bargaining). Taken together, these findings suggest the fifth proposition:

Proposition 5. As Flemming et al. (1992) argued, sponsoring agency relations will be influenced by the DA's office organizational type ("efficient firm," "reactive clan," "proactive clan") and the Chief DA's leadership style ("conservator," versus "insurgent"). Proactive clan organizational types and insurgent styles will engender comparatively more interorganizational conflict.

The balance of power between sponsoring agencies in Metro and Southwest counties illustrates the considerable degree of power and discretion judges can retain under guidelines, especially under loose guideline systems such as Pennsylvania's. Indeed, the guidelines provided Southwest judges with externally legitimated sentencing standards that helped them ward off the efforts of an insurgent DA's office. Both Metro and Southwest highlight a proposition made by Flemming et al. (1992, p. 204) that "...when prosecutors fail to take advantage of their organizational and institutional resources, the judges by default have an edge over prosecutors as long as the bench remains reasonably consensual." Despite its considerable bureaucratic control over its assistants' case processing, Metro's DA's office chose not to use their office as a "bureacratic weapon" (Flemming et al. 1992) to challenge judges' use of their sentencing discretion and lenient sentencing practices. The Southwest chief DA spurned a very potent organizational weapon for influencing sentences—the use of charge reductions as leverage for pleas agreements—because he found this ideologically abhorrent. Conversely, Rich County illustrates the degree to which DA's offices can alternately subordinate and exploit guidelines to their advantage, given the favorable resources and ideological climate to do so. The balance of power between sponsoring agencies suggests a sixth proposition:

Proposition 6. Contrary to some predictions about sentencing under guidelines (e.g., Tonry and Coffee 1987; Alschuler 1978), judges can retain considerable sentencing discretion and interorganizational power under sentencing guidelines, especially under comparatively less restrictive guidelines.

The three courts differed in their basis for going rates, and this factor is also linked to the degree of membership stability and familiarity, or the robustness of members' shared pasts (see Katovich and Couch 1992; Ulmer 1995) and the character of sponsoring agency relations. Rich County's informal organizational culture of collegial bargaining and more severe local sentencing traditions were based in robust shared pasts—extensive personal familiarity between participants. These local sentencing norms provided a way for participants to reduce uncertainty in routine negotiation and decision making. The guidelines provided only a secondary set of reference points for sentencing decisions—"a place to start from" in the words of one judge—that were drawn upon primarily in more problematic cases in which one or all workgroup participants felt that going rates could not be as easily applied.

By contrast, Southwest and Metro County exhibited less reliance on locally developed sentencing norms and more reliance on the guidelines. As mentioned, Southwest's judges used guidelines as a tool for rewarding defense attorneys and their clients for fast guilty pleas, and as an externally legitimated standard for less severe sentences than the DA's office wanted. In Metro County, the guidelines *were* the going rates. Guidelines provided ready-made sentencing standards that all participants used and manipulated in their case processing strategies. The guidelines provided a tool for reducing uncertainty that took the place of the kind of locally developed going rates based in the extensive familiarity between defenders and prosecutors in Rich County. Further, the guidelines provided the Metro DA's office leaders with a mechanism for increased control of assistants' case processing decisions.

Proposition 7. The robustness of shared pasts among court community membership combines with the degree of interorganizational consensus regarding ideological sentencing goals to influence the primary "stocks of knowledge" (Berger and Luckmann 1967) for uncertainty reduction in case processing decisions.

7a. Locally developed going rates are the primary uncertainty reduction tools under conditions of high membership stability and familiarity and high ideological consensus about sentencing goals. Reliance on formal, externally imposed norms such as sentencing guidelines will be lowest under these conditions.

7b. Under conditions of low stability and familiarity and high-to-moderate consensus about sentencing goals, formal norms such as sentencing guidelines can serve as the primary stock of knowledge for reducing uncertainty in case processing.

7c. Under conditions of high stability and familiarity and interorganizational conflict about sentencing goals, sentencing guidelines can be used as formal, externally legitimated norms that serve the strategic interests of one sponsoring agency (or a sponsoring agency coalition) over another.

These social world context factors conditioned different processual orders of workgroup case processing strategies. Table 8.2 compares the three counties in terms of their case processing orders.

First, the predominant case processing strategies differed between the three counties. Metro County's case processing order largely centered around unilateral decision making and strategic manipulations, rather than explicit guilty plea negotiations. This is reflected in the fact that open pleas were the most frequent mode of conviction. As mentioned, the guidelines were important in that they helped to reduce the uncertainty involved in these unilateral decisions, especially since ADAs and defenders lacked the kind of robust shared pasts that facilitated easy negotiation in Rich County. Inexperienced prosecutors quickly learned to rely on guidelines "like a crutch" both in their unilateral charging decisions and in their less frequent negotiated sentence agreements. Explicit judicial involvement in Metro's plea negotiations was very rare, but judges used the guidelines to establish routine plea rewards even in open plea cases and often made conviction decisions in bench trials based on the guideline sentence they felt was appropriate. Defense attorneys relied on the guidelines, plus their knowledge of the "personality of the bench," to reduce uncertainty in their usual open plea strategies, and in their less common plea negotiations as well.

By contrast, Rich County provides almost a prototypical example of what Strauss (1978a) calls a negotiated order. Court

TABLE 8.2
Processual Order of Case Processing by County

	Metro	Rich	Southwest
Predominant workgroup strategy	unilateral decisions and manipulations	negotiation	conflictive strategies, coalition formation
Predominant mode of conviction	open pleas	negotiated pleas	"last minute pleas," open pleas
Judge participation plea negotiations	very rare	frequent, explicit, and welcomed by counsel	rare in plea negotiations, but frequent invitations for defenders to plead open
Frequency and nature of sentence agreements in negotiated pleas	guideline-based recommendations are predominant concessions	recommendations based on local going rates	guidelines-based recommendations are predominant concession
Frequency and nature of charge reductions in negotiated pleas	less frequent, most charge reductions are unilateral by ADAs and by judges at bench trials	largely restricted to charges carrying potential mandatory sentences, usually conditional on defendant cooperation with police	charge reductions strongly discouraged by chief DA, occur only under defense threat of trial when prosecution case is weak
Conditions of departures below guidelines	implicit agreements for ADAs to stand silent, occasional negotiated agreements for departures by more experienced ADAs	explicit negotiations for ADA silence in return for open pleas	open pleas, DAs stand silent while disclaiming responsibility and occasionally complaining to media

TABLE 8.2 (continued)

	Metro	Rich	Southwest
Sentence severity	tendency toward leniency for all but serious violent offenses	most severe of the three counties, on average	lenient for property offenses, more severe for violent and drug offenses
Sources of extralegal sentencing differences	mitigated range and downward departure plea rewards, consideration of race-linked status and resource factors mobilized by serious prior records, gender differences smaller due to more local jail space for women	trial penalties, intervening race and gender-linked status and resource factors, community fear of influx of inner-city black offenders	bottom-standard, mitigated range, and downward departure plea rewards, gender-linked status factors, very few black defendants

community participants' high familiarity and consensus regarding local going rates and sentencing goals, based on their extensive shared pasts and joint futures (see Katovich and Couch 1992), fostered easy and collegial negotiation. Thus, the most common mode of conviction in Rich County was the negotiated plea, and local going rates were the primary tools in reducing uncertainty in case processing decisions. About half of the judges also got involved in the plea negotiation process, and this involvement was welcomed by counsel. More problematic cases were mainly resolved through open pleas. Further, even the circumstances giving rise to open pleas, and participants' roles in them were well defined by informal normative expectations.

Southwest County can be characterized as a conflict order, in that the case processing strategies of judges and defense attorneys were primarily conditioned by ongoing disputes with the insurgent DA's office. Defenders would engage in protracted haggling through last-minute pleas in order to wrest concessions from prosecutors, who granted meaningful sentencing concessions only when their cases were weak and they did not want to risk trials. Judges exerted a number of pressures to counteract the inflexible plea policies and political posturing of the DA's office, including case scheduling pressure and an alliance with the defense bar revolving around predictable, guidelines-based rewards for fast (preferably open) guilty pleas. These patterns suggest two important propositions regarding case processing strategies and the sources of norms for uncertainty reduction in case processing decisions:

Proposition 8. Court community membership stability and familiarity, interorganizational consensus regarding sentencing goals, and the strength of locally developed going rates combine to influence which workgroup case processing strategies will be predominant.

8a. Negotiative strategies (negotiated pleas) will predominate under conditions of high stability and familiarity, high consensus about sentencing goals, and strong local going rates.

8b. Unilateral decision making and manipulation (open pleas, bench trials) will predominate under conditions of low stability and familiarity, high-to-moderate consensus about sentencing goals, and weak local going rates.

8c. Conflict strategies (trials, last-minute pleas) and coalitions (e.g., bench and defense bar alliances) will predominate under conditions of high stability/familiarity, low consensus about sentencing goals, and weak local going rates.

One of the commonalities between the three courts was the predominance of sentence bargaining rather than charge bargaining in guilty plea negotiations. This coincides with a little-noticed finding of Miethe's (1987) study of Minnesota's guidelines—pleas involving charge reductions declined after guidelines implementation, while those involving sentence recommendations increased.[1] One reason for this similar finding in Pennsylvania may be that the guidelines provide detailed and complete prior record information at the time of sentencing (often rendering presentence investigations unnecessary, as illustrated by Southwest County in particular). Such a situation did not characterize sentencing prior to guidelines (see Kramer and Steffensmeier 1993, p. 358). It is likely that this lack of readily available prior record information in the guilty plea process before the guidelines conditioned much greater ambiguity in sentence bargaining. By necessitating the collection of more complete prior record information, and tying sentence prescriptions to such information, guidelines likely foster greater certainty in sentencing bargaining.

Findings from the three counties suggest that factors such as the choice of sentences within guideline ranges, the application of sentence enhancements or mitigations, and the choice to depart above or below guidelines have become the focal concern not only of plea negotiations, but of open plea decisions as well. As one defense attorney in Rich County put it, "Charge bargaining is so overrated. It's sentence bargaining that's important—you bargain for the sentence." And when defense attorneys can reasonably expect attractive guilty plea rewards from judges without a negotiated plea agreement, open pleas can become a more attractive strategy. These patterns suggest that the heavy reliance on charge bargaining predicted by Savelsberg (1992) and others (e.g., Tonry and Coffee 1987) is less likely under loose guidelines like Pennsylvania's, and as Miethe's data (1987) suggest, may not even characterize more restrictive guidelines like Minnesota's. By explicitly specifying a "menu" of sentencing ranges and options that can become the center of sentence bargaining, Pennsylvania's guidelines seem to render charge bargaining less necessary. On the other hand, findings from Rich County in particular illustrate the potential prevalence of charge bargaining in cases involving charges that carry mandatory sentences. This supports Tonry's (1992) argument that mandatory sentencing policies foster considerable charge bargaining. This is because, unlike guidelines, mandatory sentence laws remove all sentencing discretion once the defendant has been convicted of an offense to which the mandatory sentence applies. These patterns suggest a proposition about sentence and charge bargaining in guilty plea agreements.

Proposition 9. Sentencing guidelines may actually foster, rather than inhibit, implicit or explicit sentence bargaining by presenting a codified "menu" of sentencing factors that can be negotiated or otherwise manipulated. Charge bargaining is more likely when mandatory minimum sentences potentially apply to a given charge (see Tonry 1992).

Related to the predominance of sentence bargaining, the strategic importance of open pleas and the prosecutorial tactic of "standing silent" in connection with departures below guidelines are further commonalities between the counties, suggesting another proposition:

Proposition 10. Open guilty pleas and the prosecutorial tactic of "standing silent" can serve a variety of important strategic and political purposes for implicit sentence bargaining and sponsoring agency relations under sentencing guidelines.

In each county, open pleas were used for different—but equally important—purposes. Open pleas were the routine mode of conviction in Metro County, and served as an important way of by-passing the DA's office in Southwest County. By comparison, open pleas in Rich County were a technique for judge-mediated dispute resolution when negotiations became difficult between defenders and ADAs, and thus served a purpose somewhat similar to that of the bench trials in Metro County.

Similarly, prosecutors in each county stood silent at sentencing hearings where defenders argued for departures below guidelines, but the frequency and conditions of standing silent varied. In Metro County, more experienced ADAs were allowed the leeway to negotiate sentence agreements for departures below guidelines. Those with less experience had less negotiating discretion and resorted to standing silent as a substitute for an explicit sentencing agreement for a departure. On the other hand, Rich County ADAs would not agree to departures below guidelines, but did explicitly bargain for their silence in exchange for open pleas. The prosecutor's silence at the sentencing hearing, in turn, was a potent symbolic communication of their sentencing preferences to the judge. When ADAs did object to defense arguments for downward departures at sentencing hearings, the judges almost always followed prosecutorial preferences. Southwest's prosecutors' practice of standing silent represented a partial capitulation to judges' sentencing preferences, but also served as a political tactic that allowed them to disclaim responsibility for any "soft on crime" sentences.

The three-county analyses suggest some sources of sentencing differences associated with mode of conviction, race, and gender. The specific factors conditioning these differences are detailed in the respective counties' chapters, so I focus on their similarities and differences here. First, the strongest extralegal differences in each county and in the statewide analyses involved mode of conviction, especially jury trial conviction. Case processing strategies in Metro and Southwest illustrate ways in which sentencing guidelines provide mechanisms to reward both negotiated and open guilty pleas. Whether through negotiated agreements or open pleas, defendants who pleaded guilty were rewarded with sentences at the bottom of the standard ranges, mitigated range sentences, and dispositional and durational departures below guidelines. On the other hand, Rich County provides an example of more explicit trial penalties. The guidelines provide structured mechanisms with which to mete out differential leniency toward those who plead guilty, or differential punishment of those who exercise their rights to trial.

> *Proposition 11.* Given defendants with the same offense severity and prior record, sentencing guidelines provide a variety of explicit sentencing mechanisms for court actors to reward defendants who plead guilty or punish those convicted by trial (especially jury trial).

As many have observed (Sudnow 1965; Blumberg 1967; Heumann 1978), plea rewards and trial penalties hinge on a presumption of defendant guilt rather than innocence, an assumption that innocent defendants have been weeded out at earlier processing stages, and a preference to reserve trials for only the most problematic cases. While the plea rewards and trial penalties seen in the three counties do induce guilty pleas and bring more lenient sentences, consider the potential dilemma of a defendant who is in fact innocent, but who is reluctant to face a trial (a situation that may be more frequent than one might think, see LaFree 1985; Feeley 1979). If the innocent defendant goes to trial and loses, he or she gets a stiffer sentence, or at least forgoes the more lenient sentence (often probation) that would have been given as a reward for pleading guilty. However, pleading guilty also results in a conviction and a criminal record that can mobilize a number of material and personal penalties (Sampson and Laub 1993; Stebbins 1971), increased future attention from law enforcement (Farrell and Swigert 1978), and stiffer sentences if the defendant should ever be convicted of another offense in the future.

Race differences in sentencing, especially in terms of incarceration decisions, also were apparent in all three counties. These differences were apparently less pronounced in Southwest County, whose court processed very few black defendants in any case. In Metro County, race differences were concentrated among defendants with serious prior records, and race was associated with much smaller differences in state imprisonment. Race had the largest and most consistent influence in Rich County, especially in terms of state imprisonment decisions. Further, recall that county jail sentences carry significant advantages over state imprisonment in Pennsylvania, offering the possibility of early release, work release, and remaining closer to one's family and community. Compared to Metro County, then, the race differences in sentencing in Rich County represent greater lengths of actual time served for blacks, perhaps resulting in greater disruption of personal relationships, work opportunities, and other social bonds that prevent future crime (see Sampson and Laub 1993).

Despite differences between Metro and Rich, the two counties were similar in that race differences were apparently conditioned by court actors' interpretation and consideration of defendants' status and resources in sentencing decisions. Most prominent among these were employment status, family stability, education, and the ability to afford drug and alcohol or other treatment programs. These findings support Albonetti's (1991) propositions regarding bounded rationality and the use of stereotypes to reduce uncertainty regarding whether an offender is likely to recidivate or whether he or she is a candidate for rehabilitation. In conjunction with other status factors, a defendant's race may mobilize stereotypes and attributions concerning the types of offenders seen as more dangerous, "blameworthy" (see Kramer and Steffensmeier 1993), or more likely to be bad risks for rehabilitation. The race/prior record interactions for county jail incarceration and dispositional departure in Metro County support this argument. That is, a serious prior record can be one of the factors that conditions the consideration of status characteristics that are associated with perceptions of race in incarceration decisions. On the other hand, the statewide race/prior record interaction is directly the opposite of that in Metro County. This suggests the possibility that the defendant's prior record can sometimes override other defendant characteristics and lead to smaller race differences among defendants with serious prior records. Further, the findings that race differences in Rich County are greater for state imprisonment decisions, and in court actors' explanations of these decisions, suggest that race differences may sometimes be conditioned by court actors' interpretation and consideration of state prison population size and race composition, and a reluctance to send white defendants to predominantly black prisons (see also Kramer and Steffensmeier 1993). In sum, the nature of the influence of race in sentencing decisions varies between courts and is contextualized by the defendant's prior record. Furthermore, racial sentencing differences are arguably related to: (1) court actors' interpretations of defendants' "character," employment history, family status, education, resources, appearance, and demeanor, and (2) the linkage of these to perceptions and stereotypes of blacks.

The three county chapters also discussed some sources of gender differences in sentencing and suggested that they are contextualized by factors similar to the race differences. In general, the findings lend support to Steffensmeier et al.'s (1993) and Daly's (1995) arguments that gender differences in incarceration decisions are related to the consideration of intervening factors such as family status, responsibility for dependent children, and indications of remorse. These factors lead court actors to view women defendants as less blameworthy, less dangerous, better risks for rehabilitation, and thus candidates for leniency. On the other hand, gender differences varied between the three counties, with Metro and Southwest exhibiting smaller gender differences compared to Rich County and the state as a whole. The analysis suggests that gender differences may be smaller in counties with more adequate jail resources to handle women inmates (as in Metro County) and in counties where rehabilitative programs are available in local jails (as in Southwest County).

Overall, the findings regarding race and gender differences in sentencing suggest a final set of propositions:

Proposition 12a. Race and gender differences in sentencing can be conditioned by court actors' consideration of intervening status and resource factors that are associated with perceptions and stereotypes of race and gender.

Proposition 12b. Race and gender sentencing differences can be conditioned by court actors' use of race- and gender-linked attributions of offender dangerousness, blameworthiness, or rehabilitative potential.

Proposition 12c. Race and gender sentencing differences can be conditioned by court actors' consideration of prison and jail resources and population characteristics.

Proposition 12d. The influence of defendants' race and gender in sentencing decisions will depend on how court actors interpret and typify these statuses in light of defendants' prior records. In other words, prior record contextualizes race and gender sentencing differences.

Sentencing Guidelines: Possibilities, Limitations, and Dilemmas

Additionally, this book suggests important issues regarding the possibilities and limitations of sentencing guidelines as a mechanism of sentencing reform. The first issue concerns the balance of power and the distribution of sentencing discretion between sponsoring agencies under guideline systems. As noted in chapter 3, I lack the longitudinal data necessary to test the idea that sentencing guidelines cause a "hydraulic displacement" of discretion from judges to prosecutors. One would expect that such an effect would be less likely under a guideline system like Pennsylvania's, which purposefully allows more "windows" of judicial discretion (Cirillo 1986). Nevertheless, the three-county analysis suggests that the "hydraulic displacement" proposition is not necessarily incorrect, but may be incomplete. As described in chapters 1 and 2, current framings of the issue in the literature place a great deal of emphasis on prosecutorial discretion and the importance of charge bargaining, and give little attention to ways in which local court contexts provide opportunities, motives, and constraints for the exercise of prosecutorial power (for an exception, see Nagel and Schulhofer 1992).

My findings suggest that the issue should be framed more broadly, with a focus on: (1) the ways in which guidelines facilitate implicit or explicit sentence negotiation; (2) the influence of guidelines on the attractiveness of open pleas and their strategic uses; (3) the dynamics of guideline departures; and (4) the local contextual features that condition the relative resources, power, and strategies of each sponsoring agency—not just prosecutors' offices. Research could focus on the influence of local context, the opportunities and constraints faced by each sponsoring agency, and the characteristics of guidelines systems themselves that are more or less likely to influence the distribution of discretion and power within court communities in intended and unintended ways.

More generally, this analysis also highlights a fundamental dilemma of policy efforts to structure sentencing processes, and of sentencing in general. This dilemma involves what Savelsberg (1992) identifies as a key issue in the sociology of law—the dilemma between formal and substantive rationality in sentencing. The discretion allowed judges under sentencing guidelines is seen as important for two reasons: (1) to counteract the displacement of too much sentencing influence to prosecutors; and (2) to allow court actors to tailor sentences to cases that are more or less serious than "typical" ones, which are the focus of guideline recommendations (see Alschuler 1988; Steury 1989). The statistical and qualitative findings of this study show that by avoiding stringently attaching highly specific sentences to specific charges, Pennsylvania's guidelines allowed considerable discretion beyond the charging stage.

As the findings also show, however, the windows of discretion under guidelines, such as mitigated range sentences, dispositional departures, and relatively wide standard ranges, were the locus of the kinds of extralegal differences that guidelines are intended to reduce. Thus, loose guidelines allow sentences to be adapted to fit individual defendants (substantive rationality), but risk unwarranted disparity (Tonry 1987). On the other hand, severely constraining judicial sentencing discretion could not only displace the locus of disparity to prosecutorial decisions—as the hydraulic displacement proposition argues—but also risks "dehumanizing" sentencing and treating unlike offenders alike in the name of formal rationality. Both historical and more recent experiences with federal and state mandatory sentences provide examples of these effects (see Tonry 1992).

While this dilemma has not been resolved, Del Sole (1993) suggests one possible way to more satisfactorily balance the need for discretion with a desire to reduce unwarranted disparity. He argues that guidelines can and should allow various windows of judicial discretion, but that appellate courts should more proactively scrutinize departures from guidelines with an explicit concern for issues of disparity. However, Pennsylvania's sentencing appeals process has not provided such scrutiny (a complaint of Metro County's DAs). Appellate courts have set a very lax standard for guideline departures, requiring that a sentence must represent a "manifest abuse of discretion" to be overturned (*Commonwealth v. Devers*, 546 A2d. 1989).

As Walker (1993) and Savelsberg (1992) argue, the history of American criminal justice in the twentieth century—especially sentencing—is the history of the tension between two related dilemmas: formal and substantive rationality, and discretion and its constraint. Sentencing guidelines are indeed a "fascinating experiment" (Savelsberg 1992, p. 1361) in formal social control. The key question sentencing guidelines try to address is: What set of actors does society choose to trust with the discretion to determine punishments, and how will these actors be held accountable for their use of that discretion? The ways in which organizations and actors at the local, state, or national level attempt to balance formal and substantive rationality, as well as the interplay of discretion and its control, are rich topics for further social science research and policy discussion.

Broader Sociological Issues

The above dilemma also has implications for the more general problem noted by Max Weber—dilemmas of formal and substantive rationality in organizational control (Savelsberg 1992; 1994). The situation of the role of sentencing guidelines in the court communities studied here is an example of a more general organizational problem. On one hand, centralized control through formal rules aimed at achieving desired goals risks informal strategies to circumvent those rules. On the other hand, decentralized control and informal rules allow actors the discretion to adapt to situational contingencies, but risk unintended and perhaps undesirable consequences (see Daft 1989; Manning 1992; Schwartzman 1993).

Relatedly, the issue of uncertainty and its management is a central issue in organizational sociology (see Weick 1979; Weick and Browning 1986; Manning 1992; Schwartzman 1993), and has been invoked repeatedly throughout this book. The analysis reveals how uncertainty management relates to tensions between sources of authority internal and external to organizational arenas (see Katz 1977). The conflict in Southwest County between judges and DAs over locally desired versus guideline sentencing standards, and Rich County's subordination of guidelines to local traditions and going rates provide examples of tensions between local and external rules and authority. Rich County in particular provides an example of how locally developed sentencing standards and informal practices were often seen by participants as providing superior information sources and action strategies for managing uncertainty. On the other hand, the analyses of the three court communities showed many ways in which sentencing guidelines (external authority) were used to structure and manage the uncertainty involved in case processing strategies and the prediction of sentencing outcomes. For instance, the Metro County example suggests that formal, externally imposed policies like sentencing guidelines can be used by actors as primary stocks of knowledge to reduce uncertainty in routine tasks, especially when alternative uncertainty reduction tools are not available.

Relatedly, Prechel (1994, p. 725) and Daft (1989) argue that factors such as task complexity foster decentralized organizational control. The kinds of case processing tasks and decisions that courtroom workgroup actors are involved in can become highly complex, involving the consideration and interpretation of dozens of variables (Hagan et al. 1979; Flemming 1992). In fact, the complexity of case processing and sentencing decisions was one impetus behind the initial development of sentencing guidelines (Kramer and Scirica 1986). However, the example of the Metro County DA's office illustrates how organizational leaders can use externally imposed policies or rules to centralize and formalize control over members, even in organizations such as court community sponsoring agencies, whose characteristics and core activities would otherwise foster decentralization.

Another issue involves the implications of extralegal sentencing differences for the organizational concept of bounded rationality (March and Simon 1958), which deals with "cognitive limits of individual decision makers" (Prechel 1994, p. 730). Albonetti (1991) and Farrell and Holmes (1991) have argued that extra-legal sentencing differences provide an example of bounded rationality in the management of uncertainty in decision making and interaction strategies. For example, in pursuing sentencing goals of incapacitation or rehabilitation, judges and other court community actors make predictions about defendants' future behavior with very inadequate information (even under guidelines), and under significant time and resource constraints. To reduce such uncertainty, court actors use a defendant's past behavior, circumstances of offenses, sense of remorse as indicated by a guilty plea, and any other status and "character" clues. The findings of this study linking race and gender to other so-called "character" factors in sentencing, as well as the findings regarding the interactive influence of race, gender, and prior record, support this line of argument. For example, recall one Rich County judge's description of his sentencing decision making: "You rely on your sense of whether or not if you give them another chance are they really not going to commit another crime. You can get a good picture of people in just a few minutes."

These findings also have potential implications for the more general issue of the role of race and gender in other organizational decision making processes. Race and gender perceptions and/or stereotypes may come into play in a wide range of arenas through decision makers' intepretation of intervening status, resource, and career factors. Relatedly, perceptions of race and gender statuses may mobilize typifications and attributions about behavior that favor some while disadvantaging others. Obvious examples of criminal justice decision making processes in which to test these propositions would be arrest and initial charging decisions, parole board decisions, and juvenile court decisions. More generally, research could examine how race and gender may be linked to interpretations, attributions, and stereotypes about behavior, resources, and "character" in organizational decisions such as hiring and promotion.

This line of argument also suggests the implications of the interactionist conceptualization of identities for the interrelationship of micro and macro levels of social orders. This conceptualization of identities is based on the famous interactionist statement of W. I. and Dorothy Swain Thomas (1928) that what people define as real becomes real in its consequences. Stone (1977), Strauss (1969), and others (e.g., Katovich 1986) describe identities as situated transactions in which people identify, define, and place one another in social locations or positions. These social definitions and placements invoke expectations of personal characteristics and future behavior associated with those identities in people's minds. Those identities that are tied to one or another dimension of social stratification, such as race, class, or gender are known as statuses (Stone 1962). For example, a Rich County judge confronted with a young black male defendant from an inner-city neighborhood might place him in the identity of "serious, dangerous criminal" on the basis of stereotypes of personal "character" and expectations of future crime that are mobilized by the judge's interpretation of the defendant's race, age, and gender statuses. The transaction of identities thus involves the definition of people and expectations of their future behavior. The choices between action strategies that people make on the basis of others' identities and statuses and the expectations they mobilize are a crucial way in which large-scale patterns of stratification (race, gender, or class for example) become manifest, and are reproduced, at the meso level of institutional organization and the micro level of face-to-face interaction and the courses of people's lives.

Further directions for research in courts and other organizational arenas are also suggested by this study. For example, research could examine the influence of the robustness of shared pasts on the availability and ease of negotiation as an action strategy in a variety of organizational worlds (for a fuller treatment, see Ulmer 1995). Another example involves an important issue this study implies but does not examine explicitly—the role of different types of personal, structural, and moral commitments (Johnson 1991; Ulmer 1994b) in courts and other organizational arenas. Commitments, of course, are both the "glue" that holds organizations together, and also a potential source of segmentation and conflict (see Gerson 1976; Clarke 1991; Scott 1987). It follows that the development, maintenance, and change of court actors' "webs" of personal, structural, and moral commitments to constituencies in their own and other sponsoring agencies—as well as outside the courthouse—would be an important contextual factor that could influence case processing strategies and sentencing outcomes in a variety of ways.

Sentencing as Processual Order

The various formal and substantive rationalities used by the court actors in this study are, on a more abstract level, different discourses that provide sometimes overlapping, but more often divergent rules and criteria for decisions about sentencing criminal offenders. As suggested by the processual order approach, the units of analysis here have been the court communities as social worlds, and the participants' action strategies. Since the symbolic interactionist assumptions upon which the processual order approach is based hold that action is inherently communicative, this is also a study of communication strategies and their consequences. The court community participants' action strategies draw on a variety of both local and externally legitimated discourses about sentencing, as well as various ideologies about the goals of criminal justice. Embedded in the court community participants' strategies are communicative tactics of various kinds, intended for various audiences, and drawing on various formal and substantively rational criteria for sentencing, all of which are "contoured" (Eisenstein et al. 1988) or configured by local political and organizational contexts.

For decades, interactionists who study social organization and structure have argued that large-scale, macro processes are channeled through and potentially modified by local institutional and organizational arrangements, local culture (especially organizational culture, see Fine 1984; Clarke 1991), and face-to-face interaction processes (Blumer 1990). This book extends this conceptual line of reasoning to the realm of state policies, the legal and organizational cultures of local criminal courts, and the sentencing activities of courtroom workgroups. In doing so, this study expands upon the court community framework's main contribution to the sociology of law by showing that the nature and character of justice and formal social control—such as in the sentencing process—depend as much or more on the processual orders of local courts as they do on the policies and laws of larger-scale state actors. Likewise, the role and nature of broad policies such as sentencing guidelines depend not merely on the characteristics and principles of the policies, but also on how they can be used by local organizational and individual actors to serve their own interests.

In examining these issues, this analysis has illustrated the value of the processual order/social worlds analytical strategy. Use of this approach, along with the substantive concepts and propositions of the court community framework, has allowed a more detailed analysis of the linkages between court organizational contexts, the workgroup action strategies conditioned by them, and sentencing outcomes than is common in most of the sentencing literature. This symbolic interactionist theory makes explicit an analytical strategy for capturing the interrelationships of macro, meso, and micro levels in broad government policies, court community contexts, and courtroom workgroup strategies. The social worlds analytical strategy provides an explicit "checklist" of contextual levels and action strategies to be examined in research. Plus, the framework locates the specific substantive concepts of the court community framework in a more generic theory and conceptualization, enhancing the ability to generalize and produce stimulating comparative research between different types of organizational arenas. The interface between sentencing guidelines, local court contexts, and court actors' strategies are an example of more general sociological themes of social worlds contexts and processual ordering. The processual order framework is a powerful analytical strategy for studying social organization at micro, meso, and even macro levels of scale without losing sight of the fact that social organization is both a context and a product of human agency and interaction processes.

Appendix A
Pennsylvania Sentencing Guidelines

Pennsylvania Sentencing Guidelines (ranges in months)

Offense Severity Score / Prior Record Score

OSS	0	1	2	3	4	5	6
10	A = * S = 48–120 M = 36–48	A = * S = 54–120 M = 40–60	A = * S = 60–120 M = 45–60	A = * S = 72–120 M = 54–72	A = * S = 84–120 M = 63–84	A = * S = 96–120 M = 72–96	A = * S = 102–* M 76–102
9	A = 60–75 S = 36–60 M = 27–36	A = 66–82 S = 42–66 M = 31–42	A = 72–90 S = 48–72 M = 36–48	A = 78–97 S = 54–78 M = 40–54	A = 84–105 S = 66–84 M = 49–66	A = 90–112 S = 72–90 M = 54–72	A = 102–* S = 78–102 M = 58–78
8	A = 48–60 S = 24–48 M = 18–24	A = 54–68 S = 30–54 M = 22–30	A = 60–75 S = 36–60 M = 27–36	A = 66–82 S = 42–66 M = 32–42	A = 72–90 S = 54–72 M = 40–54	A = 78–98 S = 60–78 M = 45–60	A = 90–112 S = 66–90 M = 50–66
7	A = 12–18 S = 8–12 M = 4–8	A = 29–36 S = 12–29 M = 9–12	A = 34–42 S = 17–34 M = 12–17	A = 39–49 S = 22–39 M = 16–22	A = 49–61 S = 33–49 M = 25–33	A = 54–68 S = 38–54 M = 28–38	A = 64–80 S = 43–64 M = 32–43
6	A = 12–18 S = 4–12 M = 2–4	A = 12–18 S = 6–12 M = 3–6	A = 12–18 S = 8–12 M = 4–8	A = 29–36 S = 12–29 M = 9–12	A = 34–42 S = 23–34 M = 17–23	A = 44–55 S = 28–44 M = 21–28	A = 49–61 S = 33–49 M = 25–33
5	A = 12–18 S = 0–12 M = NC	A = 12–18 S = 3–12 M = 1½–3	A = 12–18 S = 5–12 M = 2½–5	A = 12–18 S = 8–12 M = 4–8	A = 27–34 S = 18–27 M = 14–18	A = 30–38 S = 21–30 M = 16–21	A = 36–45 S = 24–36 M = 18–24
4	A = 12–18 S = 0–12 M = NC	A = 12–18 S = 0–12 M = NC	A = 12–18 S = 0–12 M = NC	A = 12–18 S = 5–12 M = 2½–5	A = 12–18 S = 8–12 M = 4–8	A = 27–34 S = 18–27 M = 14–18	A = 30–38 S = 21–30 M = 16–21
3	A = 12–18 S = 0–12 M = NC	A = 12–18 S = 0–12 M = NC	A = 12–18 S = 0–12 M = NC	A = 12–18 S = 0–12 M = NC	A = 12–18 S = 3–12 M = 1½–3	A = 12–18 S = 5–12 M = 2½–5	A = 12–18 S = 8–12 M = 4–8
2	A = * S = 0–12 M = NC	A = * S = 0–12 M = NC	A = * S = 0–12 M = NC	A = * S = 0–12 M = NC	A = * S = 0–12 M = NC	A = * S = 2–12 M = 1–2	A = * S = 5–12 M = 2½–5
1	A = * S = 0–6 M = NC	A = * S = 0–6 M = NC	A = * S = 0–6 M = NC	A = * S = 0–6 M = NC	A = * S = 0–6 M = NC	A = * S = 0–6 M = NC	A = * S = 0–6 M = NC

A = Aggravated Range   S = Standard Range   M = Mitigated Range   * = Statutory limit
NC = Non-confinement

Appendix B
Examples of Interview Questions by Topic

Examples of Interview Questions by Topic

I. Community Context

1. Are most judges Democrats or Republicans? What about members of the DA's office? The PD's office and defense bar?
2. How much does the local media cover court matters? How does the local media affect the sentencing process?
3. What is the county jail situation like? Do you have an overcrowding problem?

II. Individual Backgrounds

1. Could you describe your background for me? When did you start working in (the DA's office, the PD's office, private practice)? (For judges: How long have you been on the bench? Were you a prosecutor or defense attorney prior to your position on the bench?)

II. Sponsoring Agency Organization and Relations

1. Could you describe your office to me? How many people work here? Is your office specialized in any way? How?
2. Could you describe your typical schedule for me?
3. (Judges): How do cases get assigned to you? Who is in charge of the docket list? How does the list work? Is judge shopping possible in this county? (DAs and PDs): How are cases assigned within your office? Do you have any control over what judge hears what case? Can you use this to your advantage?

4. (DAs and PDs) Does anyone review (your) plea agreements? How does this work? Are there any review policies when there is a departure from the guidelines?
5. How much personnel turnover is there in your office (or on the bench)? How long do people usually stay in their jobs? What is the average level of experience of the people in your office? In other offices?
6. (DAs and PDs): Where do people go after they leave their jobs here?
7. How well do people know each other? Do most DAs and PDs and judges know each other well?
8. How would you characterize your office's relationship with (the court, the DA's office, the PD's office, the private attorneys, the probation office)?
9. Do policies or operating procedures vary noticeably between the judges? Can you provide some examples?

III. Case Processing

1. Could you trace the guilty plea process in this county for me? What is the typical pattern of a case that ends up in a guilty plea?
2. From the statistics, it seems like there are a lot of (open pleas, negotiated pleas, bench trials). Why is that? What is the advantage to them? Do guidelines make it easier to go with them?
3. In plea agreements, are charges usually reduced, dropped, or changed? How often and in what way do initial charges differ from the final conviction charges that somebody pleads to? What is more common, charge reductions or sentence agreements? How often do plea agreements involve both charge reductions and sentence agreements?
4. Two conceptions of the guilty plea process are common. One has a lot of haggling over charges, counts, sentencing, and so forth. The other is a system of "going rates," where there is sort of a standard plea package and sentence for various offenses, and it's a "take it or leave it" proposition. Which do you think best characterizes this county?
5. How much bargaining actually goes on in guilty pleas? What types of concessions are usually made? What kinds of concessions are not made?

6. Do you have a good sense of what a particular crime is worth in terms of a plea or sentence? Where does this sense come from? Can you provide an example of an offense and its worth? Are the guidelines consistent with what most people think different crimes are worth? If not, how do you resolve this?
   Is there a strong tradition of sentencing norms, like rules of thumb about who gets what under what circumstances, *apart from the guidelines*? If so, what are these based on?
7. Do the prosecution and defense ever bargain about specific guidelines issues like the offense gravity score or the prior record score? How often? If there is disagreement over a guidelines issue, how is it usually resolved?
8. How often does the prosecution ask that guidelines enhancements be applied, such as the deadly weapon enhancement? Do they use the enhancements as a threat in the guilty plea process?
9. How would you say the guidelines help or hinder the guilty plea process? How (if at all) do the guidelines influence the type or content of plea agreements?
10. Do the DAs make recommendations for specific sentences in guilty pleas? In other cases? How often are sentence agreements a plea agreement concession? Does the judge usually follow them?
11. Do you (Do the judges) ever get involved in the plea agreement process? To what extent? Under what circumstances?
12. Have you (Has a judge) ever rejected a plea agreement? Under what circumstances?
13. Does the probation office get involved in the plea process? To what extent? How often are pre-sentence investigations usually waived? When they are waived, what kind of information is used at the time of sentencing?
14. How often are guideline departure sentences a part of plea agreements, if ever? Under what circumstances?
15. How does jail or prison capacity have an impact on the plea agreements or plea decisions made?
16. Under what conditions are plea agreements ever made to ensure that the defendant will serve time in the county jail as opposed to state prison?
17. How do sentences differ for people who plead guilty and people who go to trial? Do you perceive a trial penalty in this county? How does it work?

IV. Sentencing

1. (Judges): What are the key elements in your decision when you have to choose between incarceration and probation? (Others): What are the key factors in determining whether someone gets probation or is incarcerated?
2. Under what conditions is there (Judges: Do you grant) a non-incarceration sentence when the guidelines call for incarceration? Is this usually part of a plea agreement? Can you provide an example? Under what conditions is there any kind of departure below the guidelines?
3. For what offense(s) do sentences depart from the guidelines most frequently? Why?
4. (Judges): How cognizant are you of overcrowding in the jail or prison at the time of sentencing? How does this affect your decision? (Others): How does jail or prison capacity affect sentencing?
5. Have you ever appealed a case (Judges: Have you ever had a case appealed) based on the guidelines? What were the issues? Do you think the appellate courts have done an adequate job of reviewing appeals?
6. Has the threat of appeal based on guidelines constrained the judges? Is it used as a "stick" to keep judges in line? Has the appeals process jeopardized the (DA's, PD's) relationship with the court?
7. One of the reasons the sentencing guidelines were created was to reduce sentencing disparity. Do you see disparity in the system? Where? What impact have the guidelines had on it?
8. Around the state, statistics show that there are sometimes differences between the sentences blacks and whites get, and that whites get probation and departures below guidelines more often. Do you think that happens in this county? What might be some reasons for this?
    A similar situation exists in terms of differences between the sentences that men and women defendants get. What might be some reasons for this?
9. In general, what kind of impact have the guidelines had on the sentencing process? (If subject worked prior to guidelines: How has sentencing changed as a result of guidelines?) What benefits are there as a result of guidelines, and what drawbacks?
10. If the guidelines were eliminated tomorrow, would the system change? In what ways?

Appendix C
Descriptive Statistics: Variables in State-wide Analysis

Variables in Statewide Analysis

Independent Variables	Frequency	Percent
Offense Severity Score		
1	18,640	11.2
2	19,781	11.9
3	19,362	11.6
4	9,596	5.8
5	49,064	29.4
6	25,900	15.5
7	17,693	10.6
8	2,025	1.2
9	3,966	2.4
10	650	.4
total	166,677	100.0
Prior Record Score		
0	97,023	58.3
1	13,358	8.0
2	17,235	10.4
3	9,186	5.5
4	7,776	4.7
5	4,441	2.7
6	17,365	10.4
total	166,384	100.0
Number of Conviction Charges		
Single	122,986	73.7
Multiple	43,951	26.3
total	166,937	100.0
Type of Conviction		
Other Guilty Plea	76,505	45.8
Negotiated Plea	74,083	44.4
Bench Trial	10,251	6.1
Jury Trial	6,098	3.7
total	166,937	100.0

		Frequency	Percent
Race			
Non-black		102,317	61.0
Black		64,620	39.0
total		166,937	100.0
Gender			
Male		144,965	87.0
Female		21,972	13.0
total		166,937	100.0
Sentencing Year			
1985		21,193	12.7
1986		23,320	14.0
1987		23,245	13.9
1989		24,387	14.6
1990		36,736	22.0
1991		38,056	22.8
total		166,937	100.0

	Mean	St. Dev.	Minimum	Maximum
Offense Severity Score	4.4	2.05	1	10
Prior Record Score	1.4	2.06	0	6
Defendant Age	28.4	8.6	18	88
Court Caseload	257.9	117.6	8	571
Percent Urban	75.7	25.3	0	100
Percent Black	12.4	14.5	0	40
Percent aged 15–19	7.3	1.1	5	13
Percent Republican	42.2	16.6	19	72
UCR Index Rate	3,631.6	1,491.5	933	6,933

Dependent Variables		Frequency	Percent
Incarceration			
Nonincarceration		61,632	37.0
Jail or Prison		105,305	63.0
total		166,937	100.0
Dispositional Departure[1]			
Nondeparture		61,007	86.0
Dispositional departure		9,481	14.0
total		70,488	100.0

	Mean	St. Dev.	Minimum	Maximum
Minimum Incarceration Length (months)	9.7	17.0	0	468
Durational Departure Below[2] (N = 26,855)	.63	.32	.023	1.0

Durational Departure Above[3] (N = 33,850)	.96	1.44	.01	23.0

1. Includes only guideline cells where dispositional departures are possible.
2. Includes only guidelines cells where departure below guidelines is possible.
3. Includes all guideline cells, since departure above is possible in any cell.

Descriptive Sentencing Outcomes for Offense Categories

Homicide[4] (N = 970):	Frequency	Percent
Nonincarceration	124	12.8
Incarceration	846	87.2
Dispositional[5] Departure	11	2.0
	Mean	St. Dev.
Minimum incarceration length	57.3	43.4
Durational departure below	.41	.29
Durational departure above	.86	1.01
Kidnapping (N = 155):	Frequency	Percent
Nonincarceration	13	8.4
Incarceration	142	91.6
Dispositional Departure	13	8.4
	Mean	St. Dev.
Minimum incarceration length	55.8	38.7
Durational departure below	.54	.35
Durational departure above	.76	.63
Rape/IDSI[6] (N = 2,860):	Frequency	Percent
Nonincarceration	144	5.0
Incarceration	2,716	95.0
Dispositional Departure	144	5.0
	Mean	St. Dev.
Minimum incarceration length	53.3	30.4
Durational departure below	.50	.31
Durational departure above	.49	.99

4. Category includes third degree murder, voluntary manslaughter, and involuntary manslaughter.
5. Dispositional departure frequencies and percentages include only guideline cells where dispositional departure is possible.
6. Category combines forcible rape and involuntary deviate sexual intercourse, both of which are grade 1 felonies.

Robbery (N = 9,399):

	Frequency	Percent
Non-incarceration	1,499	16.0
Incarceration	7,900	84.0
Dispositional Departure	484	7.0

	Mean	St. Dev.
Minimum incarceration length	23.2	27.5
Durational departure below	.56	.33
Durational departure above	1.12	1.61

Aggravated Assault (N = 5,642):

	Frequency	Percent
Nonincarceration	1,411	25.0
Incarceration	4,231	75.0
Dispositional Departure	934	20.0

	Mean	St. Dev.
Minimum incarceration length	17.6	23.0
Durational departure below	.69	.32
Durational departure above	1.10	1.50

Simple Assault (N = 11,279):

	Frequency	Percent
Nonincarceration	6,767	60.0
Incarceration	4,512	40.0
Dispositional Departure	—	—

	Mean	St. Dev.
Minimum incarceration length	1.9	3.5
Durational departure below	—	—
Durational departure above	1.88	2.86

Arson (N = 9,241):

	Frequency	Percent
Nonincarceration	3,463	37.5
Incarceration	5,778	62.5
Dispositional Departure	685	14.0

	Mean	St. Dev.
Minimum incarceration length	12.8	21.0
Durational departure below	.63	.32
Durational departure above	1.13	1.57

Weapons Offenses (N = 3,213):

	Frequency	Percent
Nonincarceration	1,602	49.9
Incarceration	1,611	50.1
Dispositional Departure	474	33.0

	Mean	St. Dev.
Minimum incarceration length	4.7	7.8
Durational departure below	.72	.31
Durational departure above	1.30	1.45

Appendix C

Burglary (N = 22,464):

	Frequency	Percent
Non-incarceration	4,824	22.0
Incarceration	17,640	78.0
Dispositional Departure	2,200	13.0

	Mean	St. Dev.
Minimum incarceration length	13.6	17.9
Durational departure below	.62	.32
Durational departure above	.93	1.51

Felony Criminal Trespassing (N = 4,438):

	Frequency	Percent
Nonincarceration	1,911	43.0
Incarceration	2,527	57.0
Dispositional Departure	68	10.4

	Mean	St. Dev.
Minimum incarceration length	4.5	6.6
Durational departure below	.57	.31
Durational departure above	.69	.62

Theft (N = 39,138):

	Frequency	Percent
Nonincarceration	18,841	48.0
Incarccration	20,297	52.0
Dispositional Departure	1,313	17.0

	Mean	St. Dev.
Minimum incarceration length	4.2	7.0
Durational departure below	.65	.32
Durational departure above	.91	1.23

Retail Theft (N = 10,807):

	Frequency	Percent
Nonincarceration	4,506	42.0
Incarceration	6,301	58.0
Dispositional Departure	725	17.3

	Mean	St. Dev.
Minimum incarceration length	4.8	6.9
Durational departure below	.62	.30
Durational departure above	.70	.95

Forgery (N = 5,421):

	Frequency	Percent
Nonincarceration	2,308	43.0
Incarceration	3,113	57.0
Dispositional Departure	456	20.0

	Mean	St. Dev.
Minimum incarceration length	6.4	9.4
Durational departure below	.68	.31
Durational departure above	1.07	1.36

Drug Felonies (N = 27,006):	Frequency	Percent
Nonincarceration	4,791	18.0
Incarceration	22,215	82.0
Dispositional Departure	1,960	12.0
	Mean	St. Dev.
Minimum incarceration length	12.0	13.3
Durational departure below	.61	.33
Durational departure above	.84	1.06
Drug Misdemeanors (N = 14,904):	Frequency	Percent
Nonincarceration	9,428	63.3
Incarceration	5,476	36.7
Dispositional Departure	—	—
	Mean	St. Dev.
Minimum incarceration length	1.3	3.2
Durational departure below	—	—
Durational departure above	1.10	1.91

Descriptive Statistics: Metro County

Independent Variables	Frequency	Percent		
Number of Conviction Charges				
Single	17,654	67.7		
Multiple	8,423	32.3		
total	26,077	100.0		
Type of Conviction				
Other Guilty Plea	18,039	69.1		
Negotiated Plea	5,422	21.0		
Bench Trial	1,864	7.1		
Jury Trial	770	3.0		
total	26,095	100.0		
Race				
Nonblack	11,291	43.0		
Black	14,786	57.0		
total	26,077	100.0		
Gender				
Male	22,270	85.4		
Female	3,807	14.6		
total	26,077	100.0		
	Mean	St. Dev.	Minimum	Maximum
Offense Severity Score	4.4	2.1	1	10
Prior Record Score	1.75	2.26	0	6
Defendant Age	29.6	8.8	18	86

Appendix C

Dependent Variables	Frequency	Percent
Incarceration		
Nonincarceration	12,872	49.4
County Jail	6,594	25.2
State Prison	6,611	25.4
total	26,077	100.0
Dispositional Departure[1]		
Nondeparture	9,040	79.6
Dispositional departure	2,311	20.4
total	11,351	100.0

	Mean	St. Dev.	Minimum	Maximum
Minimum Incarceration Length (months)	10.	13.0	0	468

1. Includes only guideline cells where dispositional departure is possible

Descriptive Statistics: Rich County

Independent Variables	Frequency	Percent
Number of Conviction Charges		
Single	10,254	85.0
Multiple	1,810	15.0
total	12,064	100.0
Type of Conviction		
Other Guilty Plea	1,774	14.6
Negotiated Plea	10,079	82.9
Bench Trial	124	1.0
Jury Trial	177	1.5
total	12,064	100.0
Race		
Nonblack	6,446	53.5
Black	5,618	46.5
total	12,064	100.0
Gender		
Male	10,062	83.4
Female	2,002	16.6
total	12,064	100.0

	Mean	St. Dev	Minimum	Maximum
Offense Severity Score	4.04	1.9	1	10
Prior Record Score	1.01	1.82	0	6
Defendant Age	28.6	8.2	18	87

Dependent Variables	Frequency	Percent
Incarceration		
Nonincarceration	6,076	50.4
County Jail	4,298	35.6
State Prison	1,690	14.0
total	12,064	100.0
Dispositional Departure[1]		
Nondeparture	3,235	85.8
Dispositional departure	537	14.2
total	3,772	100.0

	Mean	St. Dev	Minimum	Maximum
Minimum Incarceration				
Length (months)	11.9	11.3	0	432

1. Includes only guideline cells where dispositional departures are possible

Descriptive Statistics: Southwest County

Independent Variables	Frequency	Percent
Violent Offenses	187	14.0
Drug Offenses	249	18.7
Property Offenses	899	67.3
total	1,335	100.0
Number of Conviction Charges		
Single	874	65.5
Multiple	461	34.5
total	1,335	100.0
Type of Conviction		
Other Guilty Plea	302	22.6
Negotiated Plea	970	72.2
All Trials	63	4.7
total	1,335	100.0
Race		
Nonblack	1,256	94.1
Black	79	5.9
total	1,335	100.0
Gender		
Male	1,110	83.1
Female	225	16.9
total	1,335	100.0

	Mean	St. Dev.	Minimum	Maximum
Offense Severity Score	3.78	1.9	1	10
Prior Record Score	1.3	2.06	0	6
Defendant Age	27.9	9.12	18	86

Dependent Variables	Frequency	Percent
Incarceration		
Nonincarceration	598	49.4
County Jail	483	31.6
State Prison	254	19.0
total	1,335	100.0
Dispositional Departure[1]		
Nondeparture	355	85.7
Dispositional departure	59	14.3
total	414	100.0

	Mean	St. Dev.	Minimum	Maximum
Minimum Incarceration				
Length (months)	10.7	11.0	0	475

1. Includes only guideline cells where dispositional departure is possible

Notes

1. Courts, Sentencing, and Sentencing Guidelines

1. On the other hand, unwarranted parity of sentences can also occur when legally dissimilar defendants receive similar sentences (Kramer and Lubitz 1985; Kramer and Scirica 1986). For example, consider two defendants, each with one prior conviction, convicted of possessing ten grams of cocaine and sentenced to a mandatory prison term of five years. However, if one defendant is a small-time street dealer and one is a multi-kilo dealer in a large supply network, sentencing them similarly would arguably constitute an unwarranted parity.

2. Further, Brereton and Casper (1981) and Eisenstein et al. (1988) argue that even jury trials do not uniformly result in more severe sentences. Rather, they argue that sentencing penalties generally occur only for defendants who insist on trials perceived by court actors as "illegitimate" (see also Heumann 1978). This leads a conceptual problem that Brereton and Casper (1981, p. 50–51) describe this way:

> . . . when sentencing differentials are most effective, they are least observable . . . Provided the [trial] penalties were large enough and certain enough, we would expect the defendants in most of these "inappropriate" cases to be convinced of the wisdom of pleading guilty, thereby leaving the "appropriate" cases heavily over-represented in the trial category...one might expect that an effectively managed sentence differential policy would minimize the number of cases in which defendants would, in fact, actually have to be punished for exercising their right to trial.

Therefore, statistical models that fail to uncover substantial sentencing differences between guilty pleas and trials do not necessarily indicate that disparity based on mode of conviction does not exist. Cases in which defendants are penalized for "illegitimate" trials need not be statistically frequent to encourage guilty pleas.

3. Other studies such as Church (1976), Heumann and Loftin (1979), and Casper and Brereton (1984) have studied court organizational arrangements and case processing strategies under other determinate sentencing systems. Miethe's (1987) study, however, is the only one

that explicitly deals with the issue of hydraulic displacement of discretion under a guidelines system.

4. For histories of the development of Pennsylvania's, Minnesota's, and other states' guidelines systems, see Austin et al. (1994).

5. Guidelines may be either prescriptive, in which recommendations prescribe normative standards for sentences that may or may not be tied to existing sentencing practices, or descriptive, in which recommendations merely reflect existing practices (though perhaps omitting extralegal considerations deemed illegitimate).

2. Court Communities as Social Worlds

1. Couch (1986) and Seckman and Couch (1989) have discussed problems in Strauss's work concerning the definition of negotiation and distinguishing it from other forms of interaction. One possible contribution of this study would be to develop analytical distinctions between negotiations and other strategies in the context of court communities.

2. It is well known that bench trials are more similar to "slow pleas" mediated by judges, despite their adversarial appearance (see Mather 1973). I include them under adversarial proceedings to distinguish them from consensus or concessions mode pleas, where going rates are more easily applied.

3. As will be explained in chapter 4, these county-level characteristics will be omitted from the models presented due to severe multicollinearity with court size.

4. For example, Alschuler (1988) notes that while guidelines afford greater potential leverage for prosecutors in charge bargaining, they also allow judges to depart from the guideline recommendations. Thus, he argues, the judge's ability to depart from guidelines is an important preserve of judicial sentencing discretion, and an important potential check on the prosecutor's plea bargaining power. Therefore, unlike other proponents of the hydraulic displacement proposition (e.g., Savelsberg 1992; Tonry 1987), Alschuler explicitly recognizes that ample opportunities for sentencing discretion exist under guidelines beyond the charging decision, should judges choose to take advantage of them.

3. Data and Analytical Strategy

1. The units of analysis in the PCS sentencing data are criminal events or *transactions*, rather than individual defendants. Thus, if a

defendant is convicted of multiple offenses in one event or transaction and receives separate sentences for each, each of these sentences will appear as cases in the data, even though only one defendant was involved. PCS in-house analyses indicate that focusing on criminal events rather than individual defendants may inflate the estimate of actual numbers of defendants by as much as 30 percent. This overestimation of numbers of defendants is relatively unimportant, since the actual number of defendants is less important for the purposes of this study than is determining the outcomes of given sentencing cases, and how those outcomes vary according to various factors.

2. The guidelines were not in effect for a six-month period in 1988 due to a Pennsylvania appellate court case (*Commonwealth v. Sessoms* 516 PA 365,532 A2d 1987), which held that the state legislature's rejection of the first set of guidelines in 1981 was unconstitutional. This meant that the second set implemented in 1982, which incorporated changes desired by the legislature, were inapplicable. The guidelines went back into effect after the PCS declared that the changes made in the second set of guidelines would have been incorporated regardless of the legislature's action. During this six-month period, however, an unknown number of courts stopped reporting their sentences to the PCS. Thus, I do not use data from 1988 because I cannot have confidence in the representativeness of the PCS cases for 1988 sentences.

3. The Pennsylvania guidelines subcategorize many serious offenses, such as robbery, burglary, assault, and others, to reflect gradations in severity.

4. The one exception to the counting of misdemeanors in the prior record score concerns weapons misdemeanors, which count as one point each.

5. The durational departure below variable theoretically ranges from zero to one, but there are actually no values of zero for durational departure below in the models, since all nondeparture sentences (which would be coded as zero) are omitted.

6. Certainly, selection bias correction is important when sentencing outcomes are measured by collapsing the incarceration decision and incarceration lengths into one overall "sentence severity" scale (for example, see Peterson and Hagan 1984; LaFree 1985; Albonetti 1991).

7. In examining this supplemental dataset, my analyses revealed that bail and defense counsel information was missing for 73 percent of the cases. Further, data on types of pleas/trials were missing for 57 percent of the cases, and data on final charges were missing for more than 90 percent of the cases.

8. Due to the coding of this supplemental dataset, even if original and final charges could be accurately distinguished, or if some simple measure of change in charges could be constructed, all this would indicate is that a charge or charges were changed to something else. One could not tell from such a measure whether the change in charges represents a reduction in charge severity due to a plea agreement, a unilateral dropping of lesser-included charges by the prosecutor, or the dropping of ancillary charges due to a lack of evidence, or police overcharging.

9. Most of the subjects consented to being recorded. When a subject did not wish to be recorded, careful notes were taken by the interviewer and later transcribed.

10. When interviews were not tape recorded and transcribed, I coded the notes taken from the interview in a similar way.

11. Nor is adequate statistical data available to conduct a preguidelines versus postguidelines analysis of changes in sentencing outcomes.

4. Statewide Sentencing Outcomes

1. Correlations of dependent with independent variables, and groups of independent variables with one another, are not shown but are available on request.

2. The type of conviction variable presents a problem in that just under 20 percent of its cases are missing. In order to avoid deleting these missing cases, I have included them in the reference category of "other pleas." This procedure seems questionable at first glance, but I feel it is justified for two reasons. First, about 91 percent of the cases are convicted by guilty pleas, and chances are that the missing cases overwhelmingly consist of guilty pleas. Descriptive statistics on these missing cases (not shown but available on request) indicate that they are virtually identical to guilty pleas (i.e., other pleas and negotiated pleas combined) in terms of average offense severity, prior record, number of conviction charges, gender, race, age, and most importantly, sentencing outcomes. The missing cases are very different in terms of these profiles compared to known trial cases. Thus, it is unlikely that the missing cases contain significant numbers of trial cases. In differentiating types of guilty pleas, I simply included the missing cases in the "other plea" category so that the category of negotiated pleas would be free of missing cases.

Thus, while the "other plea" reference category may contain some negotiated pleas and perhaps a few trials, the "predictor" categories of substantive interest remain uncontaminated by missing cases. These categories reflect *only* those cases known to have been convicted by negotiated pleas, bench trials, or jury trials.

3. The incarceration cases also include a very small number of cases (about 150) receiving sentences of confinement other than prison or jail.

4. As mentioned in the previous chapter, logistic models are considerably superior to OLS models in the case of dichotomous dependent variables. As the descriptive statistics indicate, this is especially true for incarceration decisions and dispositional departures. According to Aldrich and Nelson (1984; pp. 25–30), least-squares coefficients for dichotomous dependent variables will be systematically misleading (usually in the direction of underestimation of effects) to the extent that the dependent variable's distribution differs from an equal ("50-50") distribution. If a dichotomous dependent variable is distributed unequally between its categories, least-squares estimates will be inherently heteroskedastic (nonconstant), producing bias in independent variables' coefficients. The more unequal the dependent variable's distribution, the more biased least-squares coefficients become. Only the sign of the least-squares coefficient will be correct. Furthermore, the R-squared statistic used to estimate the fit of least-squares models will be largely meaningless, since the coefficients' error terms will be heteroskedastic and the model's sum of squared errors will be distorted accordingly.

5. The odds ratio is calculated by taking the natural antilog of the logit coefficient (Aldrich and Nelson 1984).

6. For continuous independent variables, the cumulative change in odds of incarceration is calculated by raising the odds ratio in the model to a power equal to the number of points by which the independent variable hypothetically changes. For example, suppose an odds of 1 (a 50-50 chance) for incarceration when the prior record score is 0. Going from 0 to 1 yields an odds of 1.57 for incarceration, and going from 1 to 2 yields an odds of 1.57 x 1.57, or 2.47, and so on for any value of prior record.

7. According to Hanushek and Jackson (1977) and Lichter (1989), the formula for converting odds ratios for dummy variables to probabilities is as follows: **P1 = O1 / (O1 + 1)**, where P1 is the expected probability of a member of the dummy variable category coded as "1" exhibiting the predicted outcome, and O1 is the odds ratio from the logit coefficient for the dummy variable coded as "1." To obtain the probability of the predicted outcome for the comparison category, (the dummy variable category coded as "0"), or **P2**, simply reverse the sign of the logit for the dummy variable category coded as "1," obtain the appropriate odds ratio, and repeat the above calculation. To obtain the probability difference between the two dummy variable categories, subtract P2 from P1.

For example, to compare the probabilities of overall incarceration between blacks and whites in Table 4.1, one first obtains the black probability of overall incarceration as follows: P1 = 1.57 / (1.57 + 1)
= .61

Then, one reverses the sign of the logit for blacks, yielding a logit of $-.45$ for whites, which converts to an odds ratio of .64 for whites. Thus,
$$P2 = .64 / (.64 + 1) = .39$$
Therefore, P1 − P2 = .22, which represents a .22 difference in the probability of overall incarceration between blacks and whites—with blacks 22 percent more likely to be incarcerated.

8. Blumstein et al. (1978; 1986), for example, argue that while young people are more likely to commit and be convicted of offenses, older offenders are more likely to be incarcerated, since they are more likely to have amassed a significant criminal record. I suspect that my findings regarding age stem from the fact that I include much more refined controls for criminal history than many studies.

9. In the uncorrected model (not shown), like the corrected model, the strongest influences on incarceration length are prior record, offense severity and offense type. Together, these three factors account for 96 percent of the model's R-squared value of .51. The only other variable that contributes meaningfully to the model is jury trial. Those convicted by jury trial are, on average, incarcerated 11.5 months longer than those convicted through other guilty pleas, and jury trial adds about one-and-a-half points to the model's R-squared. Importantly, race and gender exert no significant influence in the uncorrected length model, and in fact the slope of race is *negative* (i.e., blacks receive slightly shorter sentences than nonblacks.) Given the consistent race effects in favor of nonblacks for incarceration decisions, this is rather implausible, and further suggests that the uncorrected models' coefficients may be contaminated by selection bias.

10. I combined bench and jury trials in the model testing the interaction of race and trial in order to ensure adequate numbers of cases when partitioning by race and trial together, while also controlling for the other variables in the model.

11. Comparisons of logistic odds, OLS coefficients, and R-squared values between the models in Table 4.4 should be made with caution. Even though significant cross-product terms in models that included all of the offense dummy variables indicated the interaction effects discussed in the text, the models for defendants with serious prior records omit three offenses due to insufficient numbers of cases, and are not strictly comparable to the models for defendants with less serious prior records.

12. On the other hand, age is more influential among serious priors defendants. Among these defendants, a one-year increase in age is associated with an average decrease of roughly one-fifth of a month in sentence length. For example, this would amount to about an average six-month difference in sentence length between twenty-year-old and fifty-year-old defendants.

13. In models not shown, the effects of some variables also differ modestly according to court community size, though these differences in effects must be interpreted with some caution due to the dissimilar composition of caseloads between courts of different sizes. This is especially true for the effect of offense type and severity, which differs substantially between small and large courts. With this caution in mind, the most interesting differences pertain to extralegal influences. The increased incarceration chances—and sentence lengths—associated with jury and bench trials seem to be more pronounced in large courts. On the other hand, negotiated pleas seem to gain defendants significantly increased chances of getting dispositional departures only in large courts.

Race effects are somewhat greater in medium courts for incarceration, greater in small courts for dispositional departures, and greater in large courts for length. The effects of gender are similar across court sizes for incarceration, but gender seems to exert a stronger influence on dispositional departures and sentence length in small courts. The effect of age differs across courts only in terms of length, where it is moderately more influential in large courts.

Finally, a small but consistent yearly trend toward moderately greater use of incarceration, less frequent dispositional departures, and longer sentences is apparent in medium-sized courts. Although the data do not allow a definitive explanation for this apparent trend, one might speculate about changes in political climate in medium courts and how these changes may have affected sentencing practices. For example, medium courts, which also tend to be more Republican, may have been differentially affected by the decade-long political trend toward more punitive sentencing strategies (Steffensmeier 1992; Edna McConnell Clark Foundation 1993). Over time, medium counties may have made greater use of the several mandatory minimum sentences and harsher guideline recommendations for violent and drug offenses in order to satisfy local political constituencies' demands to "get tough" on crime.

5. Metro County

1. Another interesting observation of the city's culture concerns the affiliations of many court community members and defendants with the Catholic church. Our first field visit to the county coincided with the Christian holiday of Ash Wednesday. Throughout the halls and courtrooms, many attorneys, judges, administrative people, and even defendants wore ash crosses on their foreheads, indicating that they had attended mass that morning for the ritual imposition of ashes.

2. I estimated statewide models of overall incarceration, state imprisonment, incarceration length, and dispositional departure testing the following cross-product interaction terms involving a dummy variable for Metro County: Metro * jury trial, Metro * bench trial, Metro * negotiated

plea, Metro * gender, Metro * race. The differences discussed in this chapter between Metro County and the statewide models in terms of the effects of mode of conviction, gender, and race were indicated by the statistically significant interaction terms in these statewide models.

3. One judge in particular vehemently disagreed with the suggestion that the skills of public defenders were less than those of private attorneys, saying that "some of our best attorneys in the county are public defenders."

6. Rich County

1. The differences between Metro and Rich Counties in the effects of mode of conviction, gender, and race discussed in this chapter were also indicated by testing cross-product interaction terms in models combining Rich and Metro (and Southwest) cases. These tests showed statistically significant differences between the counties in terms of the effects of mode of conviction, gender, and race.

7. Southwest County

1. Differences between Metro, Rich, and Southwest Counties discussed in this chapter were indicated by statistically significant cross-product interaction terms involving dummy variables for county, race, modes of conviction, and gender in models of incarceration, imprisonment, dispositional departure, and length combining the three counties.

2. Analyses of durational departures are also omitted, because they lack explanatory power and do not differ substantially from those of the statewide analysis.

3. The term "slow plea" often refers to bench trials, which serve as the functional equivalent of a judge-mediated plea negotiation in some jurisdictions (see Eisenstein and Jacob 1977; LaFree 1985; Mather 1973). However, Southwest County conducted only sixteen bench trials from 1989 to 1991, and only seven of these involved the offense categories selected for my earlier statistical analyses. When plea negotiations failed in Southwest, the usual result was a jury trial

8. Conclusion: Court Communities and Sentencing under Guidelines

1. Miethe noted, however, that the relative frequency of charge versus sentence bargaining varied widely between counties.

References

Agresti, Alan and Barbara Finlay. 1986. *Statistical Methods for Social Scientists*. San Francisco: Dellen.

Albonetti, Celesta. 1987. "Prosecutorial Discretion: The Effects of Uncertainty." *Law and Society Review* 21:291–313.

———. 1991. "An Integration of Theories to Explain Judicial Discretion." *Social Problems* 38(2):247–66.

Aldrich, John H. and Forrest D. Nelson. 1984. *Linear Probability, Logit, and Probit Models*. Beverly Hills, Calif.: Sage.

Alschuler, Albert. 1978. "Sentencing Reform and Prosecutorial Power: A Critique of Recent Proposals for Fixed and Presumptive Sentencing." in *Determinate Sentencing: Reform or Regression*. Washington, D.C.: U.S. Government Printing Office.

———. 1988. "Departures and Plea Agreements Under the Sentencing Guidelines." *Federal Rules Decisions* 117:459–76.

Altheide, David. 1992. "Gonzo Justice." *Symbolic Interaction* 15(1):1–22.

Austin, James, Charles Jones, John Kramer, and Phil Renninger. 1994. *National Assessment of Structured Sentencing*. San Francisco, Calif.: National Commission on Crime and Delinquency.

Becker, Howard S. 1964. "Personal Change in Adult Life." *Sociometry* 27(1):40–53.

Berger, Peter L. and Thomas Luckmann. 1967. *The Social Construction of Reality*. New York: Doubleday.

Berk, Richard. 1983. "An Introduction to Sample Selection Bias in Sociological Data." *American Sociological Review* 48:386–98.

Bernstein, Ilene Nagel, Edward Kick, Jan Leung, and Barbara Schultz. 1977a. "Charge Reduction: An Intermediate Stage in the Process of Labeling Criminal Defendants." *Social Forces* 56(2):362–84.

———, William Kelly, and Patricia Doyle. 1977b. "Societal Reaction to Deviants: The Case of Criminal Defendants." *American Sociological Review* 42:743–55.

Bickle, Gayle and Ruth Peterson. 1991. "The Impact of Gender-Based Family Roles on Criminal Sentencing." *Social Problems* 38(3):372–94.

Blumberg, Abraham. 1967. "The Practice of Law as a Confidence Game: Organizational Co-optation of a Profession." *Law and Society* 1(June):15–39.

Blumer Herbert. 1954. "Social Structure and Power Conflicts." in *Industrial Conflict*, edited by A. Kornhauser, R. Dubin, and A. Ross. New York: McGraw-Hill.

———. 1962. "Society as Symbolic Interaction." in *Human Behavior and Social Processes*, edited by A. Rose. Boston: Houghton-Mifflin.

———. 1969. *Symbolic Interactionism*. Englewood Cliffs, N.J.: Prentice Hall.

———. 1990. *Industrialization as an Agent of Social Change*. New York: Aldine.

Bogan, Kathleen. 1990. "Constructing Sentencing Guidelines in an Already Overcrowded State: Oregon Breaks New Ground." *Crime and Delinquency* 36(4):467–87.

Brereton David and Jonathan Casper. 1984. "Does It Pay to Plead Guilty? Differential Sentencing and the Functioning of Criminal Courts." *Law and Society Review* 18(1):45–70.

Bridges, George S. and Robert Crutchfield. 1988. "Law, Social Standing, and Racial Disparities in Imprisonment." *Social Forces* 66:699–724.

Busch, Lawrence. 1982. "History, Negotiation, and Structure in Agricultural Research." *Urban Life* 11(3):368–84.

Casper, Jonathan and David Brereton. 1984. "Evaluating Criminal Justice Reforms." *Law and Society Review* 18:121–44.

Champion, Dean J. 1989. "Private Counsels and Public Defenders: A Look at Weak Cases, Prior Records, and Leniency in Plea Bargains." *Journal of Criminal Justice* 17:253–63.

Church, Thomas. 1976. "Plea Bargaining, Concessions, and the Courts: Analysis of a Quasi-Experiment." *Law and Society* 10:377–410.

———. 1979. "In Defense of 'Bargain Justice.'" *Law and Society* 13:509–25.

Cirillo, Vincent. 1986. "Windows of Discretion in the Pennsylvania Sentencing Guidelines." *Villanova Law Review* 31:1309–49.

Clarke, Adele E. 1991. "Social Worlds/Arenas Theory as Organizational Theory." in *Social Organization and Social Process: Essays in Honor of Anselm Strauss*, edited by D. Maines. New York: Aldine.

References

Clear, Todd, John D. Hewitt, and Robert Regoli. 1978. "Discretion and the Determinate Sentence: Its Distribution, Control, and Effect on Time Served." *Crime and Delinquency* October:428–45.

Couch, Carl J. 1986. "Structural Conditions of Intergroup Negotiations." in *Studies in Symbolic Interaction, Supplement 2*, edited by C. Couch, S. Saxton, and M. Katovich. Greenwich, Conn.: JAI.

———, and Marion Weiland. 1986. "A Study of the Representative-Constituent Relationship." in *Studies in Symbolic Interaction: The Iowa School, Vol. 2*. edited by C. Couch, S. Saxton, and M. Katovich. Greenwich, Conn.: JAI.

Daft, Richard L. 1989. *Organization Theory and Design*. Los Angeles: West Publishing.

Daly, Kathleen. 1987. "Discrimination in the Criminal Courts: Family, Gender, and the Problem of Equal Treatment." *Social Forces* 66:152–75.

———. 1995. *Gender, Crime, and Punishment*. New Haven, Conn.: Yale University Press.

Del Sole, Joseph. 1993. "Appellate Review in a Sentencing Guidelines Jurisdiction: The Pennsylvania Experience." *Duquesne Law Review* 31:479–504.

Denzin, Norman. 1989. *The Research Act*. Chicago: Aldine.

Dixon, Jo. 1995. "The Organizational Context of Criminal Sentencing." *American Journal of Sociology* 100:1157–98.

Edna McConnell Clark Foundation. 1993. "Americans Behind Bars." Edna McConnell Clark Foundation.

Eisenstein, James and Herbert Jacob. 1977. *Felony Justice: An Organizational Analysis of Criminal Courts*. Boston: Little, Brown.

Eisenstein, James, Roy Flemming, and Peter Nardulli. 1988. *The Contours of Justice: Communities and Their Courts*. Boston: Little, Brown.

Emerson, Robert. 1983. "Holistic Effects in Social Control Decision-Making." *Law and Society Review* 17:425–55.

Estes, Carroll and Beverly Edmonds. 1981. "Symbolic Interaction and Social Policy Analysis." *Symbolic Interaction* 4(1):75–86.

Farr, Kathryn Ann. 1984. "Maintaining Balance Through an Institutionalized Plea Negotiation Process." *Criminology* 22(3):291–319.

Farrell, Ronald and Victoria L. Swigert. 1978. "Prior Offense as a Self-Fulfilling Prophecy." *Law and Society* 12:437–53.

Farrell, Ronald and Malcolm Holmes. 1991. "The Social and Cognitive Structure of Legal Decision Making." *The Sociological Quarterly* 32(4):529–42.

Feagin, Joe R. 1991. "The Continuing Significance of Race: Antiblack Discrimination in Public Places." *American Sociological Review* 56:101–16.

———, and Melvin Sikes. 1994. *Living With Racism: The Black Middle Class Experience*. Boston: Beacon Press.

Feeley, Malcolm. 1979. *The Process is the Punishment: Handling Cases in a Lower Criminal Court*. New York: Russell Sage.

———. 1988. "Plea Bargaining and the Structures of the Criminal Process." in *Criminal Justice, Law and Politics*, edited by G. Cole. Pacific Grove, Calif.: Brooks/Cole.

Feeley, Malcolm and Jonathan Simon. 1992. "The New Penology: Notes on the Emerging Strategy of Corrections and Its Implications." *Criminology* 30(4):449–74.

Fine, Gary Alan. 1984. "Negotiated Orders and Organizational Cultures." *Annual Review of Sociology* 10:239–62.

Flemming, Roy, Peter Nardulli, and James Eisenstein. 1992. *The Craft of Justice: Work and Politics in Criminal Court Communities*. Philadelphia: University of Pennsylvania Press.

Frazier, Charles and E. Wilbur Bock. 1982. "Effects of Court Officials on Sentence Severity." *Criminology* 20(2):257–72.

Frazier, Charles, Donna Bishop, and John Henretta. 1992. "The Social Context of Race Differentials in Juvenile Justice Dispositions." *The Sociological Quarterly* 33(3):447–58.

Friedman, Lawrence. 1977. *Law and Society*. Englewood Cliffs, N.J.: Prentice Hall.

Gerson, Elihu. 1976. "On 'Quality of Life.'" *American Sociological Review* 41:793–806.

Giddens, Anthony. 1976. *New Rules of the Sociological Method*. New York: Basic Books.

Glaser, Barney and Anselm Strauss. 1967. *The Discovery of Grounded Theory*. Chicago: Aldine.

Goodstein, Lynne and John H. Kramer. 1989. "Case Processing and the Federal Sentencing Guidelines." in *The U.S. Sentencing Guidelines: Implications for Criminal Justice*, edited by D. Champion. Westport, Conn.: Praeger.

Griswold, David. 1987. "Deviation from Sentencing Guidelines: The Issue of Unwarranted Disparity." *Journal of Criminal Justice* 15:317–29.

Hagan, John, John D. Hewitt, and Duane Alwin. 1979. "Ceremonial Justice: Crime and Punishment in a Loosely Coupled System." *Social Forces* 58(2):506–27.

———, and Kristen Bumiller. 1983. "Making Sense of Sentencing: Race and Sentencing Outcomes." in *Research on Sentencing: The Search for Reform*, edited by A. Blumstein, J. Cohen, S. Martin, and M. Tonry. Washington, D.C.: National Academy Press.

Hall, Peter M. and Dee Ann Spencer-Hall. 1982. "The Social Conditions of Negotiated Order." *Urban Life* 11(3):328–49.

Hall, Peter M. 1987. "Interactionism and the Study of Social Organization." *The Sociological Quarterly* 28:1–22.

———. 1995. "The Consequences of Qualitative Analysis for Sociological Theory: Beyond the Microlevel." *The Sociological Quarterly* 36(2): 397–424.

Hanushek, Eric A. and John Jackson. 1977. *Statistical Methods for Social Scientists*. New York: Academic Press.

Heumann, Milton. 1978. *Plea Bargaining*. Chicago: University of Chicago Press.

Heumann, Milton and Colin Loftin. 1979. "Mandatory Sentences and the Abolition of Plea Bargaining: The Michigan Felony Firearm Statute." *Law and Society* 13:393–423.

Holmes, Malcolm, Howard Daudistel, and Ronald Farrell. 1987. "Determinants of Charge Reductions and Final Dispositions in Cases of Burglary and Robbery." *Journal of Research in Crime and Delinquency* 24(3):233–54.

Hughes, Everett C. 1958. *Men and Their Work*. Glencoe, Ill.: The Free Press.

Humphrey, John and Timothy Fogarty. 1987. "Race and Plea Bargaining Outcomes: A Research Note." *Social Forces* 66(1):176–82.

Johnson, Michael P. 1991. "Commitment to Personal Relationships." in *Advances in Personal Relationships, Vol. 3*, edited by W. Jones and D. Perlman. London: Jessica Kingsley.

Katovich, Michael. 1986. "Temporal Stages of Situated Activity and Identity Activation." in *Studies in Symbolic Interaction: The Iowa School, Vol. 2*. edited by C. Couch, S. Saxton, and M. Katovich. Greenwich, Conn.: JAI.

———, and Carl Couch. 1992. "The Nature of Social Pasts and Their Use as Foundations for Situated Action." *Symbolic Interaction* 15(1):25–48.

Katz, Jack. 1977. "Cover-up and Collective Integrity: On the Natural Antagonisms of Authority Internal and External to Organizations." *Social Problems* 25(1):3–17.

Kleck, Gary. 1981. "Racial Discrimination in Criminal Sentencing: A Critical Evaluation of the Evidence with Additional Evidence on the Death Penalty." *American Sociological Review* 46:783–805.

———. 1985. "Life Support for Ailing Hypotheses: Modes of Summarizing the Evidence for Racial Discrimination in Sentencing." *Law and Human Behavior* 9:271–85.

Kling, Robert and Elihu Gerson. 1978. "Patterns of Segmentation and Intersection in the Computing World." *Symbolic Interaction* 1(2):24–43.

Klingler, David A. 1985. "The Guilty Plea Process in Three Small Pennsylvania Judicial Districts: An Inquiry into the Nature of Rural Criminal Justice." Unpublished master's thesis, Department of Political Science, The Pennsylvania State University.

Kramer, John H. and Robin Lubitz. 1985. "Pennsylvania's Sentencing Reform: The Impact of Commission-Established Guidelines." *Crime and Delinquency* 31(4):481–500.

Kramer, John H. and Anthony Scirica. 1986. "Complex Policy Choices: The Pennsylvania Commission on Sentencing." *Federal Probation* L(3):15–23.

Kramer, John H., Robin Lubitz, and Cynthia Kempinen. 1989. "Sentencing Guidelines: A Comparison of Sentencing Policies in Minnesota, Pennsylvania, and Washington." *Justice Quarterly* 6(4):565–87.

Kramer, John H. and Darrell Steffensmeier. 1993. "Race and Imprisonment Decisions." *The Sociological Quarterly* 34(2):357–76.

Kruttschnitt, Candace and Donald Green. 1984. "The Sex Sanctioning Issue: Is It History?" *American Sociological Review* 49:541–51.

LaFree, Gary D. 1985. "Adversarial and Nonadversarial Justice: A Comparison of Guilty Pleas and Trials." *Criminology* 23(2):289–312.

Lagoy, Stephen, Frederick Hussey, and John H. Kramer. 1979. "The Prosecutorial Function and Its Relation to Determinate Sentencing Structures." in *The Prosecutor*, Vol. 2, edited by W. F. McDonald. Beverly Hills, Calif.: Sage.

Levin, Martin. 1977. *Urban Politics and the Criminal Courts*. Chicago: University of Chicago Press.

Levy, Judith. 1982. "The Staging of Negotiations Between Hospice and Medical Institutions." *Urban Life* 11(3):293–311.

Lichter, Daniel. 1989. "Race, Employment Hardship, and Inequality in the American Nonmetropolitan South." *American Sociological Review* 54(3):436–46.

Lizotte, Alan. 1978. "Extra-Legal Factors in Chicago's Criminal Courts: Testing the Conflict Model of Criminal Justice." *Social Problems* 25:564–78.

Lubitz, Robin and Cynthia Kempinen. 1987. "The Impact of Pennsylvania's Sentencing Guidelines: An Analysis of System Adjustments to Sentencing Reform." Report for the Pennsylvania Commission on Sentencing and the Pennsylvania Commission on Crime and Delinquency. Commonwealth of Penn.

Maines, David R. 1982. "In Search of Mesostructure: Studies in the Negotiated Order." *Urban Life* 11:267–79.

———. 1993. "Narrative's Moment and Sociology's Phenomena: Toward a Narrative Sociology." *The Sociological Quarterly* 34(1):17–38.

Maines, David R. and Joy Charlton. 1985. "The Negotiated Order Approach to the Analysis of Social Organization." in *Studies in Symbolic Interaction, Supplement 1*, edited by R. Perinbanayagam. Greenwich, Conn.: JAI.

Manning, Peter K. 1992. *Organizational Communication*. New York: Aldine.

March, James and Herbert Simon. 1958. *Organizations*. New York: John Wiley and Sons.

Maroules, Nick. 1991. "Fashioning Courtroom Sentences." in *Studies in Symbolic Interaction*, edited by N. Denzin. Greenwich, Conn.: JAI.

Massey, Douglas. 1993. *American Apartheid: Segregation and the Making of the Underclass*. Cambridge, Mass.: Harvard University Press.

Mather, Lynn. 1973. "Some Determinants of the Method of Case Disposition: Decision-Making by Public Defenders in Los Angeles." *Law and Society* 7:187–216.

Maynard, Douglas. 1984. *Inside Plea Bargaining: The Language of Negotiation.* New York: Plenum.

———. 1988. "Narratives and Narrative Structure in Plea Bargaining." *Law and Society Review* 22(3):449–81.

McDonald, William F. 1979. "From Plea Bargaining to Coercive Justice: Notes on the Respectification of a Concept." *Law and Society* 13:385–92.

McDonald, William F., Henry Rossman, and James Cramer. 1979. "The Prosecutor's Plea Bargaining Decisions." in *The Prosecutor*, Vol. 2, edited by W. F. McDonald. Beverly Hills, Calif.: Sage.

Meeker, James and Henry Pontell. 1985. "Court Caseloads, Plea Bargains, and Criminal Sanctions: The Effects of Section 17 P.C. in California." *Criminology* 23(1):119–43.

Miethe, Terence. 1987. "Charging and Plea Bargaining Practices Under Determinate Sentencing: An Investigation of the Hydraulic Displacement of Discretion." *Journal of Criminal Law and Criminology* 78(1):155–76.

Miethe, Terence and Charles Moore. 1985. "Socioeconomic Disparities Under Determinate Sentencing Systems: A Comparison of Pre-guideline and Postguideline Practices in Minnesota." *Criminology* 23:337–63.

———. 1986. "Racial Differences in Criminal Processing: The Consequences of Model Selection on Conclusions about Differential Treatment." *The Sociological Quarterly* 27:217–37.

———. 1988. "Officials' Reactions to Sentencing Guidelines." *Journal of Research in Crime and Delinquency* 25(2):170–87.

Moore, Charles and Terence Miethe. 1986. "Regulated and Non-Regulated Sentencing Practices Under Minnesota Felony Sentencing Guidelines." *Law and Society Review* 20:253–65.

Myers, Martha and Susette Talarico. 1986. "The Social Contexts of Racial Discrimination in Sentencing." *Social Problems* 33(3):236–51.

———. 1987. *The Social Contexts of Criminal Sentencing.* New York: Springer-Verlag.

Myers, Martha. 1987. "Economic Inequality and Discrimination in Sentencing." *Social Forces* 65(3):746–66.

Nagel, Ilene and Stephen Schulhofer. 1992. "A Tale of Three Cities: An Empirical Study of Charging and Bargaining Practices Under the

Federal Sentencing Guidelines." *Southern California Law Review* 66:501–66.

Nardulli, Peter, Roy Flemming, and James Eisenstein. 1985. "Criminal Courts and Bureaucratic Justice: Concessions and Consensus in the Guilty Plea Process." *Journal of Criminal Law and Criminology* 76(4):1103–31.

Nardulli, Peter, James Eisenstein, and Roy Flemming. 1988. *The Tenor of Justice: Criminal Courts and the Guilty Plea Process*. Chicago: University of Illinois Press.

Nelson, James F. 1992. "Hidden Disparities in Case Processing: New York State, 1985–1986." *Journal of Criminal Justice* 20:181–200.

Ouchi, W.C. 1980. "Markets, Bureaucracies, and Clans." *Administrative Science Quarterly* 25:129–49.

Padgett, John F. 1985. "The Emergent Organization of Plea Bargaining." *American Journal of Sociology* 90(4):753–800.

Peterson, Ruth D. and John Hagan. 1984. "Changing Conceptions of Race: Towards an Account of Anomalous Findings of Sentencing Research." *American Sociological Review* 49:56–70.

Prechel, Harland. 1994. "Economic Crisis and the Centralization of Control Over the Managerial Process." *American Sociological Review* 59:723–745.

Quinney, Richard. 1970. *The Social Reality of Crime*. Boston: Little, Brown.

Rathke, Stephen. 1982. "Plea Negotiating Under the Sentencing Guidelines." *Hamline Law Review* 5(2):271–91.

Rosett, Arthur and Donald Cressey. 1976. *Justice by Consent: Plea Bargaining in the American Courthouse*. Philadelphia: Lippincott.

Ryan, John Paul and James Alfini. 1979. "Trial Judges' Participation in Plea Bargaining: An Empirical Perspective." *Law and Society* 13:479–507.

Sampson, Robert and John Laub. 1993. *Crime in the Making: Pathways and Turning Points Through Life*. Cambridge, Mass.: Harvard University Press.

Savelsberg, Joachim. 1992. "Law That Does Not Fit Society: Sentencing Guidelines as a Neoclassical Reaction to the Dilemmas of Substantivized Law." *American Journal of Sociology* 97(5):1346–81.

———. 1994. "Knowledge, Domination, and Criminal Punishment." *American Journal of Sociology* 99(4):911–43.

Schur, Edwin. 1980. *The Politics of Deviance: Stigma Contests and the Uses of Power.* Englewood Cliffs, N.J.: Prentice-Hall.

Schwartzman, Helen. 1993. *Ethnography in Organizations.* Newbury Park, Calif.: Sage.

Scott, W. Richard. 1987. *Organizations: Rational, Natural, and Open Systems.* Englewood Cliffs, N.J.: Prentice-Hall.

Seckman, Mark and Carl J. Couch. 1989. "Jocularity, Sarcasm, and Relationships: An Empirical Study." *Journal of Contemporary Ethnography* 18(3):327–44.

Shalin, Dmitri N. 1986. "Pragmatism and Social Interactionism." *American Sociological Review* 51:9–27.

Shibutani, Tomatsu. 1962. "Reference Groups as Social Control." in *Human Behavior and Social Process.* Edited by A. Rose. Boston: Houghton-Mifflin.

Spitzer, Steven. 1975. "Toward a Marxian Theory of Deviance." *Social Problems* 22(5):638–51.

Spohn, Cassia, John Gruhl, and Susan Welch. 1982. "The Effect of Race on Sentencing: A Reexamination of an Unsettled Question." *Law and Society Review* 16:71–88.

———. 1987. "The Impact of Ethnicity and Gender of Defendants on the Decision to Reject or Dismiss Felony Charges." *Criminology* 25:175–92.

Spohn, Cassia. 1990. "The Sentencing Decisions of Black and White Judges: Some Expected and Unexpected Similarities." *Law and Society Review* 24(5):1197–1216.

Spohn, Cassia. 1995. "Courts, Sentencing, and Prisons." *Daedalus* 124:119–143.

Stebbins, Robert. 1971. *Commitment to Deviance.* Westport, Conn.: Greenwood.

Steffensmeier, Darrell. 1976. "Advocates of Law and Order." *Criminal Justice and Behavior* 3:273–85.

———. 1980. "Assessing the Impact of the Women's Movement on Sex-based Differences in the Handling of Adult Criminal Defendants." *Crime and Delinquency* 23:344–56.

———. 1992. "Incarceration and Crime: Facing Fiscal Realities in Pennsylvania." Report to the Pennsylvania Commission on Sentencing. University Park, Penn.: Center for the Study of Law and Society.

Steffensmeier, Darrell and Emilie Allan. 1991. "Gender, Age, and Crime." In *Criminology*, edited by J. Sheley. Belmont, Calif.: Wadsworth.

Steffensmeier, Darrell, John H. Kramer, and Cathy Streifel. 1993. "Gender and Imprisonment Decisions." *Criminology* 31(3):411–46.

Steffensmeier, Darrell, John H. Kramer, and Jeffery Ulmer. 1995. "Age Differences in Sentencing." *Justice Quarterly* 12(3):583–602.

Steury, Ellen Hochstedler. 1989. "Prosecutorial and Judicial Discretion." In *The U.S. Sentencing Guidelines: Implications for Criminal Justice*, edited by D. Champion. New York: Praeger.

Stolzenberg, Lisa and Stewart D'Alessio. 1994. "Sentencing and Unwarranted Disparity: An Empirical Assessment of the Long Term Impact of the Sentencing Guidelines in Minnesota." *Criminology* 32(2):301–10.

Stone, Gregory. 1962. "Appearance and the Self." In *Human Behavior and Social Processes*, edited by A. Rose. Boston: Houghton-Mifflin.

———. 1977. "Personal Acts." *Symbolic Interaction* 1(1):2–19.

Strauss, Anselm, Leonard Schatzman, Rue Bucher, Danuta Ehrlich, and Melvin Sabshin. 1963. "The Hospital and Its Negotiated Order." In *The Hospital in Modern Society*, edited by E. Friedson. New York: The Free Press.

Strauss, Anselm. 1969. *Mirrors and Masks: The Search for Identity*. San Francisco: The Sociology Press.

———. 1978a. *Negotiations: Varieties, Processes, Contexts, and Social Order*. San Francisco: Jossey-Bass.

———. 1978b. "A Social Worlds Perspective." In *Studies in Symbolic Interaction*, edited by N. Denzin. Greenwich, Conn.: JAI.

———. 1984. "Social Worlds and Their Segmentation Processes." In *Studies in Symbolic Interaction*, edited by N. Denzin. Greenwich, Conn.: JAI.

———. 1987. *Qualitative Analysis for Social Scientists*. New York: Cambridge University Press.

———. 1993. *Continual Permutations of Action*. New York: Aldine.

Strauss, Anselm and Juliet Corbin. 1990. *Basics of Qualitative Research: Grounded Theory Procedures and Methods.* Newbury Park, CA: Sage.

Sudnow, David. 1965. "Normal Crimes: Sociological Features of the Penal Code." *Social Problems* 12(4):255–64.

Swigert, Victoria Lynn and Ronald Farrell. 1978. "Criminal Conceptions, Legal Process, and Crime Causation." in *Social Deviance*, edited by R. Farrell and V. L. Swigert. Philadelphia: Lippincott.

Taylor, Carl C. 1947. "Sociology and Common Sense." *American Sociological Review* 12:1–12.

Thomas, Jim. 1984. "Some Aspects of Negotiated Order, Loose Coupling, and Mesostructure in Maximum Security Prisons." *Symbolic Interaction* 7(2):213–31.

Thomas, W. I. and Dorothy Swain Thomas. 1928. *The Child in America.* New York: Knopf.

Thomson, Randall and Matthew Zingraff. 1981. "Detecting Sentence Disparity: Some Problems and Evidence." *American Journal of Sociology* 86(4):869–80.

Tonry, Michael. 1987. "Sentencing Guidelines and Their Effects." In *The Sentencing Commission and Its Guidelines*, edited by A. Von Hirsch, K. Knapp, and M. Tonry. Boston: Northeastern University Press.

———. 1992. "Mandatory Penalties." in *Crime and Justice: A Review of Research* vol. 16, edited by M. Tonry. Chicago: University of Chicago Press.

———, and John Coffee. 1987. "Enforcing Sentencing Guidelines: Plea Bargaining and Review Mechanisms." In *The Sentencing Commission and Its Guidelines*, edited by A. Von Hirsch, K. Knapp, and M. Tonry. Boston: Northeastern University Press.

Uhlman, Thomas and N. Darlene Walker. 1980. "'He Takes Some of My Time, I Take Some of His': An Analysis of Judicial Sentencing Patterns in Jury Cases." *Law and Society Review* 14(2):323–41.

Ulmer, Jeffery T. 1994a. "Revisiting Stebbins: Labeling and Commitment to Deviance." *The Sociological Quarterly* 35(1).

———. 1994b. "Trial Judges in a Rural Court Community: Contexts, Organizational Relations, and Interaction Strategies." *Journal of Contemporary Ethnography* 23(1).

———. 1995. "The Organization and Consequences of Social Pasts in Criminal Courts." *The Sociological Quarterly* 35(3).

Ulmer, Jeffery T. and John H. Kramer. 1996. "Court Communities Under Sentencing Guidelines: Dilemmas of Formal Rationality and Sentencing Disparity." *Criminology* 34(3):306-332.

Unnever, James and Larry Hembroff. 1988. "The Prediction of Racial/Ethnic Sentencing Disparities." *Journal of Research in Crime and Delinquency* 25:53–82.

Walker, Samuel. 1993. *Taming the System: The Control of Discretion in Criminal Justice.* New York: Oxford University Press.

Weber, Max. 1954. *Max Weber on Law and Economy in Society*, translated by M. Rheinstein and E. Shils. Cambridge, U.K.: Cambridge University Press.

Weick, Karl E. 1974. "Middle Range Theories of Social Systems." *Behavioral Science* 19:357–67.

———. 1979. *The Social Psychology of Organizing.* Reading, Mass.: Addison-Wesley.

Weick, Karl E. and Robert Browning. 1986. "Argument and Narration in Organizational Communication." *Yearly Review of Management* 12(2):243–59.

Wilbanks, William. 1987. *The Myth of a Racist Criminal Justice System.* Monterey, Calif.: Brooks/Cole.

Zatz, Marjorie. 1984. "Race, Ethnicity, and Determinate Sentencing." *Criminology* 22(3):147–71.

———. 1985. "Pleas, Priors, and Prison: Racial/Ethnic Differences in Sentencing." *Social Research* 14:169–93.

Index

Blumer, Herbert G., ix–x, 4, 21, 35, 189
Becker, Howard S., ix, 25

Cocaine (powder vs. crack), 99
Commitments, 22, 24–25, 29, 34, 125, 135, 188
Correctional Resources, 11, 87–88, 102, 119–120, 134, 144, 158–159, 176, 181–183
County Contextual Variables (measurement of), 37–40, 50–51, 54–55, 60, 213n
Court Case Assignment Systems
 individual calendar systems, 82–83, 112, 144, 152, 166, 170–171
 master calendar systems, 83, 112–113, 166, 170–171
Court Communities
 bench, 13, 26, 82–85, 86–89, 112–114, 116–117, 135, 142–150, 168–170, 172–174
 D.A.'s Office, 13, 26
  organization, 83, 85–86, 89–93, 114–115, 116–121, 143, 145–150, 151–152, 154, 156–157, 160, 165–169
  organizational style, 167, 171–172
  organizational type, 121, 167, 171–172
 defense bar, 13, 26, 83–84, 93–96, 101, 115–116, 117–121, 143, 149–150, 151–155, 160, 165–170, 178, 214n
 definition of, ix, 4, 13–14, 25–27
 "going rates", 13, 27–29, 33–34, 86, 103–104, 105, 121, 123–125, 127, 135, 153–154, 167, 173–174, 177–178, 186
 guilty plea agendas, 29, 33–34, 85, 96, 121–124, 126–129, 135, 153–154, 167, 173–174, 177–180, 184
 political contexts, 13, 31, 75, 82–84, 105, 112, 116–117, 121, 137, 142–143, 149, 166, 168–170, 172, 184–185, 187–189, 213n
 sponsoring agencies, 13, 26, 34, 82–86, 116–118, 142–150, 165–173
Courtroom Workgroups, 13, 27–29, 121, 174–175
 case processing strategies, 5–6, 15, 19, 27–29, 33–34, 86–97, 121, 150, 165, 174–179, 188, 207n, 214n
 defense attorneys, 93–97, 122–130, 151–154, 158, 160, 174–179
 prosecutors, 89–93, 122–130, 150–152, 154, 156–157, 160–161, 174–180
 "standing silent", 92, 97, 128–129, 135, 156–157, 179–180

230   Index

Courtroom Workgroups *continued*
  judges, 86–89, 113–114, 122–130, 150–160, 173, 177, 180
  charge bargaining, 16, 32–33, 43–44, 86, 89–92, 95, 103, 123, 135, 149–152, 160, 175, 178–179, 183–184, 208n, 210n, 214n
  definition of, 26–27
  familiarity and stability (see also social pasts), 29, 33–34, 82–84, 86, 94, 103, 116–119, 121, 135, 143–146, 148, 166–168, 173–174, 177–178
  guilty plea rewards, 9–10, 53–54, 56, 59, 62, 65–69, 71–73, 79, 81, 88–89, 97–98, 102–103, 107–111, 130–132, 141–142, 152–154, 157–158, 160, 164–165, 176, 180–181
  sentence bargaining, 16, 32–33, 44, 85, 90, 92, 95–98, 104, 123–129, 130–132, 135, 150–154, 158, 160, 175, 178–181, 184, 214n
  trial penalties, 9–10, 53–54, 56, 59, 62–69, 71–73, 77, 79, 81, 89, 97–99, 103, 107–111, 131, 135, 141, 150, 158, 164, 176, 180–181

Defendant Characteristics
  measurement of, 37–39
  race, 7–9, 29–30, 37–39, 53–55, 57, 60, 62–63, 64, 67, 69, 71–81, 99–101, 103, 109–111, 132–134, 135, 141–142, 158, 164–165
  gender, 7, 9, 29–30, 37–39, 53–55, 57, 60, 62, 64, 67, 69, 71–73, 77–81, 101–103, 109–111, 134–135, 141–142, 158–159, 164–165
  age, 7, 29, 37–39, 53, 55, 57, 60, 71–73, 165
  stereotypes and, 100–103, 133–134, 159, 165, 176, 181–183, 187–188

Definition of the Situation, 24, 187

Eisenstein, James, ix–x, 3, 21, 25, passim
Ethnographic Data Coding, 45–46, 210n

Identities, 22, 187–188
Informal Norms (see also "going rates"), 3, 13, 25, 27–28, 33–34, 86, 115–119, 121, 124–125, 131, 135, 158, 177, 185–186, 189
Interaction Strategies (see also case processing strategies), 5, 22–25, 27, 33, 165, 177–178, 188–189
  appeals to higher authorities, 23, 152–153, 160–161
  coalitions, 23, 150, 152–155, 157, 160, 174, 177
  cooperation, 5, 23–24, 115–118, 121, 131, 135, 168, 177
  conflict strategies, 5, 23–25, 131, 168, 170, 177–178
  negotiations, 5, 23–25, 27–29, 90–92, 95–98, 102–104, 114, 121–130, 135, 150–154, 160, 174, 177
  unilateral decisions/manipulations, 5, 23–25, 27–29, 90–91, 93, 95–97, 102, 104, 174, 177

Index

Judge Shopping, 82–83, 103, 113–114, 166, 170–171

Kramer, John H., xi, 9, 164

Labeling Theory, 3, 6, 165, 181–183, 186–188
Logistic Regression (explanation of), 42–43, 50–51, 53–54, 58–59, 64, 211n

Maines, David R., ix
Mode of Conviction (measurement of), 37–39, 53, 210n, 212n

News Media, 82, 118–119, 142–144, 146–147, 149, 156–157, 159–161, 166, 169–170, 172
Negotiated Guilty Pleas (see case processing strategies)

Odds Ratios
  conversion to probabilities, 53–54, 211n–212n
  interpretation of, 50, 51–54, 64, 211n
Offense Severity (measurement of), 36–39, 51, 208n–209n
Offense Type (measurement of), 36–37, 51–53, 137, 199–202, 209n
OLS Regression, 43, 50, 57, 212n
Open Guilty Pleas (see case processing strategies)

Police, 26–27, 89, 94–95, 122–123, 128, 135, 148, 210n
Pragmatism, 21, 23, 35, 187, 189
Prior Record (measurement of), 37–38, 64–65, 209n

Processual Order Theory, 5–6, 21–27, 32–34, 165, 174, 188–190

Rationality
  bounded, 181, 186–187
  formal, 3, 17, 19, 163, 184–185, 188–189
  substantive, 3–4, 17, 19, 163, 184–185, 188–189

Savelsberg, Joachim, 3, 178, 184–185
Sentencing
  discretion, 1–3, 16–19, 29–33, 47, 69, 71, 84, 86–90, 97, 99–100, 102–104, 124–127, 130, 135, 146, 148–149, 152–161, 172–174, 178–179, 180–185, 189
  disparity (see also defendant characteristics, plea rewards, trial penalties), 1–4, 7–13, 29–30, 32–33, 53–57, 59–64, 67–73, 77–81, 97–103, 107–111, 130–135, 141–142, 157–159, 163–165, 176, 180–185, 187–188, 214n
  ethnographic studies of, 13–14, 47, 105
  goals, 29, 32, 83, 119, 142, 148, 159–160, 166, 168, 173–174, 177–178
    deterrence, 1, 18, 119–120, 132–133, 148, 159, 166, 169
    incapacitation, 1, 18, 159, 166, 169, 182, 186–188
    just desert/retribution, 1, 18, 83, 86, 88, 97, 102, 119–120, 148–149, 166, 169, 182–183

Sentencing *continued*
  rehabilitation, 18, 83, 86, 88, 100, 102, 148, 156, 158–159, 166, 169, 181–183, 186–187
  mandatory sentences (see also charge bargaining), 2, 91, 93, 95, 99, 101–102, 123, 127, 135, 179, 184, 213n
  selection bias and, 11, 43, 50, 57–59, 209n, 212n
  statistical studies of, 7–13, 37, 43–44, 53, 57, 213n, 214n
Sentencing Guidelines
  appellate review of sentences and, 18, 90, 93, 96, 129–130, 147, 149, 156–157, 160, 209n
  departures from, 33, 50, 75–76, 85, 95, 102, 104, 163, 184–185
    above guidelines, 18, 38–39, 42, 62–63, 69, 72, 81, 107, 111, 129, 178, 214n
    below guidelines, 9, 15, 18, 38–39, 41, 60–62, 69, 72, 81, 86, 90, 92–93, 105, 111, 127–129, 135, 153, 156–157, 178–180, 209n, 214n
    dispositional, 18, 38–39, 40–41, 49, 55–57, 64, 67–69, 71–73, 76–81, 97–98, 99–100, 103, 105, 107, 111, 127, 132, 139–141, 158–159, 164, 180, 182, 184, 214n
  Federal System's, 2, 4, 15–19, 158
  Minnesota's, 2, 4, 14–19, 40, 178
  Pennsylvania's
    history of, 17–18, 124, 186
    characteristics of, 17–19, 29–30, 36, 40–42, 62–63, 65, 103–104, 130, 156, 160, 178–180, 183–185, 191, 208n
  Pennsylvania Commission on Sentencing, xi, 17–18, 36
  judicial discretion and, 2, 16–17, 30, 31–32, 47, 84–89, 92–94, 96–101, 102–104, 124–125, 127, 130, 133, 135, 146, 152–154, 156–161, 172–173, 180, 183–185
  prosecutorial discretion and, 16–17, 31–32, 47, 83, 85–86, 89–93, 95–97, 98, 100, 102–103, 113–115, 122–125, 126–129, 130, 135, 146–149, 151–154, 156–157, 160–161, 171–173, 178–181, 183–185
Social Pasts (shared and common), 24, 29, 33, 94, 103, 165, 173–174, 188
Social Worlds (see also Processual Order Theory), 5–6, 21–27, 35, 165, 188–190
  contextual features, 24–25, 28–29, 165, 174, 189
  definition of, 22–23
Strauss, Anselm L., ix, xi, 21, 23, 25, 35, 45, 174, 187
Symbolic Interactionism (see also Pragmatism, Processual Order Theory), ix–x, 5, 21, 35, 165, 187–190

Trials (see case processing strategies)

Uncertainty (reduction of), 23, 28, 32, 34, 84–85, 94–95, 103–104, 114, 123–125, 135, 153–155, 173–174, 177–178, 181, 185–187

Walker, Samuel, 1–2, 185
Weber, Max, 3, 185